The Future Health Workforce

The Future Health Workforce

Edited by

Celia Davies

Foreword by

John Wynn Owen

First published 2003 by
PALGRAVE MACMILLAN
Houndmills, Basingstoke, Hampshire RG21 6XS and
175 Fifth Avenue, New York, N. Y. 10010
Companies and representatives throughout the world

PALGRAVE MACMILLAN is the global academic imprint of the
Palgrave Macmillan division of St. Martin's Press, LLC and of
Palgrave Macmillan Ltd. Macmillan® is a registered trademark in
the United States, United Kingdom and other countries. Palgrave is
a registered trademark in the European Union and other countries.

ISBN 1–4039–1903–8 hardback

This book is printed on paper suitable for recycling and made
from fully managed and sustained forest sources.

A catalogue record for this book is available from the British Library.

Library of Congress Cataloging-in-Publication Data

The future health workforce/edited by Celia Davies.
   p. cm.
  Includes bibliographical references and index.
  ISBN 1–4039–1903–8 (cloth)
   1. National health services–Great Britain–Administration.
2. National health services–Great Britain–Personnel management.
3. Medical personnel–Great Britain–Forecasting. 4. Medical
personnel–Government policy–Great Britain. 5. Health care
reform–Great Britain. I. Davies, Celia, 1945–

RA412.5.G7F88 2004
362.1′0941–dc22   200305958

10   9   8   7   6   5   4   3   2   1
12 11 10 09 08 07 06 05 04 03

Printed and bound in Great Britain by
Antony Rowe Ltd, Chippenham and Eastbourne

Contents

List of Tables

List of Figures

Foreword

We are at an inflexion point in healthcare – on the brink of great changes in both the healthcare system and the world in which it operates. Health systems which adequately served the limited medical options of the earlier twentieth century are unable to cope with modern complexity. Advances in biomedical sciences, new developments in genetics, pharmacology, computing and nanotechnology are generating tests and treatments which could overwhelm our economic resources. The new health economy offers us the challenge of choice: between length and quality of life; between investment in health care and in the infrastructure influencing the determinants of health – agriculture, housing, education and transportation. The features of the new health economy – new medicines, health informatics, globalisation, the internet, eHealth – are all characteristic of a knowledge-based economy. The importance of thinking through fully, and well in advance, the implications of these changes for people who work in the health service is paramount.

This collection of essays, providing a snapshot of some of the key players in the health workforce, makes a start on this important task. The book has its origins in a conference, organised under the auspices of the Policy Futures Project, supported by the Nuffield Trust and held in September 2002 at the Judge Institute of Management at the University of Cambridge. A companion volume, edited by Sandra Dawson and Charlotte Sausman and tackling the question of organisational futures, is shortly to be published.

The introductory chapter charts the changes that have been put into place since the Labour Government came into office in 1997 with its project of modernisation, and the challenges its policies present for medicine, nursing and allied health professions. The concluding essay draws on the Policy Futures Project to speculate about wider forces of change, including scientific and technological advances, and social and demographic change.

Between these two chapters is a rich array of policy analysis and critique, evidence and evaluation, focused on different groups in the workforce – doctor, nurse, dentist, care assistant, pharmacist and others. There is something for everyone to learn from in this collection – the practitioner and the policymaker, the student and the seasoned academic commentator.

There is a repeated call here for new ways of thinking, not least for enlarging the concept of the workforce in health and health care. Patients and carers are seen here as co-producers of health. Complementary and alternative practitioners are an increasingly important component of the health care workforce. Widening thinking about the health workforce has implications which, as yet, have been barely considered.

The contributors to this volume are perhaps best described as 'critical friends' of government – sympathising with overall values and visions yet questioning whether policies have the capacity to deliver the cultural and structural changes that will ultimately make a difference. Sometimes, they argue, it is the vision which is at fault and needs to be restated and renewed to fit with contemporary demands.

If plans for the NHS at this crucial period of change do not come to fruition in the ways intended, and if the new ways of working that are being developed do not quite always work out, then some of the reasons for this can be found in this volume. Its details may date but the arguments of the contributors – about the dynamics of workforce change and the factors at work – are likely to remain relevant. It is a book that deserves attention by anyone interested in the fate of the NHS and its development over coming decades.

JOHN WYNN OWEN
The Nuffield Trust, London, June 2003

Notes on the Contributors

Alison Blenkinsopp is Professor of the Practice of Pharmacy at Keele University's Department of Medicines Management. She has recently completed, with Professor Jennifer Tann, *Understanding Innovation in Community Pharmacy* (2003). In another recent study with colleagues at Aston University, *What Makes an Effective PCT Pharmacist? A study of training and development needs* (2003), she explores the emerging strategic role of pharmacists in primary care. She is currently working with the Department of Health on Guidance on Medicines Management to support National Service Frameworks.

Christine Bond is Professor of Primary Care (Pharmacy) at the Department of General Practice and Primary Care, University of Aberdeen, and Head of General Practice teaching. Her research interests are in the role of pharmacy in optimising effective use of medicines (prescribed and 'OTC'), and in contributing to the wider primary health care agenda. She is seconded part-time to Grampian NHS Board as Consultant in Pharmaceutical Public Health, and has been a member of the Scottish Executive of the Royal Pharmaceutical Society of Great Britain since 1999.

Ailsa Cameron is a Research Fellow in the Centre for Health and Social Care, at the School for Policy Studies, University of Bristol. Ailsa has been interested in changing professional roles since 1996 when she took part in an evaluation of nurse practitioner roles in the South West, with Susan Dowling and Lesley Doyal, *Challenging Practice* (1998). Ailsa was also involved in the Exploring New Roles in Practice research project which investigated the development of new professional roles for nurses and the professions allied to medicine on behalf of the Department of Health (co-edited with colleagues on the ENRiP Project) *Exploring New Roles in Practice: final report* (2001).

Angela Coulter is Chief Executive of Picker Institute Europe. A UK-registered charity, the Picker Institute works with European health care providers to obtain feedback from patients and promote patient-centred care. Angela has a doctorate in health services research from the University of London and has published widely on a variety of topics. Her two most recent books are *The Autonomous Patient* (2002) and *The European Patient of the Future* (2003).

Celia Davies is Professor of Health Care at The Open University. She is a sociologist with a longstanding interest in the organisation of health professions. Her recent research with Abigail Beach has been published as *Interpreting Professional Self-Regulation: a history of the UKCC* (2000). She led the development of The Open University's continuing professional development course for those working in health and social care and co-edited an associated book *Changing Practice in Health and Social Care* (2000).

Liz Forbat completed a doctorate on the discursive construction of care relationships at The Open University in 2001. She worked as a Research Fellow examining intersections of ethnicity and family dementia care at The Open University, and since August 2003 has been at the University of Edinburgh researching best practice in the field of learning difficulties and dementia. She is currently working on several books, including one with a provisional title of *Exploring Accounts of Care*, whilst continuing post-graduate training in systemic psychotherapy.

Jenny Gallagher is Senior Lecturer and Honorary Consultant in Dental Public Health at the Guy's, King's and St Thomas' Dental Institute of King's College London. She worked in all branches of dentistry before embarking on specialist training and an academic career in Dental Public Health. She combines an active involvement in health services research and dental education with her role as consultant to Primary Care Trusts and to the Strategic Health Authority within South East London.

Stephen Gillam is a General Practitioner in Luton, Director of Clinical Public Health teaching at Cambridge University and is Senior Adviser on Primary Care at the King's Fund. He has worked at the King's Fund on evaluation of health policy since 1997. He has written extensively on primary care. Recent publications include an edited collection with Fiona Brooks, *New Beginnings: towards patient and public involvement in primary health care* (2001) and, with Geoff Meads, *Modernisation and the Future of General Practice* (2001).

Jeanette Henderson is a Lecturer in the School of Health and Social Welfare at The Open University and course chair of *Mental Health Challenging Ideas*. Jeanette also has experience of working in voluntary and statutory sector mental health services. Her research interests are in mental health, especially meanings and constructions of 'care'. Recent publications include papers on the impact of policy on 'care' within partnerships, the use of mental health legislation and implementing change in mental health services.

Geraldine Lee-Treweek is Lecturer in Health Studies at The Open University. She is a sociologist of health and illness with interests in complementary and alternative medicine (CAM), health work occupations, paid care labour, abuse of older people, chronic illness and risk to the researcher during qualitative inquiry. An overarching concern with trust relations and ethical conduct in a variety of settings holds these interests together, and she is currently researching the ethical conduct of CAM therapists. She is also a member of a team at The Open University writing a course on critical issues and debates in complementary and alternative medicine.

Rachel Lissauer is currently Surgery Improvement and Endoscopy Project Manager at the Mayday Healthcare NHS Trust, an acute London hospital. Before moving into the health service, she was Health Policy Research Fellow at the Institute for Public Policy Research (ippr) where she was a member of the secretariat for the Commission on Public Private Partnerships and lead researcher for the Future Health Worker project. Her work on the health service workforce includes co-authorship of *The Future Health Worker* (2003) and *New Practitioners in the Future Health Service: exploring roles for practitioners in health and social care* (2003).

Abigail Masterson is an independent healthcare consultant. She works with many local, national and international health care organisations carrying out research, developing innovative educational programmes and reviewing services. Abi has both a Bachelors and Masters degree in nursing and has published widely, particularly in relation to new role development in health care.

Sarah Oerton is a Senior Lecturer in Sociology in the School of Humanities and Social Sciences, University of Glamorgan, South Wales. She has researched and published widely in the field of work and organisations, and has undertaken research on power, politics and professionalism in the field of complementary therapies, with particular reference to alternative bodywork practitioners. She teaches courses on Sex and Sexuality and the Sociology of the Body and is currently co-authoring a book (with Joanna Phoenix) entitled *Illicit and Illegal: sex, regulation and social control* (2004).

Stephen Peckham is Reader in Health Policy and Head of the Department of Sociology and Social Policy at Oxford Brookes University. His research interests include health policy analysis, primary care, public involvement, partnership working and public health. He has a particular interest in the nature of public health and has recently completed a research project exploring the relationship between primary care and local communities in addressing public health issues.

Charlotte Sausman (formerly Dargie) is a Senior Research Associate at the Judge Institute of Management, Cambridge University. She is a political scientist and is the lead researcher on the Nuffield Trust's Policy Futures Project, which looks at the future of health and possible policy responses to it. She is also co-editor of the forthcoming sister volume to this collection, *Future Health Organisations and Systems*, with Professor Sandra Dawson at the Judge Institute.

Carole Thornley is Senior Lecturer in Industrial Relations at Keele University, and is currently Joint Secretary of the British Universities Industrial Relations Association (BUIRA). An economist by training, she has recently co-edited a book, *Industrial and Labour Market Policy and Performance* (with Dan Coffey, 2003). Her research on health service and local government pay has been widely published in the academic and practitioner press and has been presented as evidence in formal pay negotiations and to numerous official pay reviews and commissions.

Anne Williams is Professor of Nursing at the University of Wales Swansea. Her most recent research and publications, including *Nursing, Medicine and Primary Care* (2000), explore changing nursing roles, identities and relationships on the boundary with medicine. Anne's background work and qualifications encompass the disciplines of nursing, midwifery and sociology. She has served on the editorial boards of the journals, *Midwifery* and *Sociology* and is currently a member of the Nursing, Midwifery and Health Visiting sub-group of the Department of Health Service Delivery and Organisation Programme.

Erica Wirrmann is currently working on her PhD at Oxford Brookes University. Her research is exploring the developing public health roles of primary care practitioners in the UK, and she is particularly interested in diverse understandings of public health. Her background is in social policy, sociology and community development.

Introduction: a New Workforce in the Making?

Celia Davies

For many people working inside the NHS, the 1980s and early 1990s felt like a period of total revolution in health care. New vocabularies of business management pervaded thinking. Markets and managerialism came to the fore, and competition and contracting were the order of the day. The challenge was profound and, to some, also profoundly distasteful. Yet, despite the new words and new employment relations, the division of labour in delivering patient care remained much the same. From a patient perspective, the GP was still the port of first call, and the long wait for an outpatient appointment remained. The day to day experience of the hospital ward was much as it always was and the uneasy join between local authority and NHS for care in the community was still evident. Historians of the mid twenty-first century may well look back and judge that period an interlude – important certainly, for shaking the complacency of those who still saw the creation of the NHS in 1948 as the jewel in the crown of British social welfare, but an interlude nonetheless. The real revolution, they might argue, came later, after 1997, when New Labour began not just to reshape once again the overall organisational arrangements of health care, but to redesign the workforce. Assumptions about the professional autonomy of doctors, about the hierarchies and divisions of labour between and among other health professions that had survived successive health service reorganisations of earlier decades began to be cast aside. The workforce of the future seemed set to look remarkably different from the workforce of the present.

Will the old distinctions between nurse and doctor break down completely? Will patients, with access to information about health and illness as never before, take charge and bypass old-style health professionals? Will high street health care become the norm – a one-stop shop for both health education and health care? Will we order our drugs from a call centre in Calcutta – or learn to love the robot pharmacist in the hospital? The chapters in this volume open up a range of possibilities – as well as putting a brake on some of the more fanciful forms of future-gazing. This introductory essay tracks the contours of policy change, asking just how far there is a coherent political vision of the future and a groundswell of support for it. Taken as a whole, the book helps to address the question: is there justification for referring to a 'workforce revolution' in health care – or is this to confuse government aspiration with practical reality?

'Investment and reform': a government bent on change

Debates about just what was 'new' about the 'new NHS' unveiled in Labour's White Paper issued six months after it took office (Department of Health, 1997) have preoccupied commentators. Whether health service change demonstrated a 'third way' between the New Right and Old Labour, whether the approach – in health as in other areas of social policy – was simply a pragmatist and populist response, have been topics of heated debate and disagreement (Lister, 2001; Powell, 2000). Once into Labour's second term, with implementation of its NHS Plan well under way, however, the depth of challenges to those who work in the NHS are becoming easier to discern. Just what lies behind the Plan's criticism of 'a 1940s system in a twenty first century world' (Department of Health, 2000b: 15) and the repeated call for 'new ways of working'?

By the time that Labour was in its second term, five key reforms had moved beyond mere rhetorical flourish. First there is the demand for *patient-centred services*. There have been repeated admonitions over the years to provide integrated care and seamless services. What is new is the focus on the 'patient journey' within and across services, and the space that has opened up to take a detailed look at where improvements can be made. Patient journey data have often unlocked radical ideas for service redesign. Large numbers of steps on a journey to surgery, for example, can be eliminated and new-style diagnostic and treatment centres can transform the patient experience and bring satisfaction to staff through seeing results much earlier. Working effectively *across* health and social care relates closely to all this. The new statutory duties in both the health and local authority sectors to promote the health and wellbeing of their shared local communities could prove significant.

Second is the determination to *focus on primary care* – and to move away from the tendency among both the public and the media to equate the hospital with the NHS. This is apparent in the speed of movement in England, for example, to primary care trusts and the channelling of resource for specialist care through them. It is also apparent in the creation of NHS Direct as a direct public access telephone advice service, in the primary care pilots that introduce new kinds of contracts and in the pressure for nurse-led walk-in centres and one stop shops for first contact care. Devolved government now sometimes means that change is faster in other parts of the UK and the emphasis on local services is one area where this plays out.

Central standard-setting is a third key reform. The roll-out of National Service Frameworks (NSFs) for mental health, care of older people, diabetes care and so on, set parameters within which local services are to be developed. The growing work programme of the National Institute for Clinical Excellence (NICE), with its guidelines and protocols, and the monitoring and inspection from the Commission on Health Improvement (CHI) suggest a fundamental shift away from clinical autonomy for the medical profession as it was understood in the twentieth-century NHS. Fourthly, there is the mantra '*what matters is what works*'. Sending patients overseas, bringing in foreign doctors to set up a 'cataract factory' and hence bring down the waiting list, finding new ways to involve private providers, setting up foundation trusts, all these and more have been tried. It is clear that government is prepared to countenance a wide array of new possibilities for the NHS in its determination to modernise and in its confrontation with escalating demand and staff shortages.

Finally, part cause and part consequence of the changes outlined above, is a determination about *engaging with the public*. A broader quest for democratic renewal, for creating government 'in touch with the people' is visible in action across the public sector and beyond. Bringing service users in at all levels of planning and service delivery is now routinely expected. The NHS Plan was developed with representatives of patient and consumer groups and they were joint signatories to the final document. Despite controversy, legislation to replace community health councils and set new structures of involvement in place has been passed. Each of the new standard-setting and monitoring and regulatory agencies created since 1997 has to have a public and patient involvement strategy. Government support for an Expert Patient Programme, supporting patients with long-term conditions, and acknowledging that many of them have built up or could build up more knowledge than professionals, was announced in 2001 (Department of Health, 2001a).

The Prime Minister took pains to praise public service workers in his foreword to the NHS Plan. The years since 1997, however, have also seen increasingly outspoken government criticisms of professional practices. Take the strategy for nursing, (Department of Health, 1999). On the face of it, this heaped praise on the profession, valuing nurses and identifying still more that they could do – opening up new work across the medicine/nursing boundary, and establishing a nurse consultant grade. All this however, was accompanied by a decision that, with an investment of almost £800 million, the Department of Health would in future 'take more direct responsibility for the shape and direction of nurse and midwife education' (ibid: para 4.13). There was an insistence

> that the requirements of the NHS are put at centre stage in the development of all nursing and midwifery curricula and of continuing professional development. We want to give a kickstart to more multi-professional learning and teaching and to ensure the systematic sharing and spreading of good practice ... (ibid: para 4.14)

Growing impatience with old-fashioned and traditional demarcations, professionals' slowness to take on an agenda of change in practice as well as education exploded onto the scene nine months later in a consultation document on workforce planning (Department of Health, 2000a). There was criticism of early specialisation and impatience that research and development findings and good practice on skill-mix were being ignored. The workforce was described in distinctly unflattering terms as 'different professional tribes' (ibid: para 1.3).

Just what was it that Labour wanted to see in place of the old workforce with its inflexible divisions and traditional demarcations? The consultation document offered an example of a new 'clinical practitioner' managing the care of eating disorder in the main in the community. A clear referral protocol would guide the GP, and a mental health nurse with the relevant 'bolt-on' learning and working to a flexible employment contract would be able to support teenagers in their own homes out of school hours (ibid: 10). Later came another possibility. Using a few keyboard strokes, a therapist of the future will be able to download the competencies needed for the next grade, check out available courses, have her request automatically routed to her manager, and even be reminded about an update module she has yet to complete (Department of Health, 2001b: 43). This was now part and parcel of a lifelong learning strategy providing opportunities for all. The vision for the NHS University, a latecomer to this policy process (Davies, 2002), was that it would map out, broker and provide learning for everyone. If it did not quite deliver 'porters to consultants', certainly it aimed to expand opportunities – providing a skills escalator for those traditionally excluded, and a later a promise of foundation degree in five years for new employees without qualifications (NHS University, 2002). A modern NHS, it was becoming clear, was going to dismantle the separate professional hierarchies of the past and offer ladders, links and bolt-on opportunities, regardless of where any member of the workforce had started their career.

What is striking is the speed and the many fronts on which this vision has been taken forward. Strategies for other professional groups followed the initial strategy for nursing. The Modernisation Agency – with its teams of change agents, toolkits and taskforces, the Leadership Centre, NICE and CHI and NSFs – all added to pressure from the top. There was funding for shared learning and for projects to implement workforce change. There was workforce planning for care groups and parallel work on job evaluation and on simplifying the pay structure. Legislative measures were also important, for example, the new prescribing powers for nurses and pharmacists under the Health and Social Care Act 2001. Human resource strategies came more to the fore as enabling new ways of working (Department of Health, 2001b: iv). Money seemed to be forthcoming – with unprecedented increases in the budget of Spring 2002. In one area after another, however, new money was tied to the need to demonstrate change in working practices. All this made sense of the contradictory messages emerging from ministers. The NHS workforce was a precious asset and the commitment and dedication of staff was not in doubt – but the NHS professions also represented one of the 'forces of conservatism',[1] holding back modernisation. Hence came the twin themes of 'investment and reform'.

An increasingly conducive climate

Just how receptive was the public and was the professional mood? The health professions were on the back foot in the years after 1997. Allegations of medical malpractice – the enquiry into paediatric surgery at Bristol Royal Infirmary, the conviction for murder of GP Harold Shipman, the removal from the register of Rodney Ledward, for example – these and other cases were rarely out of the headlines. Government ministers hardened their resolve. The culture of 'consultant as king' had to be changed. The limitations in the power both of the General Medical Council (GMC) and of local managers to address incompetent practice and arrogant attitudes in the medical profession for the first time started to be addressed. Clinical governance began to bite; contracts were scrutinised. Legislative time was found for major reforms to at least two of the regulatory bodies and negotiations began in earnest with the GMC about reshaping its constitution and powers, and making routine revalidation a requirement if doctors were to retain their registration status. In some places, the idea of a single registering body for all health professionals was mooted. In short, many of the old institutional props for autonomous professional practice seemed on a pathway to reform in a way that would have been quite inconceivable in earlier decades. The trust in professionals that built deference to medicine so firmly into the health service of 1948, was no longer a foregone conclusion.

A debate about the need for a new kind of professional began to surface in a variety of places. The Select Committee on Public Administration, in an examination of issues involved in making government work, sounded a clarion call urging the creation of a new kind of professionalism, with public accountability at its heart, rather than one that appeared to resist scrutiny and defend sectional interests (House of Commons, 2001). Sir Donald Irvine, for much of this period president of the GMC, attracted considerable public attention as he began to explore the changing climate of trust and to write about how assumptions that had long served the medical profession were now outdated and needed to change.[2] The Kennedy Report, the official enquiry into the Bristol case, added weight to this sense of needing new ways of working (Department of Health, 2001c). Arguments for less arrogant and less heroic identities and more co-operative ways of working with others were likely to find receptive ears, for example, among women doctors, younger practitioners and co-workers.

Think-tanks put all this on a still wider canvas, taking up the call for public sector renewal. They too were debating just what new style public services would look like. The Institute for Public Policy Research put a Future Health Worker Project in train, following its earlier work on the future patient (Kendall, 2001; Lissauer and Kendall, 2002). It also galvanised thinking on the future of the social care workforce – contributing in future not to stigmatised 'welfare' but to the 'well-being' of a community (Kendall and Harker, 2002). The New Local

Government Network commissioned work on a new public *service* – as opposed to a public *sector* – ethos. This argued that private as well as traditionally public services could subscribe to values if these were made overt (Aldridge and Stoker, 2002). All this added to a sense of momentum and a growing consensus that health professional practice needed to be modernised. Such developments could challenge but they could also embolden government.

Urgent practical factors also came into play. Ambitious targets to meet the shortfalls in staff numbers across all clinical groups were outlined in the NHS Plan. The short-term picture of shortages has, if anything, worsened since 2000. Faced with the European Working Time Directive and the cut in junior doctors' hours, managers have had to adapt. More of the same is often not an option. It is clear too, that work overload in many cases is bringing staff close to breaking point. Acknowledgement of this came from what might be thought to be a 'conservative' source. Writing about doctors under pressure, the Royal College of Physicians advocated a new healthcare practitioner grade, someone with a degree who would take two to three year training, and practice in acute hospitals, in A&E, and in areas of consultant shortage (Royal College of Physicians, 2000). Early in 2003, the Medical Royal Colleges signed an agreement with the Department of Health to explore shorter forms of consultant training and various grading reforms (Department of Health Press Release 20 January, 2003). It is interesting to observe that another initiative, The Future Healthcare Workforce Project, pressing, for example, for a practitioner and assistant practitioner for older people, found a more listening ear for its work in its third report (Cochrane, Conroy, Crilly and Rogers, 2002) compared with those issued earlier.

Ordinary people are starting to do things differently as far as their health is concerned. Antipathy to the Thatcher-style health service consumer has perhaps dulled perceptions of the new consumerism of an educated and informed internet generation that is now emerging. People are turning to complementary therapies for a widening range of ailments, for holistic care and for enhancements in wellbeing. The chain stores and chemists are re-positioning themselves to create and supply a new kind of demand for high street health care. A one stop shop for eye care, foot care, back care, with massage, reflexology, cholesterol testing, and antismoking programmes, makes an uncomfortable comparison with the old-style doctor's surgery, and perhaps even competes in some aspects with the more modern group practice or health centre. The private health insurance sector is still there, presenting itself sometimes as directly supporting the NHS by taking patients off NHS waiting lists. A generational effect is also important in loosening and liberating ideas. A majority of the NHS workforce now probably has little clear memory of the NHS before the Thatcher reforms, and those who can recall life before 1948 are becoming fewer. Perhaps it is not surprising that alongside new ways of working, ideas about new ways of organising – public interest corporations, mutuals, different kinds of partnerships and franchising – are also being debated.

What then is to come for the health workforce? We can expect to see a narrowing of differences between those working in health and in social care and moves towards a new sense of collective identity in the new workplaces and the new network organisations supporting them. We can expect flexible working practices and new career routes, supported, for the younger generation, by very different initial education and training – much of it shared. We can expect that patients and public will demand to participate much more fully and directly in improving their own health and wellbeing and in shaping services – and that there will be educational and development opportunities for them as well as for those in the paid workforce. In the present climate, it does seem that government's pursuit of an altogether new kind of workforce for a new kind of public service is pushing at an already half-open door. But is this really so?

The essays in this book

The authors in this book – all specialists in their fields – offer glimpses of a variety of settings and contexts of health care and the way in which they have been changing. Many of the chapters were written in the midst of the changes just described, in some cases calling on research that took place before Labour's impetus for modernisation took very firm root. With their grasp of policy change and knowledge of the contemporary scene, contributors have been encouraged to speculate on just what the future might hold ten or perhaps 20 years down the line.

Rachel Lissauer's opening chapter casts doubt on how far the multitude of reforms described in this introduction can deliver progressive and truly patient-centred care. Involved as she was with the Institute for Public Policy Research's Changing Workforce Project until late 2002, she was in a unique position to reflect on this. The overall vision, she argues, is still too much a matter of packaging care around a

clinical diagnosis rather than focusing on the needs of an ageing population or what she calls a 'continuing healing relationship'. She finds
little to persuade her of a determination to tackle health inequalities or
a clear sense of increasing the health and wellbeing of a community.

Lissauer's insistence that patients are co-producers of care finds a
ready echo in the next two chapters. Conventionally the workforce in
health has been taken to refer to the paid providers of care, not those
'on the receiving end' or their invisible and unpaid carers. Angela
Coulter charts and assesses just how far organised groups of patients
have come in making their voices heard nationally and locally and in
reshaping services both individually and collectively. Both official and
academic conceptualisations of the workforce in healthcare need to
expand to take this into account. The various policy moves to support
carers, as well as the Expert Patient Programme (Department of Health,
2001a), are steps in this direction. As yet, however, we are a long way
from planning the workforce in a manner that routinely acknowledges
that patients and health care professionals are co-producers of health
care and need help and support to acknowledge and build on this. The
chapter by Liz Forbat and Jeanette Henderson, offers important and
thoughtful cautions on what 'professionalisation' of carers might mean
for caring relationships. Yet they too would be likely to agree that
patients, patient support groups, carers and an interested and involved
public need to be seen, counted, acknowledged, encouraged and
planned for in an expanded notion of the health workforce in the
future.

Redrawing the boundaries within and across the health professions is
the theme of the next three chapters. Ailsa Cameron and Abigail
Masterson call on a series of projects, some commissioned before the
change of government in 1997 and others more recent. Focusing in the
main on allied health professions, they vividly show the unhappy join
between new roles and old mindsets and call for greater clarity in
competence, accountability and regulatory frameworks. How far an
evaluation of the government's Changing Workforce Programme
(Department of Health, 2002) will generate similar findings will be
interesting to see. Anne Williams takes a different tack. Pressures of
costs and numbers can push towards substituting nurses for doctors
rather than working to redefine roles to ensure both continuity in the
patient care experience and satisfying work for all. She reminds us that
new ways of working call for something more fundamental – a new
kind of identity – a new conception of self. Jenny Gallagher opens a
window on specialisation at the interface between medicine and

dentistry. On the one hand, there are the professional turf wars and expansions of jurisdiction that theorists of professions have long studied. On the other, there is the impact of NSFs, of EU developments and working hours legislation. External factors, she concludes, increasingly shape specialty boundaries. And whereas purely professionally-driven change fails to provide a satisfactory reconfiguration of the workforce, change that fails to involve the professions is equally problematic.

The boundary between professional and support roles is very much in the frame today. New kinds of assistants to doctors, new technical grades to help with the bottlenecks in diagnostic testing for example, new school-leaver entry routes building up experience and skills towards a pre-registration training, bridges between the conventionally professional and vocational preparations – all these are being actively pursued. But is it a case of 'right deed, wrong reason'? Carole Thornley has spent much time studying those in care assistant grades. She points to confusing titles, and a workforce, largely made up of women, whose maturity commitment and experience signal much more competency and skill than is formally acknowledged. Increasingly, care assistants are doing nursing work but their low pay puts them on the breadline and the lack of progression routes ensures they stay there. Her preferred future – a 'high road' where egalitarianism and efficiency go hand in hand requires a fundamental re-evaluation of nursing work and (echoes of Lissauer here) and a more holistic approach to care. Of all the contributors, she is the one most alert to the inequalities – particularly gender inequalities – that have long characterised the health workforce. Treatment of care assistants will provide a test case of how far government is prepared to go in creating more equal opportunities.

A further trend that cannot now be ignored is the rise of complementary and alternative medicine. Geraldine Lee-Treweek and Sarah Oerton trace growing demand and the softening of views of the medical establishment. But they also point to the obstacles to further incorporation of previously 'alternative' practitioners into the framework of NHS care and the deep problems of forging a common knowledge base with mainstream medicine.

Complementary therapists are also part of a pattern of shifts in high street health care. In the twenty-first century, what is the fate of the old-style family doctor? A GP himself, and close policy watcher with an independent think-tank, Stephen Gillam is well-placed both to predict what might happen next and what the resistances might be – as his chapter shows. A new kind of chemist's shop, where easy access, direct advice and prescribing is available from the pharmacist seems set to be the future for many of us. Alison Blenkinsopp and Christine Bond are in the midst of new research on innovation in pharmacy organisation. They trace the twists and turns of policy development. They also, in one of the chapters with a strong UK-wider remit, point to the growing argument that Scotland might have the best model here (Jafri, Jones, Taylor and Wakeling, 2003). Several authors question the place of thinking about prevention and public health in current change projects. Stephen Peckham and Erica Wirrmann give new developments close and critical attention in their chapter. Despite the identification of roles and competencies, is there enough real will and understanding to make it work? Will we get right this time the link between tackling health inequalities and working for social justice?

A small volume such as this cannot do justice to changes across so large and complex a workforce as that in the NHS. In a final chapter, Charlotte Sausman provides a sketch of the health workforce as a whole, a challenge that has rightly preoccupied the National Training Organisation – the results of whose more detailed work in mapping the workforce are shown in an Appendix. Sausman sets the book in the context of a broader range of drivers for change than found in earlier chapters. Scientific and technological advances will be important for workforce change and she summarises workforce implications of advances in genetics. She warns, however, that predictions often fail. Are we really, for example, going to see 10 per cent of surgical interventions undertaken by robots within a decade? With the help of 'informationists' will we be able to use information technology to bypass 25–30 per cent of what we now take to the GP? Developments in ICT, after all, have had a chequered history in the NHS. Sausman reminds us also, however, to look beyond the UK. International patterns of recruitment and global workforce moves have an impact, developments in nursing being a case in point.

Participants at the conference where some of the papers were first presented were charged with the task of setting out their hopes and their fears about the future workforce. Their fears were of fragmented and isolated efforts, of failure to address unanticipated consequences and defensive power plays on the part of those reluctant to change. Their hopes were for a healthier, more collaborative and less divided workforce in the future – working together towards those elusive goals of creating a healthier community and being truly patient-centred. A book like this can bring some of this into the open for discussion and debate amongst all the parties involved.

It remains to thank all those who made the production of this volume possible. The Policy Futures Project, funded by the Nuffield Trust and based at the Judge Institute for Management Studies at the University of Cambridge, provided the initial impetus for this book. Seven of the chapters here started life as papers at its conference in September 2002 – and benefited from comments from participants and from discussants Alison Kitson and Tom Smith.[3] Other contributors proved willing to join the enterprise at a much later date, and to adjust timetables and priorities to meet the tight deadlines of the book. I am grateful to them all and to Julie Stock of The Open University, who took on the task of finalising the manuscript with enthusiasm and care. For me, and I hope for readers of this volume, this work provides a new perspective on the challenges of change in the NHS workforce.

Notes

1. This phrase, much picked up in the media, was first used in a prime ministerial speech at the Labour Party Conference on 28 September 1999. For the full text, see *http://www.guardian.co.uk/lab99/Story/0,2763,202189,00.html* [Accessed on 23 June 2003].
2. As part of its Future Health Worker Project, The Institute for Public Policy Research held a seminar on 27 September 2002 on medical professionalism where a lecture by Sir Donald Irvine on the theme 'Patients, Doctors and the Public Interest' set out his ideas and a paper by Jane Salvage on New Professionalism was made available. See *http://www.ippr.org.uk/research/index.php?current=24&project=13* [Accessed on 23 June 2003]. See also Irvine (2003).
3. For a report on the conference, see *www.jims.cam.ac.uk/research/health/polfutures/polfutures_f.html* [Accessed on 23 June 2003].

References

Aldridge, R. and Stoker, G. (2002) *Advancing a New Public Service Ethos*, London: New Local Government Network.

Cochrane, D., Conroy, M., Crilly, T. and Rogers, J. (2002) *The Future Healthcare Workforce*. The Third Report, Richmond-upon-Thames: Chamberlain Dunn Associates.

Davies, C. (2002) *From Conception to Birth: a policy analysis of the NHS University*, London: Nuffield Trust, 16.

Department of Health (1997) *The New NHS. Modern. Dependable.* Cm 3807, London: The Stationery Office.

Department of Health (1999) *Making a Difference; a strategy for nursing, midwifery and health visiting*, London: Department of Health.

Department of Health (2000a) *A Health Service of All the Talents: developing the NHS Workforce. Consultation document on the review of workforce planning*, London: Department of Health.

Department of Health (2000b) *The NHS Plan. A plan for investment. A plan for reform*, London: Department of Health.

Department of Health (2001a) *The Expert Patient Programme. A new approach to chronic disease management in the 21st century*, London: Department of Health.

Department of Health (2001b) *Working Together – Learning Together: a framework for lifelong learning for the NHS*, London: Department of Health.

Department of Health (2001c) *Learning from Bristol. The Report of the Public Inquiry into children's heart surgery at the Bristol Royal Infirmary 1984–1995*. Cm 5207(1), London: The Stationery Office.

Department of Health (2002) *Changing Workforce Programme. New ways of working in health care*, London: Department of Health.

House of Commons (2001) Select Committee on Public Administration. Seventh Report *Making Government Work: the emerging issues* [online], House of Commons. Available from: *http://www.publications.parliament.uk/pa/cm200001/cmselect/cmpubadm/94/9402.htm* [Accessed 24 June 2003].

Irvine, D. (2003) *The Doctor's Tale: professionalism and public trust*, Abingdon: Radcliffe Medical Press.

Jafri, T., Jones, R., Taylor, D. and Wakeling, M. (2003) *Future Partnerships. Primary Care in 2020?*, London: Department of Practice and Policy, School of Pharmacy, University of London.

Kendall, L. (2001) *The Future Patient*, London: Institute for Public Policy Research.

Kendall, L. and Harker, L. (eds) (2002) *From Welfare to Well-being: the future of social care*, London: Institute for Public Policy Research.

Lissauer, R. and Kendall, L. (eds) (2002) *New Practitioners in the Future Health Service*, London: Institute for Public Policy Research.

Lister, R. (2001) 'New Labour: a study in ambiguity from a position of ambivalence', *Critical Social Policy*, 21, 4, 425–7.

NHS University (2002) *Learning for Everyone. A Development Plan for NHSU*, London: Department of Health.

Powell, M. (2000) 'New Labour and the Third Way in the British Welfare State: a new and distinctive approach?', *Critical Social Policy*, 7, 1, 39–60.

Royal College of Physicians (2000) *Hospital Doctors under Pressure: new roles for the health care workforce* [online], Royal College of Physicians. Available from: *http://www.rcplondon.ac.uk/pubs* [Accessed on 23 June 2003].

1

Delivering a Patient-Centred Service: Reforming Professional Roles[1]

Rachel Lissauer

Introduction

Since the publication of the NHS Plan in 2000, the government has consistently presented reforms to working practices as being critical to the process of modernising the health service. Whether or not it has considered itself to be working for or against professional interests in this process has varied. At certain times and to certain audiences ministers have talked of the need to shatter 'old-fashioned demarcations' (Department of Health, 2000a: para 2.17) – hinting at the need to overcome the vested interests of the health service professions. At other times workforce reforms have been presented as part of the aim to move towards a stronger human resources agenda: building a service that values staff, allows them to maximise their potential and that enhances the attractiveness of an NHS career (Department of Health, 2002a). In all cases, however, reform of working practices is portrayed as being central to the broad project at the heart of the Government's agenda: that of achieving a 'patient-centred' health system.

Alongside policy imperatives, there has been a range of other powerful drivers of change. Most notable in prompting innovation in clinical roles has been the ongoing professionalisation of nursing and other health care professions (HCPs). Since the development of 'new nursing', education and philosophy has sought to prepare nurses for demanding and autonomous roles (Walby *et al.*, 2002). The 1970s saw the informal development of clinical nurse specialist roles in areas such as infection control, tissue viability, stoma care, continence. Nurse practitioners in primary care developed first in the 1980s – offering services to groups previously not covered by general practitioners (GPs), such as the homeless, or providing an alternative service to GPs

(Humphris, 2000). Whilst less publicised, advanced roles have also been developed by radiographers, occupational therapists, dieticians, speech and language therapists, physiotherapists, chiropodists and other HCPs (ScHARR, 1998).

During the 1990s the introduction of the EU Working Time Directive, which began to limit the time that doctors in training were spending on the wards, acted as a powerful catalyst for government to recognise and promote the roles that many nurses and HCPs were already undertaking. An effort to permit 'flexibility' of roles and of the division of labour between NHS workers has been at the heart of Labour's agenda for workforce reform. Under the banner of 'changing the way staff work', for example, the NHS Plan announced plans to extend the numbers of nurses to be trained in prescribing (Department of Health, 2000a). It promoted the development of therapist consultant posts as well as reinforcing a commitment to the creation of nurse, midwife and health visitor consultants that had already been stated. NHS Direct and nurse-led primary medical services represent the growing acceptability of nurse-led care, particularly in a primary care setting. In all areas of the health service, the pressure of increased activity and staff shortages have proven to be a spur for considerable innovation. Emergency units facing bed shortages, for example, have found ways of using the skills of occupational therapists and physiotherapists and specialist GPs to treat patients in medical assessment units – thereby reducing waiting times and emergency admissions (Borrill and Harrison, 2002).

Operating theatres seeking to maximise efficiency have developed roles of surgical assistants and operating department technicians who have now become integral members of surgical teams. Wider usage of protocols to change working practices was heralded alongside moves for greater inter-professional education and the establishment of the Changing Workforce Programme. This programme was intended to spread best practice and implement changes in working practices at the local level (Department of Health, 2000b).

Viewed against the history of the NHS as a service in which professions have often closely guarded their boundaries of practice, these developments appear highly progressive. Yet the development of new roles and the shifting of tasks between different practitioners are not progressive measures in themselves. They are likely to be driven by a combination of financial, practical and service considerations. The question that must constantly be asked is: do these measures improve the way that patients experience health and healthcare? Shifting roles or responsibilities may or may not bring about a change in how practitioners and patients relate to one another – fostering a greater sense of involvement and ownership from patients in their own health. Likewise, there is no inevitability that delegating tasks between different elements of the workforce will reduce the problems of fragmentation of services or improve the safety of the treatments that patients receive. It may or may not mean that professionals spend more time with patients and provide the support or personalised attention needed. Changing roles and delegating tasks may mean that existing services can be perpetuated in the face of acute staff shortages, when real innovation would involve questioning existing patterns of service provision.

This chapter suggests that new light may be shed on the future direction of workforce configuration and professional values, by asking explicitly: what changes in working practices will help to ensure the delivery of patient-centred care? The understanding upon which this chapter is based is that a high-quality, patient-centred health system will:

- *promote health and well-being* – an under-valued but core feature of the patient-centred health system is that its orientation is towards ensuring that a person's health is maintained and promoted rather than treating symptoms or a disease;
- *provide timely and convenient access to services* – quick access to care is both patients' key concern and critical to improving health outcomes and overall efficiency;
- *offer integrated and seamless care* – patient-centred care emerges where different tiers of the health system and different sectors operate smoothly together in response to the inter-connected needs of the patient;
- *inform and empower patients* – a patient-centred health system is one in which high quality information is offered at every stage in the patient's journey and those patients who want to participate actively in their care are able to become genuine partners in decision-making.

Many governments have attempted to implement structural reforms as a means of embedding some or all of these characteristics of patient-centred care. However, the basis for taking the workforce as the starting point for this paper is that many of these structural reforms, from the internal market to the formation of Primary Care Trusts, have failed fundamentally to affect the critical relationship between patients and practitioners. Beginning with these relations and questioning how policies can allow these relations to develop, offers an alternative and a more fulfilling policy agenda.

Promoting health and well-being

Historically, as has been widely acknowledged, our health system has focused on treating and managing disease, rather than on promoting, restoring and preserving health. There are numerous possible reasons for this concentration on the symptoms of disease rather than the person and their health needs. Commentators point to the dominance of the medical profession in defining the scope and structure of health services; the drive of scientific and technological discovery towards ever more complex healthcare interventions or the influence of the pharmaceutical industry whose interest lies in the medicalisation of healthcare.

Whatever reason is highlighted, the result of a disease rather than health orientation is that the health service has often failed to recognise how far a person's experience of health and ill health is mediated by the other elements of their life, whether these are economic and social status, family circumstances, ethnicity or religion. Patients' needs have tended to be classified and packaged on the basis of a clinical diagnosis (Vaughan, 2002), with less tangible requirements that cannot be captured by a clinical diagnosis viewed as being beyond the realm of the NHS. Public health is the area of healthcare that has been most ready to highlight and to tackle the economic and social determinants of ill-health. But it has historically been under-resourced and under-valued. The public health approach – recognising the person as embedded within a family, neighbourhood and cultural setting – has been slow to permeate the thinking, practice and structures of the rest of the medical world.

The danger, if this focus continues, is that we will continue to miss opportunities for preventing illness. The number of years that the future population of over 65s can expect to spend in good health will be strongly affected by measures introduced now to minimise avoidable risk factors. Recent estimates suggest that high cholesterol, mainly due to diet, accounts for 43 per cent of coronary heart disease (CHD) and smoking accounts for just over 20 per cent (McPherson *et al.*, 2002). The International Union for Health Promotion and Education (1999) suggests that 25 per cent of all cancers are preventable through public health measures.

We know that these risk factors are closely linked to life-style and environmental factors, particularly socio-economic status. Analysis by the Department of Health has indicated that if all social classes were to match the incidences of limiting long standing illness found in the highest social class, hospital admission rates would fall by 6 per cent (Wanless, 2002). Without greater focus of current resources including, critically, human resources, in health improvement and in attempts to reduce health inequality – opportunities for improving quality of life and potentially for substantially reducing demand on health services will be lost.

Many have advocated a more ecological and holistic approach to health. In 1976, McKeown demonstrated that the greatest improvements in mortality rates had occurred before the introduction of modern drugs and surgical interventions (McKeown, 1976). Subsequently, the Royal Commission on the NHS concluded that 'on the basis of past experience, a substantial improvement in national and community health is more likely to be achieved by preventive measures' (Royal Commission on the NHS, 1979).

During the 1980s, the relationships between individual health and physical, social and environmental factors were underplayed. The emphasis was firmly on promoting good health as an individual responsibility (Wistow, 2001). 'Health variations' were only acknowledged towards the end of the last Conservative administration. So it was notable that Labour, elected in 1997, made considerable strides towards recognising the link between the individual and social causes of ill health. The White Paper *Saving Lives* emphasised the complex interaction between a person's genetic make-up and the behaviour of individuals and social, economic and environmental factors in the community (Department of Health, 1999). Area-based initiatives such as Health Action Zones have attempted to integrate health into wider, community regeneration.

The Wanless Report (the most significant attempt yet to define the necessary levels of expenditure on the health service in order to meet anticipated levels of demand) offered further political impetus towards preventative measures. The review constructed scenarios exploring how different drivers of cost might impact on the use and delivery of the health service in 20 years time. The core difference in health outcomes between the *fully engaged* scenario (best health outcomes and lowest expenditure) and the *solid progress* scenario (health outcomes and expenditure continue along current lines) is not explained by activities in the health service, but by public and patients' responses to health. The fully engaged scenario is stated as only being likely to come about with a step change in the way public health is viewed, resourced and delivered nationally (Wanless, 2002).

However, despite these positive policy initiatives, the reality is that the overwhelming focus of policy continues to be the health *service*. Wanless made no reference to the way in which the necessary re-channelling of attitudes or resources might be achieved and the implications for the workforce of delivering the step-change required.

One immediate hurdle is the lack of a clear sense of responsibility for the well-being of the members of a community shared by all those professionals working for a specific geographically defined population. Although different services such as an intermediate care centre and a hospital may recognise their interdependencies, the health system as a whole provides little incentive for those working in health, education, or social services to take a unified focus on maintaining their populations' health and well-being. A PCT and local authority population (where the boundaries of these authorities are coterminous) could represent this type of geographical community, however the development of PCTs has not happened together with a commitment to greater joint training and working or workforce planning between those involved in health and social care, housing, education, police services and community regeneration. Public and professional imaginations have by no means been captured by a sense of association with an organisation (such as the PCT) responsible for maintaining, promoting and restoring health.

Even those health professionals already most closely linked to the community often face hurdles in trying to move away from a traditional medical model of care fully to implement the public health agenda. Health visitors who attempt to shift from ritualised contact with children – centred on measuring the child's growth and development – can find themselves inhibited by 'rules' about professional practice and inflexible child public health programmes. Community pharmacists involved in public health measures may have little or no training in how mortality and morbidity are affected by socio-economic circumstances, race and gender. The Royal College of General Practitioners and the Faculty of Public Health Medicine (2001) have suggested that GPs may lack the skills and capacity necessary to deliver their part of the public health function.

The challenge of providing a 'health orientated' NHS goes even beyond the substantial endeavour of raising skills in and the profile of health promotion. Underpinning this endeavour is the recognition that experiences of health and illness are mediated by the other elements of a person's life: a challenge to the biomedical understanding of health and illness. The logical outcome of this recognition is a substantial shift in focus towards those aspects of professional practice that, in hospital or in a health centre, contribute to patients' experiences but cannot necessarily be measured on the basis of completed episodes of care. These include, for example, the level of emotional support provided to patients, the manner in which patients were treated, the time spent explaining and discussing with patients their condition and treatment process. Historically, aptitude or ability to meet these needs, whilst often demonstrated, has not been rewarded. One indication is the poor remuneration of nurses, therapists, health care assistants and others associated with 'caring' roles by comparison to doctors (see Thornley, Chapter 8). The primacy attached to rapid interventions as opposed to the provision of long-term and low intervention measures is also reflected by the hierarchical structure within the medical profession. Status within medicine, as indicated by merit awards, private practice opportunities and research funding, often appears to be greatest in specialties such as surgery where the presenting problem appears to be most readily affected by biomedical, physical intervention (Salvage, 2002).

Timely access to convenient services

The move towards a health promoting NHS can only ever be pursued alongside a drive towards more timely and convenient access to health services. Currently, the most frustrating experience of the NHS is that of waiting: waiting for a doctor's appointment, waiting to see a specialist, waiting in the hospital or for diagnostic tests and waiting to be discharged (Kendall, 2001). Reducing the time that patients spend waiting for access to a GP or waiting for specialist treatment has been the primary target for successive health ministers and, as expectations continue to rise, there is no indication that in future this pressure will ease.

In addition to quicker care, people continue to want and expect more convenient access to health professionals. Patients want access to GPs outside traditional working hours (Cabinet Office, 2000) so that it does not impinge on their working life and to arrange appointment and operation dates around holidays, work commitments or other events that need to be planned in advance. The government has, rightly, acknowledged that expanding the workforce is imperative if demands for quicker and easier access are to be met whilst pressures to reduce working hours for junior doctors continue to bite. Yet in the meantime, the pace at which professional roles are changing is increasing. Health professionals are entering education and training in greater numbers whilst at the same time career pathways are becoming ever more fluid and relations between the different professions open to negotiation.

In primary care, nurses' potential role as the 'first port of call' for health services is gradually becoming accepted. The BMA now acknowledges that doctors will no longer be seen as the sole gatekeepers to the care that the NHS provides (British Medical Association, 2002). The reality is that nurse practitioners have long played a prominent role in primary care and nurses already act as the first port of call for patients through walk-in centres and NHS Direct, a service that is expected to manage 30 million calls a year by 2008 (Department of Health, 2002b). So the notion of nurses as gatekeepers to the health service is not necessarily novel. Writ large, however, a situation in which senior nurses become generalists in primary care represents a noticeable contrast to the traditional career pathways for nursing, particularly in secondary care, that have tended towards specialist care (Williams, 2001; see also Williams, Chapter 8).

These developments occur alongside moves for GPs towards formal specialisation and expansion of the range of specialist services provided outside hospitals. GPs have long pursued specialist interests: individual partners within group practices have taken a lead in a particular specialty with their skills maintained through a weekly clinical assistant post in a local hospital. So far, the process has been informal with little or no attempt to co-ordinate professional interest with population need. The NHS Plan's published targets for registering 1000 GPs with special interest by 2004 provided a pressure to more fully explore how GPs with special interests are trained, remunerated and fit into the network of providers within a health economy.

If current innovators can be taken as an example of where the future might lead, many diagnostic procedures, minor surgery and outpatient consultations currently being performed in hospital may, in future, be GP provided. In Bradford, GPs now carry out much minor surgery, almost all elective endoscopy, gastroscopy and cystoscopy, a wide range of chronic disease management and extensive triage work. Patients now wait two to three weeks rather than six to seven months for endoscopy procedures. Evaluations indicate that 30–40 per cent of patients with ear, nose and throat problems usually referred to specialists could be seen by a GP with a specialist interest (GPwSI) (Sanderson, Limber, Eldret and Harrison, 2003).

This trend is not only a challenge to the generalist orientation that has defined general practice, but also to the traditional relationship between GP specialists and consultants. Whilst many consultants may be only too happy for competent GPs to take some of the burden of their routine outpatient consultations and investigative procedures, the crux will come with pay negotiations and the value that is placed on the specialist work of GPs (see Gillam, Chapter 10). Too generous a settlement may de-stabilise the balance between generalism and specialism amongst GPs, provoke resentment from secondary care specialists and threaten the cost-effectiveness of the health system: too little and the notion of GPwSIs will be a non-starter.

There are several potential outcomes of an increasing mix of generalism and specialism in both the nursing and general practice career structures. One is that, in future, training, job titles and pay may come to be negotiated between all those acting at the same level of specialisation rather than within professional silos. So a senior nurse practitioner acting as the 'gatekeeper' would be expected to demonstrate a similar level of competency in performing initial diagnoses as a GP registrar and would have similar prescribing rights based on this level of knowledge and experience. Modifications of regulation and remuneration would need to follow. Another interesting possibility is that, as the boundary between generalism and specialism shifts, the key provider unit may increasingly become the network of providers who span different tiers of the health service rather than the GP practice or hospital. So, for example, a network of urology providers within a health economy including district nurses providing catheter care, the GPwSI providing a prostate assessment clinic and diagnostics, the cancer nurse specialist and secondary care consultants – might all undertake continued professional development together, pool equipment and resources, develop shared management arrangements or even work on the basis of a shared contract with the PCT.

Evolution of roles in primary care must be seen alongside developments in secondary care. In all NHS Trusts clinical nurse specialists, nurse consultants and nurse practitioners now play pivotal, albeit highly varied, roles. The next major challenge facing professionals working in secondary care is likely to arise from the separation of emergency and elective work and the continued pressure to increase the amount of day case surgery. Diagnostic and Treatment Centres

(DTCs), providing low risk, high volume elective surgery and diagnostic procedures are intended by government both to bring down waiting times and to be test-beds for reconfiguring working practices. DTCs will be expected to make the most of skills in order to ensure maximum efficiency.

Re-thinking access

So far, discussion has focused on the accepted notion that accessing health care for the patient involves being granted the time for a face-to-face encounter. Currently, a visit is often the only legitimate format for care and the only form that is compensated and measured in the health care world as 'productivity'. A patient-focused perspective may lead us to question this dogma. As access to electronic communication increases and as the disease burden shifts towards chronic diseases, the concept that face-to-face encounters are the only means of providing care may need to be challenged.

Patients want relief from suffering and uncertainty, knowledge about what is wrong and about what can be done to change and manage an outcome. Although much of the time this can only be provided through visits, many needs could and should be met through other forms of care. The Institute of Medicine has called for a new 'rule' of continuous access to information, care and support, 24 hours a day, 365 days a year (Institute of Medicine, 2001). The suggestion is not that people necessarily need more visits to health professionals, but that they would benefit from having a wider range of ways to communicate with practitioners and with other patients.

This may take the form of greater use of telemedicine and home-testing kits so that, for example, asthma sufferers can measure their peak flow rate and blood pressure and people with diabetes can measure their blood glucose and can communicate this over the internet to professionals without the need for an appointment. It may take the form of increased electronic communication between practitioners and their patients or more regular use of internet chat rooms. In many cases the technology that would allow for more convenient access to professional advice for patients exists, but has not been adapted as a routine part of practitioners' work. If the NHS is to keep pace with the increasing plurality of ways of communicating and finding information then the existing situation in which many health professionals have only limited access to a computer must be challenged.

Integrated and seamless services

Where patients are asked about their experiences of care one of the over-riding factors mentioned repeatedly is a lack of co-ordination (Kendall, 2001). Surveys indicate that UK patients are more likely to report a lack of organisation of their care than patients in other countries. In one study, 37 per cent of patients in the UK said their care was poorly organised, compared to 18 per cent in Switzerland, 20 per cent in Germany and 26 per cent in the USA. Twenty-three per cent of UK patients said that staff gave them conflicting information (Coulter and Cleary, 2001). Qualitative work supports these findings: patients feel that they have to struggle to get all parts of the system to work together effectively and to get different parts of the system to share and communicate the information they hold about the same person (Edwards, 2001). These problems are often even more pronounced when a person comes into contact with a range of different agencies from different sectors.

A lack of integration between agencies or between practitioners in one institution is often attributed to the difficulties of inter-professional working: differences in language, culture, values and history that inhibit effective understanding and communication. The boundaries created by differences in training and background may have become even greater over recent decades, as the healthcare work-force has become increasingly specialised. There are now 25 sub-specialties within the general physician specialty and the Royal College of Nursing has 80 special interest forums. Whilst specialisation is undoubtedly necessary as a response to increasing levels of detailed knowledge and understanding, with it comes the danger of an absence of any holistic sense of the needs of the person or any one person able to bring the range of different professional perspectives together from the patients' point of view.

Co-ordination, however, is a slippery concept. There are noticeable differences between a 'light touch' form of co-ordination in which sep-arate groups try to take the activities of other groups into account and a somewhat deeper form of collaboration, involving working together to achieve something that neither agency nor professional could achieve alone. So, inter-professional boundaries can be confronted, on the one hand, through relatively painless attempts to raise awareness of the activities of different professionals. On the other hand, breaking down boundaries can also be pursued through far tougher measures that include, at the most extreme, the 'merging' of separate professions or agencies. In almost every case it is possible to identify similar tensions arising from these proposals. Concerns centre around the question of identity and its potential loss through immersion in a wider and less well-defined group.

One of the key debates for the future is likely to centre on the value or otherwise of developing and expanding the shared elements of knowledge and skills between different professional groups. Hitherto, professional status has often been linked to claims of a distinctive approach, shared by all members of a profession and grounded in a unique theoretical perspective. In future the emphasis may shift away from distinctiveness and towards an interest in shared competencies and aspects of knowledge between those professionals working within a provider network or involved in the care of a particular patient group and towards an increasing permeability between separate professional career pathways.

Recent developments begin to signal a move in this direction. Local initiatives are seeking to develop new types of workers whose skills cut across traditional professional divides. The Isle of Wight Healthcare NHS Trust, for example, has amalgamated the roles of nursing assistants, physiotherapy helpers and occupational therapy helpers to improve services for patients with long term rehabilitation needs. The government is keen to promote shared learning as part of the experience of all undergraduates training to enter the health professions. St George's Medical School and Southampton University are pioneering substantial elements of shared teaching for first year undergraduates. The outcomes and lessons of such projects will continue to be important in shaping the speed and direction of these developments.

'Patient-focused care' projects

During the early 1990s, following the *NHS and Community Care Act* (1990) the management concepts of 'business process re-engineering' and 'patient-focused care' became used to describe the radical reconfiguration of services around the needs of the patient (Garside, 1993). The concept of re-designing care around the patient was developed and advocated by USA management consultants and was adopted by a range of Trusts including the Central Middlesex, St Helier, Kingston and Hillingdon. The characteristics of patient-focused care sites were the restructuring of services by regrouping staff and equipment; redesigning work by restructuring teams and multi-skilling the staff caring for patients and the development of care protocols for clinical conditions (National Health Service Executive, 1996).

The introduction of competition between trusts for patients was a key driver of these initiatives. A study of the introduction of patient-focused care in Kingston Trust notes that the attainment of Trust status brought with it the realisation that the hospital was in competition with 23 acute hospitals, all located within a 15-mile radius (Newman, 1997). A study of eight pilot sites in the UK notes the recurrence of 'the survival issues' as a motivation: hospitals discovered that they were in an over-bedded catchment area in which purchasers and patients demanded a more responsive service (National Health Service Executive, 1996).

Practice focused on intense analysis of patient experience and the ways in which these could be improved. The aims were to reduce delays due to poor co-ordination, fragmentation of services and the 'progression of faces' for the patient, time spent by clinical staff in non-clinical activities and the absence, for patients, of any one person with accountability for the patient experience. In asking why staff working practices had developed in such a way as to create this type of fragmentation, staff at Kingston reported it to be unrelated to legislation: staff work practices were set by professional boundaries and practice which were endowed with the power of legislation (Newman, 1997).

Some of the developments that had been occurring in these pilot sites were, meanwhile, being recorded and analysed in association with an independent group, funded by the National Health Service Executive (NHSE) called the Future Healthcare Workforce Programme. This group set out with the goal of identifying what, if they were going to design the workforce today for tomorrow's service, it would look like. A series of reports each developed a scenario for the future service including projections of the impact of changes in technology and drug therapy and then aimed to design the roles required to deliver high quality services to patients within these scenarios. Their conclusions were that, in most settings, the broad shape of the future workforce would be a structure containing three groups: specialist staff (consultants, GPs, senior registrars, specialist healthcare practitioners and clinical scientists), healthcare practitioners and junior doctors and healthcare assistants (Cochrane, Conroy, Crilly and Rogers, 2002).

The controversy generated by these reports centred on the implication that professional identities could simply be 'dissolved'. This notion conflicted with the project of professionalisation that nurses, amongst others, had been pursuing for many years. As such it was dismissed by many as another simplistic solution to the problem of nursing shortages. Yet the reality is that many of the measures adopted and used in these patient-focused sites: the development of protocols and the notion of a single, co-ordinator and point of contact for patients, for example, are widely applied as measures to reduce fragmentation and improve pathways of care role out within the wider health service. Deconstructing the series of processes that occur over the course of a single patient journey from, for example, referral from a GP to first outpatient appointment and identifying how to streamline this process is now a technique used in all modernisation initiatives being led by the government's Modernisation Agency.

The current policy approach is one of letting 'a thousand flowers bloom'. The Changing Workforce Programme, part of the Modernisation Agency, has a database of the 'new roles' that are in the process of being developed. Royal Colleges are proposing their own solutions. The Royal College of Physicians has expressed an interest in the further development of physicians' assistants (Royal College of Physicians, 1999). The physicians' assistant, as envisaged by the RCP might carry out a range of duties including: ordering and in some cases undertaking diagnostic tests; introducing intravenous cannulae, flushing cannulae and setting up IV lines as directed by medical staff and giving first doses of antibiotics and some other drugs. Some of these roles overlap with those proposed for the healthcare practitioner and those tasks that currently carried out by a nurse practitioner – yet the physicians' assistant would certainly be trained and would practice along the medical model.

The challenge will be to ensure that new roles, where they are developed, contribute towards streamlining and integrating the patients' pathway of care, rather than further adding to the fragmentation that already exists.

Informing and empowering patients

At the level of individual patients and practitioner relations – significant practical and cultural changes are needed if patients are to be treated as autonomous and involved individuals, rather than passive recipients of care.

The need to individualise patient care and to focus on the elements of quality that matter to patients has partly emerged out of a recognition that patient expectations have risen. Patients expect similar levels of personalised attention from the health service as they do from other types of service they receive in day to day life. Banks and retailers offer

24/7 instantly accessible personalised care and information. Patients make comparisons across different countries and different service sectors (Kendall, 2001). Individualised care is also a response to evidence of widespread dissatisfaction amongst patients with current levels of support, information and the involvement in decision-making.

The Picker/Commonwealth Program for Patient-Centred Care has been highly influential in highlighting the significance of communication, information and involvement in decision-making for patients' experiences. It aimed to explore patients' needs and concerns as patients' themselves define them (Beatrice, Parks Thomas and Biles, 1998). The Harvard team designed a patient feedback programme designed to find out what patients value about the experience of receiving healthcare and what they considered unacceptable (Edgman-Levitan and Cleary, 1996). This research programme resulted in the development of survey instruments designed to elicit reports from patients about concrete aspects of their experience.

The surveys and questionnaires developed using this methodology have subsequently been used to measure patient-centred care internationally. In all countries that have been surveyed the most commonly reported problems concerned communication of clinical issues. Patients recorded that they did not have enough say about treatment; had insufficient information in emergency rooms; were not given adequate explanation of test results or told adequately about the effects of their medication and treatment (Coulter, 2002; Coulter, Chapter 2). The implication is not simply that patients need more information: they often seek greater influence and involvement in the process of care although, of course, patients differ in the level and nature of involvement they seek with culture, age and stage of a person's condition all affecting their desire for engagement.

Within professional and policy circles the need to move away from treating patients as passive recipients of care is widely acknowledged. The GMC has now made communication skills the highest priority for the five year validation reports for existing doctors. Communication skills are becoming a core part of undergraduate training (Department of Health, 2000a). Yet medical education still operates under the shadow of a paternalistic era. Time is a scarce commodity and, since many patients often appear comfortable with a directive style, many clinicians see little need for change (Coulter, 2002). Even where doctors understand the importance of a patient-centred approach some evidence seems to suggest that this is seen as imparting information rather than building patients' own involvement and capabilities. Research into education for asthma patients shows that professionals tend to focus on what they believe patients need to know, such as the basic mechanisms of the disease and the correct choice of drugs, rather than attempting to help patients develop the skills they need to become effective managers of their condition (Clark and Gong, 2000). Professionals are irritated and threatened by the modern patient arriving 'armed' with internet diagnosis and treatment plan obtained from a website which, they argue, are often based on inaccurate or highly biased information (Sastry and Carrol, 2002). Coulter (2002) highlights the dangers of this wariness in fostering passivity, sapping self-confidence and reinforcing dependence on health professionals.

By contrast, where patients are actively involved in care, either through self-management or shared decision-making, the health benefits are clear. The Chronic Disease Self-Management Course (CDSMC), for example, was shown to lead to an increase in self-efficiency (perception of disease control), reduced health distress and fatigue, reduction in anxious mood, improved symptom control and shortness of breath and improved mental health (Fishwick and Letts, 2002). There is now a large body of evidence showing that educational interventions which enhance people's self-efficacy can reduce demand for medical intervention, leading to cost savings (Vickery and Lynch, 1995). Responding to these findings, and fostering a sense of patients as partners or 'co-producers' in their own healthcare, is not easy. It places new requirements on professionals. It also involves the development of a new conceptual framework as well as new skills.

Where professionalism is based on the notion of a specialised knowledge and skills that the public will wish to use (Merrison, 1975), common access to public information about health issues can appear to challenge the essence of professional status. Fostering a new form of patient–professional relations requires a new understanding of professionalism that enables professionals to recognise the knowledge and expertise that patients' bring to their own health and healthcare and to admit to the limits of their own certainty. This form of knowledge has to be accepted as growing and developing from the fusion of expertise and experience, the formal and the intuitive (Davies, 1996). It rests on widespread acceptance of an approach to health care knowledge that values things other than the formal and abstract, the scientific and measurable (ibid). Training and education are critical in instilling this approach to the variety of knowledges that different professionals and patients bring.

The onus is not just on health professionals. If clinicians are to be honest – sharing risks and admitting mistakes – patients must be prepared to take increased responsibility for the decisions that are made. The *British Medical Journal* has called for a new 'contract' or 'compact' between patients and doctors, where doctors share greater information on the basis that patients begin to understand the risks and decisions being made (*British Medical Journal*, 324, 6 April 2002: Editor's Choice). This type of contract, negotiated between patients and professionals, may be particularly helpful for patients with a chronic condition whose own actions will have an important bearing on their health outcomes.

Conclusion

The chapter has begun to draw together some of the many implications that the delivery of patient-centred care may have for the healthcare workforce. It points to the need for new skills from the future health workforce. In a health service geared towards the promotion of health and wellbeing, practitioners will need an understanding of the root causes of ill health and the relationship between an individual patient's needs and those of the wider community (Bissell and Jesson, 2002). They will be required to work collaboratively, forming strong links between the different professionals involved in treatment of the same patient group. Health practitioners will need to become skilled in techniques to share decision-making and communicate the risks as well as the benefits associated with different interventions. They will need the capability, the time and equipment to use new forms of technology to communicate with patients beyond the face-to-face encounter. The theme underpinning these suggestions is that the dominance of the biomedical understanding of health and traditional understandings of professionalism need to be challenged. The starting point must be a willingness to explore the characteristics of a patient-centred health system and to work with the people, rather than the structures, needed to provide it.

Note

1. This chapter draws on ideas developed through the Institute for Public Policy Research (ippr) *Future Health Worker* project and recently published. See Liz Kendall and Rachel Lissauer *The Future Health Worker*, London: ippr.

References

Beatrice, D. F., Parks Thomas, C. and Biles, B. (1998) 'Grant Making with an Impact: the Picker/Commonwealth patient-centred care programme', *Health Affairs*, 17, 1, 236–44.

Bissell, P. and Jesson, J. (2002) 'Health Inequalities: a neglected area of pharmacy policy and practice', *Pharmaceutical Journal*, 269, 7227, 819–821.

British Medical Association (2002) *A New Model for NHS Care.* Health Policy and Economic Research Unit Discussion Paper 9, London: British Medical Association.

Borrill, Z. and Harrison, B. (2002) 'Organisational Issues in Acute Medical Care', *Clinical Medicine*, 2, 2, 161–4.

Cabinet Office (2000) *Delivery of Public Services, 24 Hours and Day, Seven Days a Week (24x7) People's Panel*, London: The Stationery Office.

Clark, N. and Gong, M. (2000) 'Management of Chronic Disease by Practitioners and Patients: are we teaching the wrong things?', *British Medical Journal*, 320, 572–5

Cochrane, D., Conroy, M., Crilly, T. and Rogers, J. (2002) *The Future Healthcare Workforce. Third Report*, Richmond-upon-Thames: Chamberlain Dunn Associates.

Coulter, A. (2002) *The Autonomous Patient. Ending paternalism in medical care*, London: The Nuffield Trust.

Coulter, A. and Cleary, P. (2001) 'Patients' Experiences with Hospital Care in Five Countries', *Health Affairs*, 20, 244–52.

Davies, C. (1996) 'A New Vision of Professionalism', *Nursing Times*, 92, 46, 54–6, 13 November.

Department of Health (1999) *Saving Lives*, London: The Stationery Office.

Department of Health (2000a) *The NHS Plan: A Plan for Investment – a plan for Reform*, London: The Stationery Office.

Department of Health (2000b) *Investment and Reform for NHS Staff – taking forward the NHS Plan*, London: The Stationery Office.

Department of Health (2002a) *Human Resources in the NHS Plan. Consultation Paper*, London: The Stationery Office.

Department of Health (2002b) *Delivering the NHS Plan: next steps on investment, next steps on reform*, London: The Stationery Office.

Edgman-Levitan, S., and Cleary, P. D. (1996) 'What Information do Consumers Want and Need?', *Health Affairs*, 15, 42–56.

Edwards, L. (2001) *The Future of Healthcare: the patient perspective in England*, London: Institute for Public Policy Research.

Fishwick, S. and Letts, M. (2002) 'The "Lay" Person as Practitioner', in R. Lissauer and L. Kendall (eds) *New Practitioners in the Future Health Service*, London: Institute for Public Policy Research.

Garside, P. (1993) *Patient-focused Care: a review of seven sites in England on behalf of the NHSME*, unpublished.

Humphris, D. (2000) 'New Role Development: taking a strategic approach', in A. Masterson and D. Humphris, *Developing New Clinical Roles: a guide for health professionals*, Edinburgh: Churchill Livingstone.

Institute of Medicine (2001) *Crossing the Quality Chasm: a new health system for the 21st century*, Washington: National Academy Press.

International Union for Health Promotion and Education (1999) *The Evidence of Health Promotion Effectiveness: shaping public health in a new Europe*, Report for the European Commission, France: International Union for Health Promotion and Education.

Kendall, L. (2001) *The Future Patient*, London: Institute for Public Policy Research.

McKeown, T. (1976) *The Role of Medicine: dream, mirage or nemesis?*, Leeds: Nuffield Provisional Hospitals Trust.

McPherson, K., Britton, A. and Causer, L. (2002) *Coronary Heart Disease: estimating the impact of changes in risk factors*, London: The Stationery Office.

Merrison, A. (Chair) (1975) *Report of the Committee of Inquiry into the Regulation of the Medical Profession*, London: Her Majesty's Stationery Office.

National Health Service Executive (1996) *Progress with Patient – Focused Care in the UK*, Leeds: National Health Service Executive.

Newman, K. (1997) 'Towards a New Health Care Paradigm. Patient-focused care. The case of Kingston Hospital Trust', *Journal of Management in Medicine*, 11, 6, 357–71.

Royal College of General Practitioners and the Faculty of Public Health Medicine (2001) *Public Health in the New NHS Structures: the Primary Care perspective*, unpublished discussion paper.

Royal College of Physicians (1999) *Skill-mix and the Hospital Doctor*, London: Royal College of Physicians.

Royal Commission on the NHS (1979) *Report of the Royal Commission on the National Health Service*, London: Her Majesty's Stationery Office.

Salvage, J. (2002) *Rethinking Professionalism: the first step to patient-centred care?*, London: Institute for Public Policy Research.

Sanderson, D., Limber, G., Eldret, C. and Harrison, K. (2003) 'To the ENT Degree', *Health Service Journal*, 27 February 2003.

Sastry, S. and Carrol, P. (2002) 'Doctors, Patients and the Internet: time to grasp the nettle', *Clinical Medicine*, 2, 2, 131–3.

ScHARR (1998) *Exploring New Roles in Practice*, Sheffield: ScHARR.

Stewart, M. (2001) 'Toward a Global Definition of Patient-centred Care', *British Medical Journal*, 322, 24 February, 444–5.

Vaughan, B. (2002) 'The Intermediate Care Practitioner', in R. Lissauer and L. Kendall (eds), *New Practitioners in the Future Health Service*, London: Institute for Public Policy Research.

Vickery, D. M. and Lynch, W. C. (1995) 'Demand Management: enabling patients to use medical care appropriately', *Journal of Occupational and Environmental Medicine*, 7, 551–7.

Walby, S. and Greenwell, J., with Mackay, L. and Soothill, K. (2002) *Medicine and Nursing. Professions in a Changing Health Service*, London: Sage.

Wanless, D. (2002) *Securing our Future Health: taking a long-term view. Final report*, London: The Stationery Office.

Williams, A. (2001) 'Blurring the Boundaries: the nursing role in 2022', in *Health Trends Review*: Proceedings of a conference held at the Barbican Centre, London, 18–19 October.

Wistow, G. (2001) 'Modernisation, the NHS Plan and Healthy Communities', *Journal of Management in Medicine*, 15, 5.

2
An Unacknowledged Workforce: Patients as Partners in Healthcare[1]

Angela Coulter

Introduction

The patient's role as a key player in producing health, coping with acute episodes of ill-health and managing chronic disease, is often ignored in discussions about health policy. The fact is that patients themselves and their carers provide the majority of healthcare. In this role they require training and support just like other members of the workforce. Strategies to strengthen and modernise the healthcare workforce will fail if they ignore the important role played by lay people.

Patients can play a distinct role in their own care by diagnosing their problem and caring for themselves (self-care), by choosing the most appropriate form of treatment for acute conditions in partnership with health professionals (shared decision-making), or by actively managing chronic diseases (self-management). Recognising these roles and seeking to strengthen them is fundamental to securing a more patient-centred approach to healthcare delivery, the central aim of the NHS Plan (Department of Health, 2000). This chapter looks at each of these roles in turn and considers how they can be supported and the barriers that must be overcome if the goal of a more patient-centred system is to be achieved.

Self-care

Self-care – actions that lay people take to recognise, treat and manage their own health problems independently of the medical system – is the most prevalent form of healthcare. Most of us cope with minor illnesses without recourse to professional help. We go to the chemist or take ourselves off to bed when we have coughs, colds, flu, headaches, stomach pain or other minor problems which make us feel miserable but which we know are not dangerous and are probably self-limiting. If we do feel the need for advice, the doctor is not necessarily the first person we turn to. In looking after themselves and their family members, lay people provide a far greater quantity of healthcare than do health professionals. Hannay used the metaphor of an iceberg to illustrate the point that health professionals, even those working in 'first contact' care such as general practice, see only a small fraction of the afflictions that could potentially trigger a consultation (Hannay, 1979). Estimates have suggested that a majority of medical care (perhaps as much as 85 per cent) is self-care (Vickery *et al.*, 1983).

There is a wealth of lay knowledge about illness and how to treat it and many people prefer to consult their family or friends before going to see a health professional (Popay and Williams, 1996). Nevertheless, GPs often feel besieged by patients who do not really need their help. They report that a relatively high proportion of their daily consultations are for conditions that people could treat themselves (Dunnell and Cartwright, 1972). There is a vicious circle at work here. Struggling to cope with the large numbers of patients who queue in their surgeries every day, few GPs have the time, or perhaps the inclination, to help their patients to help themselves. Instead, by providing tests and prescriptions for minor everyday illnesses they reinforce the notion that doctor input is necessary, and in the process undermine patients' confidence to cope with these problems themselves.

A variety of factors influences the decision to seek medical care, including ability to assess the problem and its severity, perceptions about the effectiveness of medical treatment, perceptions of one's own state of health, and feelings of confidence or self-efficacy. These perceptions are influenced by age, gender, educational level, cultural norms, social networks, co-morbidity and the attitudes of health care professionals. If health professionals act in a way that undermines people's coping skills, they can expect to see patients calling on their services with increasing frequency. On the other hand, if they could help their patients to help themselves they might be rewarded by fewer unnecessary consultations.

There is now a large body of evidence showing that educational interventions which enhance people's sense of self-efficacy can reduce the demand for medical intervention, leading to cost savings (Crow *et al.*, 1999). Studies carried out in North America confirm that information and public education can have an effect on health service utilisation. For example, in Idaho, a self-care manual describing what to do about common health problems was distributed to every household in the state and people were encouraged to phone a helpline if they wanted more advice. The originators of the programme claimed that it led to substantial improvements in the appropriate use of services (Kemper, 1997). A similar, much earlier, programme which distributed educational self-care manuals and a monthly newsletter to people living in Rhode Island, USA, resulted in statistically significant decreases of around 17 per cent in ambulatory visit rates (Vickery *et al.*, 1983). Comparable initiatives have been introduced elsewhere in the USA, with similar reported effects (Kieschnick, Adler and Jimison, 2002; Thompson, Gee and Larson, 2001).

Recently policy makers in the UK, concerned to secure best value for the resources expended on health care, have taken a number of initiatives to capitalise on this knowledge. These have aimed to educate patients about when to seek professional help and when it is not necessary. The promotion of self-care and appropriate use of health services was a main impetus behind the establishment of the government-funded telephone helpline, NHS Direct. NHS Direct was launched in 1998 to provide healthcare information and advice to the public in England and Wales through a telephone helpline and website. National coverage for the telephone service was achieved in November 2000. Staffed by nurses, it is the world's largest provider of telephone healthcare advice, handling more than half-a-million telephone calls and half-a-million internet visits every month. By 2006, it is expected to handle 16 million calls a year and to be the main gateway to out-of-hours care (Department of Health, 2003). The online service provides information on health conditions and treatments, healthy living, and details of local services. This is to be supplemented by a digital TV service to be launched in 2004. It is hoped that this will reach groups such as men and low-income families who are hard to reach by other means. Basic information is also available via touch screen information points in public libraries and other places.

Investment in these services is a key part of the strategy for managing demand in the NHS. By providing information to ensure that patients make appropriate use of services and by encouraging self-care, it is hoped that demand for GP services and outpatient visits will decline. The Wanless report, commissioned by the Treasury, was bold enough to put an estimate on the potential impact of this strategy:

> visits to GPs could decline by over 40 per cent and outpatient visits by 17 per cent as a result of increased self care ... for every £100 spent on encouraging self-care, around £150 worth of benefits can be delivered in return. (Wanless, 2002)

It remains to be seen if these ambitious targets will be achieved. An evaluation of the pilot sites, published in 2001, concluded that the telephone service 'is appreciated by callers and, to date, has not been unhelpful to other services' (Munro *et al.*, 2001). In January 2002, the National Audit Office was more bullish, estimating that the NHS Direct telephone service was off-setting around half of its running costs by encouraging more appropriate use of NHS services (National Audit Office, 2002).

Even if self-care did not result in a reduction in the use of health services, it would be worth supporting because of the strong desire among many people to help themselves and avoid over-dependence on doctors. The growing market in over-the-counter medicines is testimony to this, as is the huge popularity of complementary therapies. In 2001 people in the UK spent £1710 million in pharmacies on over-the-counter medicines (*http://www.pagb.net/*, accessed 19 May 2003). Much of this expenditure went on preparations for pain relief, skin treatments, coughs, colds and sore throats, and vitamin pills, but growth in sales of hay fever remedies and pills, patches and other preparations to aid smoking cessation reflect the trend towards making a wider range of products available direct from the pharmacist instead of requiring them to be prescribed by the doctor.

Total expenditure on complementary therapies was estimated at £450 million in 1998 (Thomas, Nicholl and Coleman, 2001). The typical European user of complementary medicine is young or middle-aged, female, well-educated and health-conscious (Coulter and Magee, 2003). Complementary therapy users are often looking for help with problems such as back pain, asthma, arthritis, migraine, menopausal symptoms, and anxiety or stress, for which conventional medicine has been tried and found wanting. Complementary therapies are also used by people with life-threatening diseases such as cancer and AIDS (Barnett, 2002). Many users of complementary therapies do not tell their doctors that they are simultaneously seeking help from alternative practitioners or taking remedies available from chemists or health food shops. The fact that they seek out alternatives emphasises the general reluctance to play the role of passive victim in response to health problems. Most of us want to feel that we have some control over what happens to us and self-help gives us the sense of empowerment that conventional medicine often fails to acknowledge.

Knowledge represents power in medical care just as in any other field. Patients' demands for more and better information about health problems and treatments are indicative of a desire to redress the power imbalance in medical consultations. This need for more information can best be addressed by incorporating information provision into everyday medical practice. For example, an American group, the Centre for Information Therapy, has been established to promote the idea that information can have a therapeutic role in helping patients to manage their symptoms or health problems. They are encouraging clinicians to offer an 'information therapy' prescription to the patient or carer at every clinic visit, for every medical test or surgical procedure, for every hospitalisation and for continuing care (Centre for Information Therapy, 2002).

Educational initiatives such as these are a good idea, but unless they are accompanied by a change in the way health professionals respond to patients they are unlikely to have a sustained impact. It is understandable that doctors are reluctant to challenge their patients about wasting time, but failure to suggest self-help alternatives to medical treatment only perpetuates the problem. Reaching for the prescription pad because this appears to be what the patient wants rather than because a prescription is necessary only stores up problems for the future (Cockburn and Pit, 1997). Unfortunately this is often the easiest and quickest way to end a consultation, but the net effect is to increase the total workload, thus compounding the problem.

Shared decision making

It used to be assumed that doctors and patients shared the same goals and that only the doctor was sufficiently informed and experienced to decide what should be done. Patients are now much more likely to challenge the notion that 'doctor knows best'. Failures in communication of information about illness and treatment are the most frequent source of patient dissatisfaction (Coulter and Cleary, 2001). A majority of patients want to be involved in decisions about their care. In a survey of 8000 people in eight different European countries 74 per cent of respondents felt they should have a say in treatment choices, but many were critical of the availability of information to support informed choice (Coulter and Magee, 2003).

Not everyone wants to be actively involved in choosing treatments. Certain patients, especially older ones, may prefer a paternalistic consulting style. For example, a study by a British GP found that his patients were more satisfied when he adopted a 'directing' style than when he emphasised 'sharing' (Savage and Armstrong, 1990). Even if some people are more comfortable with the old-fashioned approach, there are signs of increasing frustration with the paternalistic attitudes frequently encountered in the NHS. In a survey of 2249 patients discharged from hospital in the UK, 20 per cent said staff did not always treat them with respect and dignity, 29 per cent said that doctors sometimes talked about them in front of them as if they were not there, and 59 per cent said they were not given enough say in treatment decisions (Coulter, 2001).

Desire for participation has been found to vary according to age, educational status, disease severity and cultural background. A study of 256 American cancer patients found that younger patients were more likely to want active participation in decisions about their care, but a substantial proportion of older patients also wanted to be involved: 87 per cent of patients aged under 40 expressed a desire to participate, compared to 62 per cent of those aged 40–59 and 51 per cent of those aged over 60 (Cassileth, Zupkis, Sutton-Smith and March, 1980). Some people prefer to leave the final decision about treatment options to the doctor, but they may still want some involvement in the decision-making process. A study of a group of older patients with coronary heart disease revealed considerable dissatisfaction about the fact that they were given very little encouragement or opportunity to participate in decisions about their care and little attempt had been made to inform them about the treatment options (Kennelly and Bowling, 2001). These patients felt that this implied a lack of respect for their views on the part of the doctors.

An age-related trend has been found in a number of studies – younger and better educated people are more likely to want to play an active role (Deber, 1994; Ende, Kazis, Ash and Moskowitz, 1989; Krupat *et al.*, 2000; Stiggelbout and Kiebert, 1997). This raises the interesting question of whether this is simply an age effect or whether it is a cohort effect. In other words, is it the case that older people are naturally more passive than younger people, or does it indicate that the preference for active involvement is increasing over time, suggestive of a cultural change? Cross-sectional studies such as these cannot provide a definitive answer, but it seems very likely that the latter is true, perhaps reflecting greater knowledge of the potential harms as well as the benefits of medical care and decreased willingness to submit to the authority of clinicians.

Despite the association between age and decision-making preferences, age on its own is not a reliable predictor of a patient's preferred role. Older people are particularly likely to suffer from the presumption that they are incapable of taking decisions or unwilling to face choices about their medical care. Care of patients at the end of life is a case in point. National guidance requires that do-not-rescuscitate orders should not be applied without first discussing the issue with patients and/or their relatives, yet there is evidence that this does not happen in two-thirds of cases (Bowling and Ebrahim, 2001). Respect for autonomy is just as important at the end of life as at any other time and arguments that the patient cannot comprehend the choices they face are not defensible as a reason for avoiding the attempt to involve them (Doyal, 2001).

People's preferences may vary according to the stage in the course of a disease episode and the severity of their condition. A Canadian study found a much greater desire for active participation among a randomly selected population sample than among a group of newly diagnosed cancer patients, pointing to the difficulty in predicting the level of involvement desired when serious illness strikes (Degner and Sloan, 1992). There may also be important cultural differences. Studies comparing responses in different countries found that British breast cancer patients were less likely to prefer an active role than Canadian ones (Beaver *et al.*, 1996; Richards *et al.*, 1995). However, trials in the UK of interventions designed to inform patients and promote shared decision-making by patients and clinicians have been well received by British people in all social groups (Kennedy *et al.*, 2002; Murray *et al.*, 2001a; Murray *et al.*, 2001b).

In shared decision making the intention is that both the process of decision-making and the outcome – the treatment decision – will be shared. This is a partnership approach based on the notion that two types of expertise are involved. The doctor is, or should be, well informed about diagnostic techniques, the causes of disease, prognosis, treatment options, and preventive strategies, but only the patient knows about his or her experience of illness, social circumstances, habits and behaviour, attitudes to risk, values and preferences. Both types of knowledge are needed to manage illness successfully, so both parties should be prepared to share information and take decisions jointly. Shared information is an essential prerequisite, but the process also depends on a commitment from both parties to engage in a negotiated decision-making process. The clinician must provide the patient with information about diagnosis, prognosis and treatment options, including outcome probabilities, and the patient must be prepared to discuss their values and preferences. The clinician must acknowledge the legitimacy of the patient's preferences and the patient has to accept shared responsibility for the treatment decision.

Evidence exists that many patients have strong treatment preferences, that these are not always predictable, and that doctors often fail to understand them. Patients cannot express informed preferences unless they are given sufficient and appropriate information, including detailed explanations about their condition and the likely outcomes with and without treatment. Consultation times are limited – there is often insufficient time to explain fully the condition and the treatment choices. Health professionals may themselves lack knowledge of treatment options and their effects. Patients find it hard to know what questions to ask.

A solution to this problem is to ensure that patients have access to good quality written or audiovisual material, to inform themselves and to use in discussion with health professionals. A recent survey of patient information materials currently in use in the NHS found that the quality of most materials was poor: many leaflets or audiovisual aids contained inaccurate and out-of-date information; topics that patients considered important were omitted; much information was biased, giving a one-sided and often optimistic view of the benefits of medical interventions, risks and side-effects were inadequately described, controversies and uncertainties were glossed over, and information about treatment effectiveness was often missing or unreliable (Coulter, Entwistle and Gilbert, 1999).

If decision-making is to be shared, the information to inform decisions must also be shared. Patients must be given help to obtain the information they need. Given the short consultation times experienced in most busy clinics, it is often unrealistic to expect clinicians to provide full information about the risks and benefits of all treatment options. This information is not always readily available to clinicians, let alone to lay people. If patients are to be able to express their preferences, they require help in the form of user-friendly information packages or decision aids.

Research into the use of decision aids for patients has shown that they can be an effective solution to these problems. When patient participation is facilitated by using specially designed decision aids, their knowledge and satisfaction with the decision process is increased (Estabrooks *et al.*, 2001; O'Connor *et al.*, 1999).

Decision aids help people make specific informed decisions about disease management and treatment options, prevention or screening. They use a variety of media to present the information in an accessible form to patients, including leaflets, audiotapes, workbooks, decision boards, computer programmes, interactive videos, web sites, structured interviews, and group presentations. The content is based on reviews of clinical research and studies of patients' information needs. They are very different from standard health education materials because they are not didactic or prescriptive – they do not tell people what to do. Instead they help patients clarify their own values and preferences and weigh up the potential benefits and harms of alternative courses of action. Decision aids have been developed to cover a variety of types of medical decision; for example, conditions where there is more than one possible treatment option (for example, benign prostatic hypertrophy (BPH), back pain, breast cancer, menstrual problems, and so on); interventions where patient's choice is paramount (for example, circumcision, contraception, and so on); diagnostic tests or screening programmes (for example, amniocentesis, PSA, mammography); preventive therapies or behaviours (for example, HRT, vaccinations, risk factors for coronary heart disease, and so on); the management of chronic diseases (for example, arthritis, diabetes, asthma, and so on); and end-of-life decisions (for example, resuscitation). Decision aids are not required in every situation. They are not necessary when there is strong evidence in favour of a specific intervention and there are no appropriate alternatives, in emergency situations, or when a patient has made it clear that they do not want to participate in decisions about their care.

When efforts are made to provide patients with unbiased evidence-based information about treatment options and likely outcomes, they often make choices which are more conservative than those of the doctors in charge of their care. For example, American patients, given full information about the pros and cons of prostate specific antigen (PSA) screening for prostate cancer, were less likely to undergo the test than those who were not fully informed (Volk, Cass and Spann, 1999). Prostatectomy rates fell when patients had the opportunity to view an interactive video programme outlining the risks and benefits of this surgical procedure (Wagner *et al.*, 1995), and a British trial of an information package for women referred for hysterectomy found that hysterectomy rates dropped significantly when women learnt about alternative treatments (Kennedy *et al.*, 2002). It seems that patients are often more risk-averse than the clinicians they consult.

Self-management

People with long-term health problems often become quite expert in managing their treatment and management of chronic diseases usually depends on patients playing an active role. For example, people with diabetes have to monitor their blood sugar levels and give themselves regular injections, people with asthma must become knowledgeable about inhalers and use them appropriately, and people on long-term medication must take their pills at regular intervals. We would not expect health professionals to take on these responsibilities without education and training, but patients are usually expected to do it without such support. A survey carried out for the Audit Commission found that a significant proportion of people with diabetes did not understand about key elements of diabetes care (Raleigh and Clifford, 2002). When asked if their HbA1c had been measured in the past year, 40 per cent of a national sample of 1400 people with diabetes said they didn't know. Older people, those with type two diabetes, and ethnic minority respondents had particularly low levels of knowledge of how to care for themselves.

There is now a substantial body of evidence that shows that enhancing patients' role in self-management of chronic diseases and reducing dependence on health professionals can produce very beneficial results. Given appropriate training and clinical support when necessary, patients with long-term conditions can look after themselves most effectively and their quality of life can be much improved. An example comes from some interesting work with arthritis patients carried out under the auspices of Arthritis Care. In the *Challenging Arthritis* programme, patients are invited to attend training courses during which they learn the techniques of self-care, including use of medication, pain control methods, how to handle emotional, social and work problems, and how to monitor changes in symptoms and disease progression and take appropriate action. Reports from more than 70 studies of arthritis patient education suggest it can be effective in improving knowledge, health-related behaviour, psychosocial status and health status (Lorig, Konkol and Gonzalez, 1987).

A distinctive aspect of the arthritis self-management courses is that they are run by fellow sufferers. These volunteers are encouraged to act as facilitators rather than tutors. Using teaching methods based on Bandura's self-efficacy theory (Bandura, 1977), participants learn strategies to enhance self-efficacy such as weekly action planning and feedback, how to reinterpret the causes of symptoms, different management techniques, group problem-solving, setting personal goals and monitoring progress. Rigorous evaluation of these training programmes in the US has shown that they succeeded in greatly increasing patients' knowledge, but more importantly, patients reported improvements in symptom severity including levels of distress, fatigue, disability and ability to participate in everyday activities and they were less likely to be admitted to hospital (Lorig *et al.*, 1999).

Similar educational programmes have been established for patients with a range of chronic diseases, including diabetes, chronic lung disease, heart disease, stroke, depression, chronic pain, insomnia, sickle cell disease and multiple sclerosis. A number of these programmes have been independently evaluated, with largely positive results. For example, studies have documented benefits for children and adults with asthma (Gebert *et al.*, 1998; Lahdensuo *et al.*, 1996). A systematic review of 22 randomised controlled trials of asthma self-management programmes found that they led to reduced hospitalisation rates, fewer emergency room visits, fewer unscheduled visits to the doctor, fewer days off work or school and fewer disturbed nights due to inability to sleep (Gibson *et al.*, 2000). The National Institute for Clinical Excellence (NICE) has recently published guidance on education for patients with diabetes (National Institute for Clinical Excellence, 2003). This described self-management as the cornerstone of diabetes care. Carried out effectively it could make a substantial impact on control of vascular risk factors, including blood glucose, blood lipids and blood pressure, management of complications, and quality of life. There is also striking evidence that self-management programmes can be remarkably cost-effective. One self-management programme claimed savings of $11 in normal care for every $1 spent on the programme (Lahdensuo, 1999).

This evidence of cost-effectiveness has attracted the attention of the Department of Health in England which has recently launched *The Expert Patient* initiative (Department of Health, 2001). This initiative aims to promote the idea that patient expertise should be a central component in the management of chronic conditions. Patients' organisations are developing patient-led self-management courses and primary care staff are being actively encouraged to refer their patients to these programmes. The hope is that self-management will help patients to regain a sense of control of their health by effectively managing specific aspects such as pain, complications and medication use; they will be less severely incapacitated by fatigue, sleep-deprivation, low levels of energy and the emotional consequences of their illness; their self-esteem will improve and they will feel more empowered in their relationship with health professionals. The government is also hoping that these attempts to promote self-care will result in considerable savings. As noted earlier, a recent report for the Treasury cited estimates that for every £100 spent on encouraging self-care, around £150 worth of benefits could be delivered in return (Wanless, 2002).

The new enthusiasm for self-care risks disappointment and disillusion if it is assumed that it will automatically lead to a dramatic reduction in demand for health services (Rogers, Hassell and Nicolaas, 1999). This certainly will not happen unless there is also a significant change in the way patients and professionals interact with each other. Health professionals will require training in how to support self-management and how to work in partnership with patients to help the latter to regain a sense of self-efficacy.

Future trends

Public expectations are changing and clinical practice and the organisation of health care delivery must change too if the consensual basis for publicly-funded health care systems is to survive. Paternalistic approaches to communication will no longer be tolerated by patients, and clinicians will find that they need to devote far more time to explaining and negotiating. More staff will be required to meet these demands and they will require new skills. Medical and nursing education will need to place more emphasis on communication skills training, on support for shared decision-making, and on helping patients to play an active role in managing their own care. Clinicians will need to ensure that patients understand the basis for their recommendations and must be willing to accept that patients' priorities and values may differ from theirs.

Patients will need help to enable them to become more discriminating consumers of health care. It will be important to ensure that high quality, reliable information is made available to patients via electronic media or by other means. This should be accompanied by public education programmes which focus on how to understand and deal with health risks, how to manage health problems and where to find appropriate information and help.

The patient of the future will be better informed, less deferential, and less willing to tolerate poor quality care. Patients will expect more involvement and more choice when it comes to their own care and that of their families. Meeting these needs will place considerable pressures on the NHS. Ignoring them may make the current system unsustainable. Paternalistic attitudes are still very common in today's NHS. The modernisation agenda will have failed if it does nothing to tackle these outdated ways of thinking about patients. Support for self-care, shared decision-making and self-management clearly make sense – the problem now is to get these adopted in mainstream clinical practice. This will require a real culture change. Clinicians will have to learn to accept that patients' preferences must play a key role in medical decision-making and in disease management. Patients must be allowed, indeed encouraged, to express their views and to question health professionals if they want to gain a better understanding of what is being proposed. Skills in education and communication and the principles of shared decision-making must be given much greater priority in clinical training schemes. Registration and reaccreditation programmes should include assessment of these skills and competencies. It will be especially important to underpin these efforts with increased investment in good quality information for patients and for the public in general.

At the current rate of growth, it seems likely that by 2010 the majority of patients will be internet users and a high proportion will have sought information from health-related websites. The numbers who use IT proactively to communicate with health professionals via e-mail is also likely to increase. The rapid spread of multiple television channels and the convergence of digital television, e-mail and other computer-based technologies will greatly enhance the potential for interactive communications. Members of the public will be able to make their own diagnoses, inform themselves about treatment options and risks, seek and receive medical advice, and educate themselves about self-management of their condition, all without stirring from their armchairs. By the time they reach the doctor's clinic they will be much more knowledgeable than today's patients and quite likely to have formed their own views about what should be done. They will expect a different type of relationship with the clinicians they consult and they will be more likely to want to be actively involved in managing their own care. Adapting professional training to meet these new needs is the greatest challenge facing those responsible for developing the workforce of the future.

Note

1. This chapter draws on my monograph, *The Autonomous Patient*, published by The Nuffield Trust, London, 2002. Sections from this book are reproduced here with kind permission of The Nuffield Trust.

References

Bandura, A. (1977) 'Self-efficacy: toward a unifying theory of behavioral change', *Psychological Review*, 84, 191.

Barnett, H. (2002) *The Which? Guide to Complementary Medicine*, London: Which? Ltd.

Beaver, K., Luker, K. A., Owens, R. G., Leinster, S. J., Degner, L. F. and Sloane, J. A. (1996) 'Treatment Decision Making in Women Newly Diagnosed with Breast Cancer', *Cancer Nursing*, 19, 8–19.

Bowling, A. and Ebrahim, S. (2001) 'Measuring Patients' Preferences for Treatment and Perceptions of Risk', *Quality in Health Care*, 10 (supp 1), i12–8.

Cassileth, B. R., Zupkis, R. V., Sutton-Smith, K. and March, V. (1980) 'Information and Participation Preferences among Cancer Patients', *Annals of Internal Medicine*, 92, 832–6.

Centre for Information Therapy (2002) *http://www.informationtherapy.org/* [Accessed 19 May 2003].

Cockburn, J. and Pit, S. (1997) 'Prescribing Behaviour in Clinical Practice: patients' expectations and doctors' perceptions of patients' expectations – a questionnaire study', *British Medical Journal*, 315, 520–3.

Coulter, A. (2001) 'Quality of Hospital Care: measuring patients' experiences', *Proceedings of the Royal College of Physicians of Edinburgh*, 31, 34–6.

Coulter, A. and Cleary, P. D. (2001) 'Patients' Experiences with Hospital Care in Five Countries', *Health Affairs*, 20, 244–52.

Coulter, A., Entwistle, V. and Gilbert, D. (1999) 'Sharing Decisions with Patients: is the information good enough?', *British Medical Journal*, 318, 318–22.

Coulter, A. and Magee, H. (2003) *The European Patient of the Future*, Buckingham: Open University Press.

Crow, R., Gage, H., Hampson, S., Hart, J., Kimber, A. and Thomas, H. (1999) *The Role of Expectancies in the Placebo Effect and their Use in the Delivery of Health Care: a systematic review*, Southampton: Health Technology Assessment, NHS R&D HTA Programme.

Deber, R. B. (1994) 'The Patient–Physician Partnership: decision making, problem solving and the desire to participate', *Canadian Medical Association Journal*, 151, 423–7.

Degner, L. F. and Sloan, J. A. (1992) 'Decision Making During Serious Illness: what role do patients really want to play?', *Journal of Clinical Epidemiology*, 45, 941–50.

Department of Health (2000) *The NHS Plan: a plan for investment, a plan for reform*, London: Department of Health.

Department of Health (2001) *The Expert Patient: a new approach to chronic disease management for the 21st century*, London: Department of Health.

Department of Health (2003) *Developing NHS Direct*, London: Department of Health.

Doyal, L. (2001) 'Informed Consent: moral necessity or illusion?', *Quality in Health Care*, 10 (supp 1) i29–33.

Dunnell, K. and Cartwright, A. (1972) *Medicine Takers, Prescribers and Hoarders*, London: Routledge and Kegan Paul.

Ende, J., Kazis, L., Ash, A. and Moskowitz, M. A. (1989) 'Measuring Patients' Desire for Autonomy: decision-making and information-seeking preferences among medical patients', *Journal of General Internal Medicine*, 4, 23–30.

Estabrooks, C., Goel, V., Thiel, E., Pinfold, P., Sawka, C. and Williams, I. (2001) 'Decision Aids: are they worth it?', *Journal of Health Services Research and Policy*, 6, 170–82.

Gebert, N., Hummelink, R., Konning, J., Staab, D., Schmidt, S., Szczepanski, R., Runde, B. and Wahn, U. (1998) 'Efficacy of a Self-management Program for Childhood Asthma – a prospective controlled study', *Patient Education and Counseling*, 35, 213–20.

Gibson, P. G., Coughlan, J., Wilson, A. J., Abramson, M., Bauman, A., Hensley, M. J. and Walters, E. H. (2000) *Self-management Education and Regular Practitioner Review for Adults with Asthma (Cochrane Review)*, The Cochrane Library [Issue 4], Update Software.

Hannay, D. R. (1979) *The Symptom Iceberg – a study of community health*, London: Routledge and Kegan Paul.

Kemper, D. W. (1997) *Healthwise Handbook, 13th Edition*, Idaho: Healthwise Inc.

Kennedy, A. D. M., Sculpher, M. J., Coulter, A., Dwyer, N., Rees, M., Abrams, K. R., Horsley, S., Cowley, D., Kidson, C., Kirwin, C., Naish, C. and Stirrat, G. (2002) 'Effects of Decision Aids for Menorrhagia on Treatment Choices, Health Outcomes, and Costs', *Journal of the American Medical Association*, 288, 2701–8.

Kennelly, C. and Bowling, A. (2001) 'Suffering in Deference: a focus group study of older cardiac patients' preferences for treatment and perceptions of risk', *Quality in Health Care*, 10 (supp 1), i23–8.

Kieschnick, T., Adler, L. J. and Jimison, H. B. (2002) *Health Informatics Directory*, Baltimore: Williams and Wilkins.

Krupat, E., Rosenkranzz, S. L., Yeager, C. M., Barnard, K., Putnam, S. M. and Inui, T. S. (2000) 'The Practice Orientations of Physicians and Patients: the effect of doctor-patient congruence on satisfaction', *Patient Education and Counseling*, 39, 49–9.

Lahdensuo, A. (1999) 'Guided Self Management of Asthma – how to do it', *British Medical Journal*, 319, 759–60.

Lahdensuo, A., Haahtela, T., Herrala, J., Kava, T., Kiviranta, K., Kuusisto, P., Peramaki, E., Poussa, T., Saarelainen, S. and Svahn, T. (1996) 'Randomised Comparison of Guided Self Management and Traditional Treatment of Asthma over One Year', *British Medical Journal*, 312, 748–52.

Lorig, K., Konkol, L. and Gonzalez, V. (1987) 'Arthritis Patient Education: a review of the literature', *Patient Education and Counseling*, 10, 208–52.

Lorig, K. R, Sobel, D. S., Stewart, A. L., Brown, B. W., Bandura, A., Ritter, P., Gonzalex, V. M., Laurent, D. D. and Holman, H. R. (1999) 'Evidence Suggesting that a Chronic Disease Self-management Program can Improve Health Status while Reducing Hospitalization', *Medical Care*, 37, 5–14.

Munro, J., Nicholl, J., O'Cathain, A., Knowles, E. and Morgan, A. (2001) *Evaluation of NHS Direct First Wave Sites: final report of the phase 1 research*, Sheffield: University of Sheffield, Medical Care Research Unit.

Murray, E., Davis, H., See Tai, S., Coulter, A., Gray, A. and Haines, A. (2001a) 'Randomised Controlled Trial of an Interactive Multimedia Decision Aid on Benign Prostatic Hypertrophy in Primary Care', *British Medical Journal*, 323, 493–6.

Murray, E., Davis, H., See Tai, S., Coulter, A., Gray, A. and Haines, A. (2001b) 'Randomised Controlled Trial of an Interactive Multimedia Decision Aid on

Hormone Replacement Therapy in Primary Care', *British Medical Journal*, 323, 490–3.

National Audit Office (2002) *NHS Direct in England*, London: National Audit Office, HC 505.

National Institute for Clinical Excellence (2003) *Guidance on the Use of Patient-education Models for Diabetes*, London: National Institute for Clinical Excellence.

O'Connor, A., Fiset, V., DeGrasse, C., Graham, I. D., Evans, W., Stacey, D., Laupacis, A. and Tugwell, P. (1999) 'Decision Aids for Patients Considering Options affecting Cancer Outcomes: evidence of efficacy and policy implications', *Journal of the National Cancer Institute Monographs*, 25, 25, 67–80.

Popay, J. and Williams, G. (1996) 'Public Health Research and Lay Knowledge', *Social Science and Medicine*, 42, 759–68.

Raleigh, V. S. and Clifford, G. M. (2002) 'Knowledge, Perceptions and Care of People with Diabetes in England and Wales', *Journal of Diabetes Nursing*, 6, 72–8.

Richards, M. A., Ramirez, A. J., Degner, L. F., Fallowfield, L. J., Maher, E. J. and Neuberger, J. (1995) 'Offering Choice of Treatment to Patients with Cancers', *European Journal of Cancer*, 31A, 112–6.

Rogers, A., Hassell, K. and Nicolaas, G. (1999) *Demanding Patients? Analysing the use of primary care*. Buckingham: Open University Press.

Savage, R. and Armstrong, D. (1990) 'Effect of a General Practitioner's Consulting Style on Patients' Satisfaction', *British Medical Journal*, 301, 968–70.

Stiggelbout, A. M. and Kiebert, G. M. (1997) 'Patient Preferences Regarding Information and Participation in Clinical Decision-making', *Canadian Medical Association Journal*, 157, 383–9.

Thomas, K. J., Nicholl, J. P. and Coleman, P. (2001) 'Use and Expenditure on Complementary Medicine in England: a population-based survey', *Complementary Therapies and Medicine*, 9, 2–11.

Thompson, M., Gee, S. and Larson, P. (2001) 'Health and Loyalty Promotion Visits for New Enrollees: results of a randomised controlled trial', *Patient Education and Counseling*, 42, 53–65.

Vickery, D. M., Kalmer, H., Lowry, D., Constantine, M., Wright, E. and Loren, W. (1983) 'Effect of a Self-care Education Program on Medical Visits', *Journal of the American Medical Association*, 250, 2952–6.

Volk, R. J., Cass, A. R. and Spann, S. J. (1999) 'A Randomized Controlled Trial of Shared Decision Making for Prostate Cancer Screening', *Archives of Family Medicine*, 8, 333–40.

Wagner, E. H., Barrett, P., Barry, M. J., Barlow, W. and Fowler, F. J. (1995) 'The Effect of a Shared Decision Making Program on Rates of Surgery for Benign Prostatic Hyperplasia: pilot results', *Medical Care*, 33, 765–70.

Wanless, D. (2002) *Securing our Future Health: taking a long-term view (final report)*, London: HM Treasury.

3
The Professionalisation of Informal Carers?

Liz Forbat and Jeanette Henderson

Introduction

The 2001 census indicated that there were 5.2 million carers[1] in England and Wales with over one million of these providing more than 50 hours of care per week. The work of this 'unsung army of carers' (Brown, 1999) is estimated by Carers UK (2002: i) to save the government £57.4 million per year (based on care costs in 2000). Statistics such as these vary between sources but even conservative estimates suggest that informal caring is now a significant component in family life. Reflecting and responding to this, there has been an increase in the number of government policies relating to the position of carers in recent years. We argue this has generated a number of messages about the position of carers in society and how they seem increasingly to be understood almost as a part of the health care workforce.

In this chapter, we firstly outline the growth in recognition of carers within UK health and social care policy, and indicate how this has been played out within society and health care systems. Secondly, some examples of carer initiatives are outlined, where ideas about what we call the 'professionalisation' of carers are being put into practice. The third section offers some speculation about the future – and the possibilities and potentials for extending localised examples of facilitative and enabling practice to wider contexts.

The starting assumption is that the two positions of professional carer and informal carer are becoming progressively more blurred. Increasingly, it seems, carers are expected to take on more and more of the professionals' role (though remaining outside the career structure of paid employment). This is manifest in many ways including administering medication, monitoring and surveillance of the cared-for person (Szmukler and Holloway, 2001). In the light of this, carers might readily be identified as professionalised – a central component in the *de facto* health care workforce.

One of the key questions we seek to address in this chapter is: 'with this increasing emphasis on the carer, where does this leave the process of care?' Allied to this, 'what happens to the triadic relationship between formal carers, informal carers and cared-for people?'

Informal carers: an evolving product of the twentieth century?

Authors diligently continue to note that carers and caring emerged as a policy concern in the twentieth century. The act of people taking care of each other has, of course, a much longer history. However, with the introduction of community care into policy development, and then common parlance, the meaning and position of care in society has undergone a significant change. To summarise, the changes might be noted as moving between three domains:

i)   from family care as normal part of living
ii) to family care as warranting additional support and recognition (labeled informal care)
iii) to informal care as a professionalised component of family life.

It is the movement between these three domains which is examined in this section of the chapter.

Qureshi and Walker (1989) suggested that the mid-1970s saw the growth of a belief that families were less willing to care for their older relatives. They found no evidence to support this hypothesis, and observed in their study of 306 carers that:

> We were struck, first by the universal nature of the acceptance of their primary role in the provision of care for elderly relatives and second, by the tremendous normative pressure on them to do so. (Qureshi and Walker, 1989: 2)

Carer lobbies, however, challenged this straightforward construction of care as normative within families; and indeed continue to do so forcefully for minority ethnic groups (Department of Health, 1998). Such challenges are the hallmark of the movement to the second domain.

One key distinction between the first domain, where family care is seen as normative and the second, where it is construed as informal care and as warranting additional support, is that of 'caring for' and 'caring about'; creating a difference between the linked caring positions (Ungerson, 1983). Graham (1983) theorises the difference as labour and love. These distinctions suggest that care has two conceptually different forms: one where emotional involvement is prioritised, and one where instrumental tasks predominate. In a similar vein, other writers have demarcated care *in* the community as conceptually different from care *by* the community (Bayley, 1973).

The importance of carers as a distinct group of people is driven home by estimates of the saved cost to the government by family provision of care-services. Indeed, it has been suggested that policy which supports the maintenance of informal care networks is largely a cost-saving exercise (Lewis and Meredith, 1988; Morris, 1993). Further professionalisation of informal carers will surely enhance this positive financial outcome for the government. Indeed, over the past ten years there has been increased attention from government to the roles and rights of informal carers (Department of Health, 1995a/b). This understanding of care as cost driven, and brought about by lack of appropriate alternatives such as residential facilities, or adequately resourced homecare workers, is starkly ideologically adrift from care that is prompted by familial obligations.

Carer lobbies, together with academic interest in the field have driven the recognition of informal carers in supporting community care policy. Research into care stemmed from the work of feminist theorists who expressed concern about the unpaid and unvalued role of women in informal care (for example Finch, 1989; Finch and Groves, 1983; Twigg and Atkin, 1994) and its relation to normative family obligations. Indeed, support for carers stemmed from an organisation that was originally set up for single women (the National Council for the Single Woman and her Dependants), which extended membership to men in 1982. After some time, lobbying by carers resulted in the government taking their demands seriously, giving them due recognition. Indeed, the *1995 Carers (Recognition and Services) Act* (Department of Health, 1995a/b) does just this. The 1995 Act was the first specific instance of the government recognising informal care as different from standard family obligations, and it can be seen to form the beginning of the new discourse of professionalisation. It indexes care as something qualitatively and quantitatively different from family responsibilities (in a fashion similar to the ideas articulated by Qureshi and

Walker, 1989), by covering the provision of 'regular and substantial' care. Exact definition of these terms, however, is left to local authority discretion. Importantly, the Act also introduces the possibility of carers being service users; something which is rarely recognised for professional practitioners (though see Forbat, under review, for research which has explored this dimension).

The Act clearly spells out a new role for the government and local authorities in supporting carers to 'provide or continue to provide care' (Department of Health, 1995a). The practice guidelines set out ideas for whether carers provide 'regular and substantial' help by offering the following core questions to consider:

> What type of tasks does or will the carer undertake? How much time does or will the carer spend providing assistance? How much supervision does the user require to manage his/her life? Is this [...] a continuing commitment for the carer? (1995b: 2)

Each of the questions posed by the guidelines points to a construction of the carer as someone who is disengaged emotionally and relationally from the cared-for person; mirroring a more 'professional distancing' by defining care in non-relational terms.

The Act also suggests a need to 'recognise carers' knowledge and expertise' (1995b: 3) which again starts to position carers within a professional domain. Research is beginning to suggest that this idea has gained growing acceptance, and family caregivers are now considered part of the care team (Szmukler and Holloway, 2001). This moves us into the third domain of informal care – as a professionalised component of family life. Szmukler and Holloway (ibid.) stress the often-troubled process of involving carers due to restrictions stemming from confidentiality agreements between formal carers and the cared-for person. Particular issues are likely to become apparent in mental health as the caree's ability to give informed consent for carers to be fully briefed may change over the course of the illness (Henderson, 2002).

Further policy documents have bolstered the notion of care as of a different order from regular family obligations. The *National Strategy for Carers* (Department of Health, 1999a) constructed carers as family members, aware of their own identities as carers, co-workers, and as commodities. These features resonate with Twigg's (1989) and Twigg and Atkin's (1994) model of how carers are incorporated into service systems, for example, as 'resources', 'co-workers', and 'co-clients', and with their observation that this was an early indicator of how carers were becoming increasingly professionalised.[2] In this notion, care 'is formulated as a 'joint care enterprise, in which the traditional divisions between formal and informal care are transcended' and they observe that 'such attempts often prove problematic' (Twigg and Atkin, 1994: 14). The tensions in boundaried positions between formal and informal care are taken up in further detail later in this chapter, where we question and problematise the impact of this increasing professionalisation of carers.

The introduction of National Service Frameworks is another, and more recent, indication of the government's welcoming approach to carers. The strategy document for Mental Health (NSF/MH) (Department of Health, 1999b) identifies a standard pertaining to carers that largely promotes the carer's rights under the 1995 Act. Carers are presented as people who may themselves require health or social care services if they are not adequately supported in their role. What is implicit, however, is the pivotal role that carers occupy in maintaining good mental health in the people for whom they care. A notable silence in the framing of carers here is around the roles of surveillance, monitoring and control that they take on within mental health care. Each of these can be understood as moving the carer from domain ii) to iii) and thus signalling an increased professionalisation as they mimic the monitoring roles traditionally associated with health care workers. We would argue that carers have taken on roles of surveillance in the community, roles previously ritualised through the asylum system of care.

Turning to the NSF for Older People (NSF/OP), the Foreword notes that it was constructed through consultation with older people, professionals and also carers (Department of Health, 2001a). In this way, the document positions carers almost as professionals and indicates the responsibilities that they have to ensure that the needs of older people are met. This might be experienced as a welcome opportunity to add perspectives to the experience of care, or it may be disempowering as it moves emphasis and control away from the service user, to the 'professionalised' family carer.

Carers are also identified as playing a core role in the implementation of the standard of the NSF/OP around person-centered care. The document notes the carer's need for expert information about the person they care for. The sharing of this information – with the cared-for person's consent – marks it out as slightly different from professional care. The need for information and knowledge, however, again constructs it as significantly apart from family care where caregiving approaches would tend to be more intuitive rather than 'fact' driven.

Additionally, involvement in the older person's assessment seems to build on the discourse of carer as part of the professional team, responding to and averting crises. The need for a balance between carers as professionals and carers as potential service users is accepted here:

> Carers should be identified and offered either the opportunity to be involved in the older person's assessment, or where appropriate, informed of their right as part of a holistic assessment to an assessment in their own right. (Department of Health, 2001a: para 2.37)

This offer of support is broadly reminiscent of clinical supervision, and the overall positioning underlines the uncomfortable juncture between the carer as service user and as service provider.

The notion of adequate and appropriate support for professional carers (with, for example, clinical supervision) is addressed in the NHS Plan (Department of Health, 2000a). Speculation about the support of staff here leads to questioning the extent to which this maps onto similar promises for informal carers. Support has become a carer's right.

The growth of direct payments, which places the person in need of assistance at the centre of the purchaser–provider relationship in the care market, has also contributed to important dialogue on the rights of people involved in informal care. Professionalisation is particularly called into question since the use of direct payments impacts on the status and responsibilities of the personal assistants that are employed. In this development, standards are brought onto the agenda for people receiving care, as well as those providing it. The use of direct payments has recently (2003) been extended to the employment of spouses or other close relatives; indicating the critical nature of relatives in care and their need for remuneration. Direct payments thus also embodies the move between family care as an expected component of life toward marking it out as something distinctive and in need of recognition. It also begins to raise questions around the knowledge and skills which such carers are anticipated and expected to have.

Carers have also been explicitly identified as 'partners' in recent policy. This move is visible in the White Paper *Valuing People* (Department of Health, 2001b) which sets out a vision for supporting people with learning disabilities in England. The document notes that carers have 'training needs', an idea which seems to draw very clearly on ideas of increasing skill, in a manner reminiscent of professionals. Indeed, their knowledge is further underlined by the encouragement to professionals to use carers as a resource:

> Professional staff can learn a great deal from their experience and expertise. (Department of Health, 2001b: para 5.17)

Thus, a range of policy documents has now set up ideals around empowering and valuing carers. A by-product of this seems to be a professionalisation of the role and a blurring between formal and informal care. Demarcating the nature of the associations, differences and overlaps between formal and informal carers has become increasingly tricky.

These themes are already appearing in empirical work. Simpson (1997) describes a project where carers of people with dementia held documentation and notes at home. He suggests that in making written contributions to care plans, professional notions of care are vividly called forth:

> carers might be empowered to function in equal partnership with professionals in the care of their relative with dementia. (345)

This notion of building 'equal partnerships' can easily be bolstered by the stereotypical notion of the stigmatised and spoiled identity of people with dementia as being passive recipients of care. Though many user groups have vehemently challenged such conceptualisations, similar moves are rather more embryonic within dementia care. Ideas underpinning equal partnership, however, do seem to call up notions of the professionalisation of carers particularly forcefully.

Implications when family carers take on professionalised roles

Though it seems increasingly apparent that informal carers are being subtly and quietly incorporated into the health workforce, this professionalisation of the carer role has not been widely problematised (Daly, 2002; Williams, 2001). In this section we set out some of the pressing concerns which we feel the professionalisation of carers brings about. The argument moves between three inter-related concerns: the meaning of being and becoming a carer, notions of professional roles/status and personal connectivity in care. In each of these, there are further levels of complexity when considering the constant impact of the triadic relationship between formal carer, informal carer and caree.

Underpinning this section is a thesis that the increasing professionalisation of carers sets up a potentially problematic tension within the caring relationship. It serves to separate the people within a care relationship, constructing them as occupying distinct and separate roles. This is in opposition to an often articulated understanding by carers and carees themselves, that they are people who are in partnership – where the positions of carer and caree blur and are understood as flexible constructs.

Turning to the first concern – around understandings of being and becoming a carer – in a recent study, both carers and carees were interviewed about their relationship (Forbat, 2001). One finding was that people would more frequently refer to themselves as giving care than receiving it. Even people recovering from strokes, people with cancer and dementia, who traditionally might be thought of as *receiving* care, all positioned themselves as carers.

One example of this was Colin[3] who, while still recovering from a stroke, talked about himself, not as a care-recipient, but very definitely as a carer. Colin notes:

> I can't help it. I am a born carer unfortunately. However you look at it, my doctor said I was a born carer.

Why might this be? Why would carees want to label themselves as carers when someone close to them thought themselves to be the carer? One possible answer is that, as indicated above, to be a carer is a highly prized position. The label of 'carer' is more prestigious and powerful than that of 'cared for'. Carers are currently (rhetorically at least) given a more recognised social position. They have support groups to draw on, legislation to support them and government funding for taking time off from caring. To be a carer can open up the possibility for very positive identities, hence the weaving of dynamic movement between being a carer and a caree in accounts that are given of care.[4]

This has implications for considering notions of professionalisation, in particular, in relation to assumptions about the inherent reciprocity of relationships. It poses the question of what the place of reciprocity is when the family or informal relationship ceases to be the main contextual cue, and 'professional roles' take over. Connected to this, what does it mean for their relationship if one partner becomes identified explicitly as an expert in caring for the other? One of the major differences between informal and formal carers (and indeed, one of the obstacles to informal carers becoming totally professionalised), is the intimate relational history, and the dilemmas of providing care in an attached/detached manner.

Issues of coercion or co-operation come to the fore here, and understandably, authors urge caution about involvement based on coercion (Kirk and Glendinning, 1998). Unpicking the dynamics in such relationships is complex and often messy. It is important to be able to highlight in each instance: what coercion looks like, how informal carer, formal carer and caree experience it, and how each member brings it into being within this relationship triad.

A second concern pivots on how formal carers experience the changing balance of roles and responsibilities and in particular the impact on their perceptions of professional power and status. Role erosion may be a delicate area for practitioners who fear a loss of hands-on care, and movement into more managerial tasks. Understanding formal and informal care as qualitatively (and perhaps quantitatively) different, may enable practitioners to maintain their status. However, under scrutiny, distinctions may be difficult to uphold. Allan (2000), for example, describes a number of tense exchanges between formal and informal carers in a hospital setting, where the nature of caregiving was contested and professionals felt that their position was being usurped.

Thus, for each participant in the care triad, there is an important question of who is able to *choose* to care. For formal carers, there may be reduced opportunities for care. For informal carers, there may be conflicting pressures to provide, and not provide, assistance. A variety of factors such as availability of alternatives, concerns about providing adequate care, and ability or desire to manage several different roles within the relationship, will influence carers' decisions. Each of these invites different responses from formal carers.

Personal connectivity provides a third concern arising from problematising the emphasis on professionalising carer roles. Professionalisation is positioned within a complex matrix of research which indicates that technically competent treatment without a personal connection in care is often ineffective (Nolan, Davies and Grant, 2001). The relationship, not just the task, needs to be placed centrally. The nature of the relationship is qualitatively different for informal carers and professional carers. As Kirk and Glendinning (1998: 374) note, family carers are 'learning skills which were formally considered the province of trained professionals, but unlike professionals they are performing what may sometimes be painful procedures on people they may care for and love'. Similarly, the care of people with mental health problems may have significant repercussions where the 'mental illness can have a major impact on carers, families and friends' (Department of Health, 2002: 8).

Sustained discourse on the professionalisation of carers also generates questions around intimacy. If the carer role is professionalised, then perhaps the relationship must be asexual – since sex with patients or clients is not acceptable (Stanley, Manthorpe and Penhale, 1999). Policy which continues to recruit family carers into conceptualising their role as more formal, may then have consequences for what is arguably a fundamental element of many informal (adult) care relationships. Professionals are bounded by ethical guidelines on sexual contact with clients, and discourses around 'taking advantage' and 'misconduct' enable distinctions to be made between appropriate and inappropriate acts. For informal carers, however, the leaps between carer and lover are more complex. The image of 'naughty nurse' to some extent plays on this paradoxical move between frameworks of carer and lover, and highlights the juxtaposition of roles, with implied moral judgements attached.

Thus when thinking about how the health workforce is adapting to changing ideas of care, it is essential to be mindful of the complex and conflicting array of implications for each member of the care triad.

Inviting new thinking for care policy

The section above has emphasised the importance of understanding the impact of care on relationships and the impact of relationships on care. Indeed, there is a very real need for relationship-based social policy (Henderson and Forbat, 2002). In this section we develop ideas, drawn from our own empirical research, which bring together care, relationships and professionalisation.[5]

The field of mental health care provides a starting point where professionalisation may be particularly pertinent. As noted above, carers may be involved in the process of a relative being detained under the 1983 Mental Health Act. They may be expected to take on the task of professional monitoring within their relationship and the NSF/MH formulates carers as people in need of support. This document neglects, however, to make space for reflection on these roles. Its silence is particularly marked when the experiences of carers are taken into account. Indeed, carers have much to say about these subjects and often conceptualise themselves as formal carers.

The shift in role for carer between periods of distress and wellbeing is illustrated by carers' reflections on their experiences of monitoring their partner and of being monitored by others. One person, for example, spoke of how he tried not to take up what he called the 'semi-professional mask of the carer' at all. Another resisted the construction of a professional role for carers, but also struggled with the contradictions of this. The extract below came in response to a question about what the term 'carer' meant to him:

> I was being pushed in that direction even before the term was invented. It was something you were supposed to do, turn into some sort of policeman/nurse sort of in the situation. And obviously there is always going to be a bit of that. I mean you do have to make sure that disasters don't occur and things when she's ill, but she, it was her who explained to me just how damaging that was, how I would turn from being her husband into her carer and that would be the end of it.

This interviewee quite explicitly draws out the implications for the relationship where mental health problems dominate the need for care. Ensuring that his partner was safe and not putting herself at risk, became a dominant feature of their relationship, at the points where he moved from husband to carer mode.

Carers often speak about their interactions and relations with professionals, constructing themselves and their partners as distinct and separate from professionals within this wider system. One interviewee spoke at length about his caring role:

> I suppose they, they want me to confirm how Elaine is behaving. Especially at times when they feel they can't trust her word and her description of it, they want to hear from me just what she's doing on a day to day basis and whether it strikes me as normal. And they also, probably more latterly, have wanted me to try and influence her and participate a lot in this negotiating business.

The speaker later noted that he preferred to take his lead from Elaine, and what he thought she would want when well.

Resistance to professionalisation, as illustrated in these extracts must also be queried in the field of young carers. They fall under the remit of the 1995 Act, and are thus recognised for the services they provide, but there must be caution in fostering professional identities here. This argument may appear to mimic well-rehearsed concerns about role reversal in young carers, where the child assumes adult responsibilities and the adult becomes reliant on the child. Although this simplistic model has been severely criticised (Keith and Morris, 1995; Morris, 1995), ideas of the child parenting the parent remain pervasive. To foster professionalised identities in young carers who are assumed to have taken on more adult positions produces a risky situation for statutory services. It is necessary to maintain more clearly defined boundaries between formal and informal care, alongside clear policy guidance that reflects the complex dynamics of young child–parent relationships where care is provided.

Professionalisation in action

In this section we explore some ways that carers, and to some extent services, are adapting to the need to know more and understand more of the caring process. While this might be framed as 'good practice', it is perhaps more helpful to think of it as an evolving, collaborative and changing enterprise. Through interacting with various practice issues, carers can be enabled to provide better, or more appropriate, care.

Many of the initiatives discussed fit clearly with policy pushes, noted above, towards increasing the knowledge base of carers. Rather than aiming for a reliance on informal carers in place of professional interventions – on a simple substitution model – a more fundamental suggestion is that through interactions with various practice settings, caring relationships can be made more rewarding for those involved (Brechin, 1998). Allied to this is a call for better theorising of the ways in which carers can be enabled in their provision of care and their support needs can be better recognised. The following examples relate to developing and enhancing informal care practice.

Relationships and *Relate* in informal care

Relate (formerly known as marriage guidance counselling) in Milton Keynes has adopted a novel approach to informal carers. In association with the local Carers Project (a joint funded organisation which supports carers in the Milton Keynes area), it has begun offering short courses for carers. It places the relationship in the centre of enabling carers to get on with the business of caring. This is about giving carers a chance to develop insight into how they respond to relational difficulties and to build a repertoire of coping strategies.

Training is based around a series of group sessions focussing on the individual's responses to stress. Plotting out the physiological and psychological dimensions to this, the course enables carers to recognise when they are feeling stressed, and offers adaptive methods of coping.

The approach also promotes valuable ideas about the social model of disability and indicates a role for carers in educating others about the disabling effects of society on people with impairments. *Relate* notes that it can be exhausting for carers to be constantly 'working away at challenging attitudes; and challenging prejudices while fighting an on-going battle for resources ... or facilities for the people they care for' (Relate, 2001: 11–12). The parallels for practitioners, who also struggle to change attitudes and, especially in care management roles in social work, who juggle resources, are apparent.

A subsequent feature addressed by the *Relate* training, which invokes notions of professionalism, is associated with developing and reflecting on communication. There has been a substantial drive for health and social care practitioners at all levels to demonstrate 'good communication skills'. Conceptualising communication as something to be learnt as a skill places it in a similar domain to task-focused elements of care and, arguably, a more professionally managed exchange. The centrality of the relationship, as featured in this training, knits neatly into our concerns around increasing professionalisation

Skills training

Other initiatives have offered training that enables carers to respond more effectively in crisis situations – in particular those where, traditionally, professional carers might have been involved. An example is drawn from a recent research project (Forbat, 2001) and illustrates how care can be enhanced by taking on and embracing a more professionalised role for carers.

The extract below comes from one participant in the research, Janice, who had complex health and social care needs. Her husband, Bob, is her full time carer.

I'm fortunate in ... that Bob had to look after his mum for so long because that gave him a ... basic knowledge when I was first taken ill ... I had various accidents so Bob took a first aid course so he knew how to cope ... but it's surprising that not any carers that we know have even had a basic first aid course. I mean when I scalded my leg last year, Bob knew immediately what to do. I wasn't very happy because I'd had my hair done and he put me under a cold shower.

Janice clearly marks out this pivotal moment where Bob drew on his formal training in first aid. She underlines how this is unique amongst their care-circle and how such training has an important place in their care relationship. This level of professionalisation seems to be one which celebrates his abilities. Such affirmative accounts of training have important implications for resources in primary care and perhaps indicate a potential increase in the take-up of schemes such as the first aid training referred to here.

Sharing expertise

New technologies, such as the internet, are further enabling carers to share their expertise and develop their knowledge of illness and care. DIPEx is one such example (*http://www.dipex.org* [accessed on 10 June 2003]). This is a web based resource which stores personal accounts of health and illness. The accounts are aimed at a range of people, including people with specific illnesses and their carers. Much of the site is organised around a study principle, where conditions such as prostrate cancer and hypertension are explained and discussed in bite-sized modules. The web pages offer personal stories with video, audio and transcripts taken from interviews with people who have had the illness in question. There are also many links to more medicalised descriptions, including details on physiology, prognosis and treatment options. Specific sections are also devoted to friends and relatives, and to enabling them to understand the illness.

Websites such as DIPEx contribute to developing newly skilled and informed carers. One outcome of these sites is building capacity for carers to connect with the professional discourses used to talk about illnesses. New technologies enable informal carers to link with and share this ubiquitous medicalised language, and become part of a discourse community whereby they can increase their abilities to converse with professionals in professionalised terms. Recent projects in California have also drawn on these ideas and led to education for carers in communicative competency in GP consultations in the UK (Alzheimer's Association, 2002). The aim of this scheme is to provide carers with insight into how to put a case across to GPs. Sharing expertise is thus extended beyond knowledge to interactional competence, in ways analogous with much professional training.

What might the future hold?

If the professionalisation of informal carers is continued and worked more fully and explicitly into the health workforce, there will be implications for working across the newly created boundaries between practitioners and informal carers. What needs to be central to this, is work which fosters adaptive and useful relationships between members of the care triad (Santos-Eggimann, Zobel and Clerc Bérod, 1999). Formal and informal carers will need to work towards a position where there is mutual support of each other, since focusing attention purely at the level of the carer–caree relationship may pose real problems for workforce thinking. Indeed, there are implications for the implementation of government level priorities in considering the changing nature of the workforce. Take, for example, *No Secrets* (Department of Health, 2000b), which outlines the multi-professional guidance and responses to abuse in domestic care settings, as one example. If informal carers are increasingly seen as professionals, then their involvement in 'multi-professional' responses to abuse will need to be clearly marked out. Developing clarity over the triadic relationship between the formal carer, informal carer and cared-for person will be crucial in effective working of the *No Secrets* guidance.

For the workforce to embrace and gently develop notions of professionalisation, the NHS will need to make this a carefully carved out goal. Recent services commissioned by the Department of Health (2002) have resourced 700 carer support workers. The NHS Plan, however, failed to acknowledge the full complexity of carers' roles, and to provide a worked up vision of the future picture of health care and division of health labour.

The reduced provision for homecare services by one-quarter since 1997 (Brindle, 2003) will be accompanied by increased reliance on family members sustaining their relatives in the community. This may be of particular significance for considering the future of people from minoritised ethnic communities, where the prevalence of family care is high, due to continued stereotypic generalisations about 'looking after their own' and the failure of the statutory sector to provide culturally informed services. To what extent will informal carers from minoritised backgrounds feel increasingly encouraged to gain further skills and to continue caring for their relatives at home? Related to this is a question of how further professionalisation may add to the already pressured position of continuing home based care, since culturally sensitive alternatives are not always available.

The prospect of professionalisation is dilemmatic; it offers helpful solutions (enabling relatives to stay at home and receive care which is culturally informed), yet may simultaneously disengage the statutory sector from developing services appropriate to the community's needs. For future service systems to incorporate informal carers into the workforce in a helpful way, priority needs to be given to developing a range of models of care. In particular, social, psychological and complementary approaches need to work alongside or in place of the dominant bio-medical approach that informs health care and carer training/information needs. Bond (1992: 18) has offered a word of caution in connection with the tendency to medicalise care needs. In the field of dementia care, he suggests there has been an increase in 'the political dependency of those receiving care through the professionalisation of informal caregivers'. He highlights the need for political and ideological objectives to be attended to in conceptualising carers as workers in future healthy communities.

Conclusion

From a policy and statutory provider perspective, the informal carer is increasingly construed as part of a care package, a valuable resource – needing to be supported, but with minimal (if any) public cost. This focus on the public purse shifts attention away from what is arguably the very key to successful care – the relationship itself. We have sought to demonstrate in this chapter that the partners in a relationship may consider that they each care for the other in ways that are particular to their own relationship and are only distantly connected with monetary concerns. The increasing professionalisation of the informal carer sets up potentially problematic tensions in this regard.

These tensions are played out in a number of areas. The case study of Janice and Bob illustrates how carers and carees may positively experience the uptake of training in professionalised tasks such as advanced first aid. Meanwhile, carers in mental health may actively resist taking on professionalised surveillance and monitoring roles. Innovative programmes from *Relate* have taken the step of emphasising relationships, whilst recognising and building on discourses of case-management within social services.

Much policy discourse underlines the need to arm carers with information. This acts as reinforcement for the increased emphasis on enhancing knowledge – whilst subtly promoting bio-medical approaches to mental and physical needs for care. This information dimension of professionalisation has been harnessed by new technologies where carers can share their experiences and knowledge. However, both fruitful and problematic features are created by this kind of professionalisation. For some carers, gaining skills and knowledge may be helpful. For others, this process may feel as if it blocks them from gaining appropriate help – encouraging a feeling that they should be able to manage without statutory assistance.

The roles, rights and responsibilities of carers continue to be created, changed and written into statute. Policy seems to indicate that the increasing involvement of informal carers into health care provision is part of a vision for the future. How this may come about is yet to be clearly articulated, but it seems evident that much more thought needs to be given to the impact of professionalisation on the triadic relationship between professional carers, informal carer and care-recipient.

Discoursing carers into being was a twentieth century enterprise. The current project appears to be creating discourses and concepts that naturalise and promote the idea of informal carers as health care workers. Our dream is that the relationships between the three participants in care can be illuminated in this process, and that the spotlight will function as a catalyst to promote more functional and rewarding care exchanges. Whether this will be realised in future remains to be seen.

Notes

1. The term 'carer' is often used for both paid and unpaid workers – which highlights the overlap stemming from increased professionalisation of informal carers, and contributes to the muddying of distinctions between the two. In this chapter, the term 'carer' or 'care' is used to refer to informal care unless otherwise specified. We use a range of terms to refer to the person receiving care, including service user and caree.
2. Though Twigg and Atkin mooted the idea of the carer as co-worker, few people, with the exception of Kirk and Glendinning (1998), have taken their ideas on board. In this chapter, we update the ideas Twigg and Atkin presented and problematise the co-worker concept in terms of its impact on relationships in care.
3. All names are pseudonyms to preserve interviewees' anonymity.
4. This movement between positions also sets up the potential for difficulties and struggles within family power dynamics.
5. Liz Forbat's research explored accounts of informal caring using discourse analysis. Jeanette Henderson's research was a phenomenological study of

care partners where one member had a diagnosis (whether accepted or not) of bi-polar disorder. Both studies were based on interviews with adult care dyads, and included people from diverse backgrounds – varying in terms of sexuality, ethnicity, class and age.

References

Allan, D. (2000) 'Negotiating the Role of Expert Carers on an Adult Hospital Ward', *Sociology of Health and Illness*, 22, 2, 149–71.

Alzheimer's Association (2002) *Working With Your Doctor When You Suspect Memory Problems*, London: Alzheimer's Association.

Bayley, M. (1973) *Mental Handicap and Community Care*, London: Routledge Kegan Paul.

Bond, J. (1992) 'The Politics of Caregiving: the professionalisation of informal care', *Ageing and Society*, 12, 1, 5–21.

Brechin, A. (1998) 'What Makes for Good Care?', in A. Brechin, J. Walmsley, J. Katz and S. Peace (eds) *Care Matters*, London: Sage, 170–87.

Brindle, D. (2003) 'Downward Spiral', *Guardian*, 2 April, 4.

Brown, C. (1999) 'Unsung Army of Carers to get £50 Pension Bonus', *Independent*, 8 February, 8.

Carers UK (2002) *Without Us … ? Calculating the value of carers' support*, London: Carers UK.

Daly, M. (2002) 'Care as a Good for Social Policy', *Journal of Social Policy*, 31, 2, 251–70.

Department of Health (1995a) *Carers (recognition and services) Act. Policy Guidance*, London: The Stationery Office.

Department of Health (1995b) *Carers (recognition and services) Act. Practice Guidance*, London: The Stationery Office.

Department of Health (1998) *They Look After their Own don't They? Inspection of community care services for Black and ethnic minority older people*, London: Department of Health/Social Services Inspectorate.

Department of Health (1999a) *Caring about Carers: a national strategy for carers*, London: Department of Health.

Department of Health (1999b) *National Service Framework for Mental Health*, London: Department of Health.

Department of Health (2000a) *NHS Plan: a plan for investment, a plan for reform*. London: The Stationery Office.

Department of Health (2000b) *No Secrets: guidance on developing and implementing multi-agency policies and procedures to protect vulnerable adults from abuse*, London: The Stationery Office.

Department of Health (2001a) *National Service Framework for Older People*, London: Department of Health.

Department of Health (2001b) *Valuing People*, London: Department of Health.

Department of Health (2002) *Developing Services for Carers and Families of People with Mental Illness*, London: The Stationery Office.

Finch, J. (1989) *Family Obligations and Social Change*, Cambridge: Polity Press.

Finch, J. and Groves, D. (eds) (1983) *A Labour of Love: women, work and caring*, London: Routledge.

Forbat, L. (2001) *Exploring Care Relationships: two sides to the story*, Milton Keynes: Unpublished PhD, The Open University.

Forbat, L. (under review) 'Practitioner Voices on Service User Involvement: rhetoric and contradictions', *Journal of Mental Health*.

Graham, H. (1983) 'Labour of Love', in J. Finch and D. Groves (eds) *A Labour of Love: women, work and caring*, London: Routledge.

Henderson, J. (2002) 'Experiences of "Care" in Mental Health', *Journal of Adult Protection*, 4, 3, 34–45.

Henderson, J. and Forbat, L. (2002) 'Relationship Based Social Policy: personal and policy constructions of care', *Critical Social Policy*, 22, 4, 665–83.

Keith, L. and Morris, J. (1995) 'Easy targets: a disability rights perspective on the "children as carers" debate', *Critical Social Policy*, 15, 44/45, 36–57.

Kirk, S. and Glendinning, C. (1998) 'Trends in Community Care and Patient Participation: implications for the roles of informal carers and community nurses in the United Kingdom', *Journal of Advanced Nursing*, 28, 2, 370–81.

Lewis, J. and Meredith, B. (1988) *Daughters who care. Daughters caring for mothers at home*, London: Routledge.

Morris, J. (1993) *Independent lives. Community care and disabled people*, London: Macmillan, now Palgrave Macmillan.

Morris, J. (1995) 'Creating a Space for Absent Voices: disabled women's experience of receiving assistance with daily living activities', *Feminist Review*, 51, Autumn, 68–93.

Nolan, P., Davies, S. and Grant, G. (2001) *Working with Older People and their Families. Key issues in policy and practice*, Buckingham: Open University Press.

Qureshi, H. and Walker, A. (1989) *The Caring Relationship. Elderly people and their families*, London: Macmillan, now Palgrave Macmillan.

Relate Milton Keynes (2001) *Caring for Yourself. (A Carer's Guide)*, Milton Keynes: Relate (Carer's Project).

Santos-Eggimann, B., Zobel, F. and Clerc Bérod, A. (1999) 'Functional Status of Elderly Home Care Users: do subjects, informal and professional caregivers agree?', *Journal of Clinical Epidemiology*, 52, 3, 181–6.

Simpson, R. (1997) 'Carers as Equal Partners in Care Planning', *Journal of Psychiatric and Mental Health Nursing*, 4, 5, 345–54.

Szmukler, G. and Holloway, F. (2001) 'Confidentiality in Community Psychiatry', in C. Cordess (ed.) *Confidentiality and Mental Health*, London: Jessica Kingsley, 53–70.

Twigg, J. (1989) 'Models of Carers: how do social care agencies conceptualise their relationship with informal carers?', *Journal of Social Policy*, 18, 1, 53–66.

Twigg, J. and Atkin, K. (1994) *Carers Perceived. Policy and practice in informal care*, Buckingham: Open University Press.

Ungerson, C. (1983) 'Why do Women Care?', in J. Finch and D. Groves (eds) *A Labour of Love: women, work and caring*, London: Routledge.

Williams, F. (2001) 'In and Beyond New Labour: towards a new political ethics of care', *Critical Social Policy*, 21, 4, 467–93.

4
Reconfiguring the Clinical Workforce

Ailsa Cameron and Abigail Masterson

Introduction

The last decade has seen a rapid transformation in the roles of the various professional groups involved in the provision of health care. Most notably the profession of nursing has experienced the creation of new clinical roles, such as nurse endoscopist, and the expansion of traditional roles, such as that of night sister into night nurse practitioner. These developments are not confined solely to nursing. Other health care professions such as pharmacy, radiography and physiotherapy have gone through a similar process and others, such as ambulance staff, are under pressure to change. Such is the significance of these developments that the government's modernisation strategy outlined in *The NHS Plan* contained a raft of proposals for new service developments based on a reconfigured workforce (Department of Health, 2000a). More importantly, the *Plan* explicitly signalled the government's desire to break down the traditional barriers between the various professional groups in health and social care.

In this chapter we open by exploring the factors driving the emergence of new health care roles. These include: recruitment and retention difficulties, funding pressures and specific policy initiatives. We then discuss the contribution of the professionalising agendas of nurses and the allied health professions and advances in technology as enablers of change. Following this, we draw upon empirical work from a variety of national and local projects enquiring into new role development, and take a systems theory approach in reviewing the findings to illustrate some of the benefits and drawbacks linked to the reconfiguration of the workforce. We conclude that the tensions this analysis exposes in relation to assessment of competence, accountability, regulation and professional aspirations are unlikely to be amenable to solutions devised by individual Trusts or by the different professional and regulatory bodies working alone. National solutions will need to be found if the health labour force is to be reshaped appropriately and coherently to meet the challenges that lie ahead.

Drivers for change

Recruitment and retention difficulties

The drivers behind these professional developments are many and varied (Doyal and Cameron, 2000; Cameron and Masterson, 2000). Perhaps the most pressing of these relates to the problems faced by the NHS *vis-à-vis* the recruitment and retention of staff. The success of the NHS depends on the availability of an appropriately trained workforce, able to perform its role effectively and efficiently. There are currently almost one million people working for the NHS in England, of whom approximately three-quarters work in direct clinical care (Department of Health, 2000b). Geldman (2002) notes that every year 9 per cent of the workforce leaves, forcing the NHS to find almost 100,000 replacements annually. Although some of those who leave do so because they have reached retirement age, increasingly significant numbers are resigning as a result of stress and low morale. At the same time, shortages of trained staff – both nationally and locally – mean that finding the necessary replacements, particularly for specialties such as midwifery and radiology, can be difficult. As a response to these challenges, many Trusts have drawn on the skills of other professionals as a means to fill some of the gaps in provision. For example, some Trusts have enhanced the role of radiographers in X-ray by instituting 'red dot schemes'. These enable radiographers to identify possible fractures as a means of speeding up the reporting process and allow radiologists to concentrate on the more urgent and complicated cases.

The recruitment and retention problems faced by the NHS cannot solely be explained by increasing levels of stress and poor morale. As the British economy moves towards 'full employment', careers in the statutory welfare sector have arguably become less attractive. Indeed, for some clinical professions, such as physiotherapy, there are increasing opportunities to move into private practice. For others, particularly those professions like nursing that have recently begun to offer degree level qualifications, newly qualified professionals may consider employment opportunities in the wider graduate labour market. Some attempts have been made to improve career opportunities for nurses and the allied health professions. The development of specialist and consultant roles has meant that experienced professionals can be rewarded appropriately and build credible careers without having to move away from direct clinical care. Such developments, it is hoped, may help persuade students to join the profession whilst also encouraging experienced professionals to stay within the NHS (Department of Health, 1999 and 2000c).

Funding

Another major challenge facing the NHS is funding. Although there appears to be a broad consensus that spending on health care should increase, there is little agreement about how this funding should be raised (McKee, Dixon and Mossialos, 2002). Some commentators propose that the financial burden on the NHS could be reduced by the introduction of private insurance schemes whilst others argue in favour of social insurance (Irvine and Green, 2002). However, the government stated in *The NHS Plan* that although it considers that the funding of the NHS is not beyond reform, there are no plans to alter it at present. An increased investment to the system at an annual rate of 6.3 per cent was promised.

Despite the government's reluctance fundamentally to alter the funding structure of the NHS they have acknowledged that the system is inefficient and have set upon a course of modernisation. To underpin this, they have announced a series of initiatives to improve performance, including the introduction of performance assessment frameworks to drive efficiency. Inevitably, concerns about funding and the need to improve efficiency have led individual Trusts to re-evaluate the manner in which they deliver services and to seek ways of delivering them in a more cost-effective manner. Undoubtedly this has led to an examination of skill mix and debates about which is the most appropriate professional to undertake particular roles and procedures.

Although both staffing and funding concerns present separate challenges to the NHS they are also inter-related. Neither funding nor staffing problems are likely to be resolved in the short to medium term and may indeed worsen. Funding concerns mean that the government at the macro level, and individual Trusts at the micro level, are under pressure to make the NHS system more efficient. Labour shortages, particularly in key specialties, mean that at both levels alternative staffing strategies must be considered. One of the most obvious ways to meet the challenges is to maximise the contribution of all professional groups. In other words, reconfiguring the workforce by developing new roles and extending traditional roles is merely a pragmatic strategy, born out of necessity.

Specific policy initiatives

Whilst staffing and funding problems in general are important drivers behind the need to reconfigure the workforce, there is another set of important influences. Many of the changes in professional roles have emerged as a response to a myriad of policy initiatives which have encouraged individual Trusts, as employers, to re-evaluate the contribution that specific professional groups make to the delivery of care.

The most significant of these policy initiatives, perhaps, was the Conservative Government's attempt to reduce the hours of work of junior doctors. The policy guidance (Department of Health, 1991) urged employers to make best use of the skills of nurses and other allied staff as a means to help reduce junior doctors' workloads and ultimately their hours of work. To enable this to happen, the government established Junior Doctors' Task Forces in each of the regions and allocated them funding to support a variety of service developments. In many instances this funding was used to pump prime the establishment of new professional roles, mainly but not exclusively for nurses. For example, the Trent Regional Task Force used the funding to support and evaluate 32 new nursing posts (Read and Graves, 1994), whilst the South West Region funded the development and evaluation of four nurse practitioner posts (Dowling, Doyal and Cameron, 1998).

Other specific policy initiatives which have driven the introduction of new professional roles include the Calman–Hine Report on cancer care (1995). This report identified that one of the ways in which cancer care could be improved was to ensure that patients had access not only to specialist doctors but also to nurses with specialist skills. These, for example, might be in the management of lymphoedema or expertise in related areas such as symptom control or psychosocial support. Significantly, the Calman–Hine Report noted that nurses who had completed post-registration education in oncology should lead such developments. Developments in professional roles were also envisaged for appropriately qualified therapy radiographers. Undoubtedly, such guidance encouraged the development of new ways of working for health care professionals.

The election of the Labour Government in 1997 provided a further catalyst to such professional developments. The White Paper *The New NHS: Modern, Dependable* (Department of Health, 1997) set out the bare bones of the government's modernising agenda, the details of which were spelt out in the NHS Plan (Department of Health, 1999). The Plan announced boldly that 'radical changes are needed in the way staff work to reduce waiting times and deliver modern, patient centred services' (ibid: para 9.1). It went on to describe how the traditional patterns of professional practice were effectively holding back innovation and how their plans would effectively 'shatter old demarcations which have held back staff and slowed down care' (para 9.5). Plans were announced to support these developments, including funding to support training and development. This vision of a reconfigured workforce has been echoed in subsequent policy such as that relating to emergency care (Department of Health, 2001). The Audit Commission noted, for example, that 80 per cent of people attending accident and emergency departments are discharged straight from those departments and suggested that many of these patients could potentially be treated and discharged without the need to see a doctor (Audit Commission, 2001). In order to advance this work, the government has proposed a raft of developments including the development of Walk-in Centres and Minor Injuries Units as well as a radical reconceptualisation of professional roles in pre-hospital care.

Enablers of change

The professionalisation agenda

Many of the developments already described would not have been possible had the various health professions not sought over the recent past to advance their professional practice and status. Within nursing, one of the most important of these developments was the publication by its regulatory body of *The Scope of Professional Practice* (United Kingdom Central Council for Nursing, Midwifery and Health Visiting, 1992). This emphasised nurses' professional accountability and placed decisions about assuring competence and setting the boundaries of practice in the hands of individual registrants. Undoubtedly, *Scope* was a catalyst in terms of the reconfiguration of the workforce because it helped demolish unhelpful barriers between the healthcare professions. As a result, nurses could develop their practice into areas that previously had been the domain of medicine – thereby encouraging the development of innovative practice.

Similar developments within the wider healthcare workforce have encouraged the development of specialisms and specialist roles for allied health professionals. For example, in common with other health professions, radiography has moved over the last 10 years from a diploma to a degree based profession with two distinct branches: diagnostic and therapeutic radiography. There has also been a whole host of 'new' or extended radiography roles including radiographers taking breast biopsies, and radiotherapists giving clinical advice, support and counselling to patients. In the recent past, the profession has also witnessed the emergence of a further branch, that of ultra-sonography. In addition, at the assistant level, there are examples of the emergence of mammography technicians developing their own area of expertise as a means to improve the efficiency of the service.

Role developments are also occurring in other areas of health care. For example, a wide variety of personnel are currently involved in pre-hospital and hospital emergency care. These include: ambulance care assistants, technicians, paramedics, nurses and doctors. Roles and responsibilities vary, and commentators have noted areas of duplication and overlap. Organisations such as the Audit Commission (1998) and the Joint Royal Colleges Ambulance Liaison Committee (JRCALC) (2000) have suggested the development of a new hybrid role – the generic emergency care worker. Such a practitioner would be qualified to work in any emergency care setting and could rotate between settings to meet service needs. Education would be based on a three year undergraduate programme incorporating shared learning with other healthcare students followed by a probationary fourth year of practice placements when core practical skills would be learned and assessed. Already in some areas paramedics are assessing patients on behalf of GPs and performing simple technical procedures in patients' homes which prevent the latter having to attend their GP surgery or A&E department. Elsewhere, graduate nurse practitioners (NP) with extensive A&E experience are being used to respond to 999 calls (Walsh and Little, 2001).

Although it can be argued that these role developments represent the natural advancement of these professions, it is also important to acknowledge the importance of the wider political and economic context. The majority of developments have occurred at a time when successive governments have been exhorting health service managers to make more of the skills and expertise of the wider workforce in order to improve the efficient running of the NHS. It might therefore be prudent to acknowledge an element of serendipity in terms of the relationship between professional advancements and the reconfiguration of the health workforce.

Technological advances

Clearly many of the role developments so far discussed could not have happened without advancements in health care technology. Innovations in medical and surgical procedures and clinical technologies have ensured that some procedures have become technically rather than medically based and are therefore no longer seen as the preserve of the medical profession. These advances have enabled new roles to emerge across all professional groups. For example, technological developments in radiographic practices have permitted diagnostic radiotherapists to undertake intra-operative ultrasounds. Similar developments have enabled nurses and physiotherapists to work with greater professional autonomy and to cross traditional professional boundaries.

One interpretation of these technical advances is to argue that they have changed the very nature of particular interventions from what was thought of as solely a 'medical' task (the preserve of a medical doctor), to a 'technical' task – thus allowing any appropriately trained worker to perform it. An example of this 'technocratic' fix is endoscopy, which is now commonly performed by nurses who have undergone further training. Whilst this trend has enabled doctors to focus their attention on other clinical areas or priorities, it has had wider implications for the health care workforce. It has meant that other 'clinical' tasks are now regarded as technical and in some senses 'up-for-grabs', encouraging competition between professions about who is the most appropriate to carry them out. For example, some physiotherapists and midwives are now routinely using ultra-sound which in the past has been the preserve of radiographers. In most instances this task drift has been used as evidence of further professional advancement. But sometimes it has merely encouraged or allowed doctors and others to drop tasks that they disliked performing.

Exploring the impact of reconfiguration

To date, much of the literature on the reconfiguration of the health-care workforce has focused on describing the extent of new role development and on exploring some of the associated professional issues. Little attention has been paid to developing a theoretical framework through which policy makers, professional leaders and service managers can begin to anticipate some of the consequences of these changes. However, systems theory can be a useful lens through which to view these developments. Given the complexity of modern health care, systems theory has much to offer in the exploration of organisational change particularly since the impact of professional developments can rarely be predicted, understood or solved by classical linear cause and effect thinking (Balle, 1994).

Provision of effective health care requires different elements of the health service to work synergistically. Systems theory seeks to explain the complexity and inter relationships between different parts of systems and between systems. For example, in the healthcare system there is a close working relationship between A&E departments and diagnostic radiography departments – but although their work overlaps they are often viewed as separate entities. Changes in one of these departments will have an impact on the other and systems theory offers a useful means of exploring these relationships. Systems theory encourages us to view healthcare as a nested system, consisting of a super or supra system, the system itself and its subsystems. The advantage of viewing healthcare as a hierarchy of systems is that it might show, for instance, that improvements in performance may require action to be taken in the supra-system. For example, if health care professionals are to continue to expand their roles, this is likely to require further changes in legislation and regulation at a national level, as has happened with initiatives to allow nurses to prescribe from a limited formulary. Thus systems theory helps us acknowledge the relationship between these micro systems and the wider health economy in which they exist.

Let us now turn our attention to some empirical data that illustrate how the health care workforce is being reconfigured.

Case study 1

The following case study derives from empirical data gathered from the Exploring New Roles in Practice Project, funded by the Department of Health as part of their Policy Research Programme's Human Resources and Effectiveness Initiative (Read *et al.*, 2001). Although the Trust described here is fictional, each of the new professional roles included was identified in at least one of the hospitals that took part in the research. The drivers for these developments were varied, but included: efforts to reduce the hours of work of junior doctors in order to meet the requirements of the European Working Time directive, and shortages in the local and national labour markets. All of the role developments were possible because of educational, clinical and technological changes within nursing and the allied health professions.

In order to identify the range and purpose of new roles for nurses and the allied health professions, a mapping exercise was carried out in a 20 per cent sample of acute Trusts in England. In the first stage of the research, information on new roles was sought using a combination of methods – beginning with interviews with Nurse Executive Directors and other senior staff and then by interviewing individual practitioners. In the second stage, we explored the operational and professional issues these new roles raised in more detail. A variety of methods was used for this, including observation, interviews and analysis of the reflective diaries kept by the practitioners for a period of four working weeks.

This case study graphically illustrates how developments in one part of the health care system can have unintended consequences elsewhere. Whilst the Trust had solved pressing problems, they had also created new problems but they were not always aware of this. Some of these problems could have been identified and solved locally by adopting a 'whole systems' approach (Fulop, Allen, Clarke and Black, 2001; Jessop and Boyle, 2001) which recognises the overlaps between sub systems. For example, concerns about whether or not the pre-op assessment nurses were inappropriately requesting X-rays could have been anticipated and very easily have been resolved through the provision of local training and the development of protocols. Similarly, those radiographers who voiced concerns about taking part in the 'red dot' scheme could have been exempted from it in the short term until the process had bedded down.

However, a number of the problems identified in the case study require national consideration. These include: training and the assessment of competence; accountability; and regulation – each of which is now considered in more detail.

Training and the assessment of competence

Previous research (Dowling, Doyal and Cameron, 1998) identified the *ad hoc* nature of the training and preparation provided to many nurses and allied health professionals working in new roles. The majority of postholders in the case study received some form of further training. However, the extent of this varied. Most was in-house and tailored to the post itself rather than being generic and transferable. For instance, all the radiographers who were expanding their roles by adding the skill of injecting contrast media were taught how to do so either by a doctor or nurse in their own Trust. The physiotherapist working as the rheumatology clinical specialist received training from the consultant who led the team and was then only assessed on completing specific procedures, such as joint injections, rather than on other core skills such as information-giving. In other words, the training these post holders received was focused on the acquisition of particular clinical skills rather than assessment of the individual's competence in performing the complete role.

Case study 1 – developments within an acute Trust

An inner city teaching hospital in the South of England decided that in order to meet targets for reducing the hours worked by doctors in training they would establish a range of new roles for a variety of different professions. Whilst the immediate driver was clear, they also hoped that these developments would help reduce their surgical waiting lists and A&E waiting times.

The new roles developed included: pre-op assessment nurses who, following training in physical health assessment, undertook preoperative assessments for surgical patients with a range of conditions – thus speeding up the system and allowing doctors to focus their attention on surgery. In the rheumatology service, physiotherapists were trained as clinical specialists in order that they could run their own clinics, where they assessed and treated patients without direct medical supervision. In the radiography department, diagnostic radiographers were trained to mark X-rays using a red dot system to identify potential fractures thus hastening the reporting process. Radiographers were also trained to administer a contrast medium by IV injection and rectally (a task traditionally performed by nurses or doctors), thus reducing the number of staff involved in carrying out these sorts of procedures. Reactions to these new developments are summarised below.

Pre-op assessment nurses – whilst patients and senior doctors were thought to be satisfied with nurses undertaking pre-operative assessments and reductions were noted in the number of late theatre cancellations, these developments were not without problems. Doctors in training, for example, reported that their opportunities for learning core clinical skills, such as taking routine bloods and performing electrocardiographs – were significantly reduced by this development. Radiologists were also concerned that although these developments may have led to improved performance within the surgical directorate, they were having a negative impact on the workload of the X-ray department because nurses were reportedly requesting unnecessary X-rays.

Rheumatology clinical specialists – postholders reported tremendous job satisfaction in taking over the total care of some rheumatology patients. However, discussion with the senior physiotherapy manager identified concerns that because this initiative was led by doctors and had developed outside the physiotherapy service, little consideration had been given to professional issues. For example, no strategies had been put in place to ensure professional physiotherapy development, supervision and peer support. Concerns were also raised by general physiotherapists, that despite the postholders' professional backgrounds, the job title did not make it clear that the patient was consulting a physiotherapist rather than a doctor.

Red dot radiographers – following appropriate training, most radiographers were happy to mark potential fractures using a red dot system and managers reported that waiting times for X-rays had improved. A minority of radiographers was unhappy about these developments, because they felt it was unclear who ultimately held responsibility for clinical decisions.

> *Radiographers administering IV injections and barium enemas* – all of the radiographers who were trained to administer IV injections were keen to do so because it allowed them greater autonomy and clearly contributed to improvements in the continuity of care. However, they were less happy about performing barium enemas. Whilst there appeared to be advantages to the patient in terms of continuity of care, and doctors and nurses were reported to be glad they no longer performed this task, radiographers were sceptical about claims that extension of their role in this way constituted professional advancement.

One way to overcome this 'local' approach to training would be to develop nationally set, competency-based assessment systems. Work currently being undertaken by 'Skills for Health' the sector skills council for health, may help. They are in the process of developing a variety of national occupational standards and competencies for the health workforce. However, the implementation of this work is likely to be contentious as health professionals have historically resisted the notion of cross-professional, competency-based assessment systems (Masterson, 2002).

Accountability

Several of the posts described above pose serious challenges to established notions of, and institutional arrangements for, operationalising individual professional and managerial accountability. For example, the rheumatology clinical specialist post highlights the often complex patterns of accountability and line management experienced by those working in new roles. This post holder was not managed by a member of her own profession and did not regard herself as professionally accountable to her own profession's senior manager. Notions of clinical accountability were similarly complex for many of the post holders in the case study. The majority traced their clinical accountability to the consultant with whom they worked and only sometimes to a manager from their own profession. Although in practice they appeared pragmatically to develop a matrix approach to understanding and allocating accountability, this approach could often be unwieldy and could raise serious professional issues (Dowling *et al.*, 1996). Potentially these concerns could be addressed by the harmonisation of regulatory frameworks intended to result from the inception of the Council for the Regulation of Health Care Professionals.

Regulation

All of the posts so far described raise questions about the nature of professional regulation. In fact, the regulatory implications of new role development have challenged the regulatory body for nursing, midwifery and health visiting – the Nursing and Midwifery Council (NMC) and its predecessor the United Kingdom Central Council for Nursing, Midwifery and Health Visiting (UKCC) for nearly a decade. At what stage does a new role become so distinct from the individual's previous professional background and training that a new or additional layer of regulation is required? Should that regulation be profession-specific or cross-professional? Early attempts to regulate different levels of practice have been firmly tied to the acquisition of higher levels of education. However, extensive work with patient representative groups commissioned by the UKCC, highlighted that the public expects that regulation should be on the basis of competence rather than achievement of education qualifications (United Kingdom Central Council for Nursing, Midwifery and Health Visiting, 2001).

Case study 2

Debates about how best to provide care across the acute/community interface have generated a range of new role developments. Drivers for these initiatives include changing attitudes with regard to where care should be provided, a desire to avoid unnecessary admissions to A&E, professionalising aspirations of ambulance staff and debates about how to fund out-of-hours care. The following case study draws on empirical data collected as part of a feasibility study investigating the development of a new role in pre-hospital care funded by Kent Surrey and Sussex Workforce Development Confederation (Humphris, Crouch, Masterson and Davey, 2002).

This project involved 10 focus groups with staff from the local health economy and user and carer representatives, and 20 interviews with key local and national figures involved in similar professional developments. An extensive review of paramedic pre- and post-registration curricula was also completed.

Adopting a systems approach highlights many actual and possible difficulties of developments such as those in the case study as they impact on the wider health and social care economy. For example, poor response times might well be interlinked with deficiencies in health and social care provision locally – particularly in relation to service provision for frail older people and people with mental health

Case study 2 – a new role in pre-hospital care

In response to concerns about meeting government targets for response times to 999 calls, a large ambulance service trust in the South of England investigated the feasibility of developing a new role in pre-hospital care. The proposed Practitioner in Emergency Care would be highly skilled in advanced trauma and life support skills and could treat and discharge patients at the scene. The role as envisaged by the Trust would enable a shift from the traditional 'swoop and scoop' function of the ambulance service to a treat and discharge service for those patients who did not require A&E or hospital admission. Practitioner in Emergency Care (PEC) – paramedics with extra training at foundation degree level – were to be dispatched to 999 calls where they would undertake a full assessment and discharge, or refer on to the most appropriate agency (acute, mental health services, GP, community nursing, social services and voluntary organisations). For example, if an elderly person had fallen out of bed, the PEC would check to see whether or not there were signs of trauma and following that assessment would organise home care or admission to A&E.

Consultation with the various key groups highlighted a number of challenges. Consumer representatives and doctors reported concerns about the level of the paramedics' skills and competencies. They doubted whether these were adequate enough to undertake the full physical assessment and treatment and referral decisions traditionally undertaken by general practitioners. Community nurses were concerned about the potential for role overlap, whilst representatives from social service departments said that they would be reluctant to accept referrals from the PEC. Ambulance personnel themselves were unwilling to acknowledge the need for a higher level of academic preparation to undertake such a role. Concerns about how the new service would be funded were also raised. For example, Primary Care Trusts were reported to be reluctant to invest scarce resources in the new service, whilst Acute Trusts were thought unlikely to invest unless significant reductions in unnecessary A&E admissions could be demonstrated. Finally, there were logistical problems in attempting to decide how many PECs were needed, how to ensure a 24/7 service, and how to manage the impact of the new role on other Ambulance Trust personnel, in relation to career development, status and remuneration.

As a result of the feasibility study it was decided not to progress this initiative in its current form. Instead, key stakeholders signalled that they wished to review the whole system of pre-hospital care. They hoped that by involving all of the organisations involved in the delivery of pre-hospital and immediate care, a more appropriate approach could be found to improve access and service quality across the pre-hospital care system including ambulance response times.

problems, rather than the speed and type of response provided by the ambulance service *per se*. In addition, any change to the role of ambulance service personnel would have implications for ambulance service training locally. It would also impinge on and overlap with existing roles in the pre-hospital care system such as District Nursing, GP, and Nurse Practitioners.

The feasibility study brought into sharp relief some of the national issues that need to be addressed if such developments in pre-hospital care are to become commonplace. These include training and the assessment of competence of ambulance staff and funding the reconfiguration of the workforce.

Training and the assessment of competence of ambulance staff

Ambulance staff are currently the only health professional group who, in most parts of the country, are trained completely outside of the higher education system, and have limited opportunities for additional post-registration education and training. At the same time, practical experience is limited with each paramedic on average only seeing one case of serious trauma per month and only a few cases of cardiac arrest per year. Concerns have been expressed about how paramedics are taught the necessary skills to assess patients accurately, make effective clinical judgements and how these skills are retained. The Audit Commission (1998) took the view that if ambulance staff were to have an extended role in pre-hospital care, then they would require a much greater depth of understanding of basic medical sciences. This view was echoed by the Joint Royal Colleges Ambulance Liaison Committee which proposed that paramedics should move towards a graduate entry profession (Walsh and Little, 2001). The Ambulance Service Association is also supportive of developing a structured pathway to degree level, combined with a restructuring of the workforce to enable jobs to be allocated to the professional with the most appropriate expertise and skills.

To meet some of the requirements for changes in professional practice, several universities are already offering a variety of degree courses for pre- and post-registration paramedics. Each course is unique, they have varying objectives and most recruit existing ambulance staff rather than providing a career foundation. There is no doubt that if such roles are to be developed nationally, further work is required in relation to establishing appropriate national intra- and inter-professional standards and awards. However, this work may now be easier to progress since paramedics have been required since April

2000 to be registered with the Health Professions Council which approves professional courses for the purposes of registration.

Funding the reconfiguration of the workforce

Whilst the development of new roles in pre-hospital care could potentially make a major contribution to improving the quality and accessibility of services, the issue of funding remains unresolved. Historically, the cost of training ambulance service staff has been excluded from the non-medical education and training levy and the feasibility study highlighted local concerns and even reluctance from some quarters about how to fund these developments. However, with the establishment of Workforce Development Confederations as the lead commissioners of education for all healthcare staff including ambulance staff in England, and their incorporation into Strategic Health Authorities, there are likely to be opportunities for systematic change.

Developing new roles – fix or fudge?

At a micro level, the case studies described above offer an illustration of how individual hospitals, directorates and other organisations view the development of new professional roles as a means to resolve local service difficulties. As such, new role developments can be seen to represent a pragmatic solution to pressing problems – a 'fix', perhaps. However, as previous research has demonstrated, many of these developments have occurred without any rigorous consideration of their wider implication either at a micro or macro level (Cameron, 2000; Humphris and Masterson, 2001; Masterson, 2002). Indeed, it can be argued that at the macro level these developments are a classical example of Lindblom's 'muddling through' approach to policy making (see Cameron and Masterson, 2000). Whilst they may appear to be a very rational response in order to cope with a range of pressures faced in the delivering of healthcare, they do not tackle underlying problems such as recruitment and retention. Seen in this light, moves to 'reconfigure' the workforce may be less of a 'fix' and more of a 'fudge', diverting attention away from the underlying problems.

Our analysis is not intended as a condemnation of these professional developments. Indeed our research has demonstrated the benefits to be accrued when experienced and appropriately trained staff are empowered to maximise their contribution to healthcare. However, we would argue that at some stage in the future, key stakeholders, collectively, will have to take a bolder course of action and consider whether or not the current range of professionals can meet the clinical, and hence workforce, needs of the NHS. Have some roles changed so much that they might more usefully be considered to constitute a new profession? Does it make sense to continue to resist the development of a generic health worker? Until such radical questioning is adopted, there will only ever be incremental changes made to the way health professionals work. As a consequence, employers will inevitably lead developments, whilst the regulatory bodies, professional associations, education institutions and indeed the government itself, will continue to respond reactively, tidying up the ensuing muddle whilst imposing a *post hoc* rationale for the creation of new professional roles.

Systems theories offer a useful means to understand why new roles develop and the effect of their emergence on different parts of the health care system. This type of approach is useful because it focuses attention on the inter-relationships both within the organisation being studied and between it and other organisations. Using this approach allows both the anticipated consequences of changes in practice and the unanticipated ones to be mapped. It also allows an exploration of the effect of these developments at a local and national level, and enables consideration of how the local impacts on the national and vice versa. For example, whilst individual Trusts may develop their own schemes for assessing competencies of those undertaking new roles, in total such individual initiatives may well challenge the very existence of some professions as currently constructed.

The way forward

The professional developments we have discussed in this chapter have played an important part in demonstrating the potential contribution of nurses and allied health professionals to delivering new patterns of health care. Such is their potential contribution that the government has confirmed its commitment to the reconfiguration of the workforce as a key plank of its modernisation strategy. In order to progress this work the government has established the Changing Workforce Programme supported by the Workforce Taskforce as a means to help employers redesign staff roles and ensure that new ways of working are embedded throughout the NHS (Department of Health, 2002).

As we have demonstrated, these developments are not without difficulty, and raise important questions about current professional boundaries, training, assessment of competence, accountability and regulation. Some of these tensions have the potential to be addressed under the present governance arrangements. The newly established Council for the Regulation of Health Care Professionals, for example, has been urged to streamline the processes of regulation across member professions and institute a strong focus on periodic revalidation linked to fitness to practice. Similarly, in response to growing public concerns about the practice of health professions, the government's review of the regulatory bodies of nurses and the allied health professions has highlighted the need for greater lay representation. Finally, concerns about competence and national standards of practice have the potential to be resolved through *Agenda for Change – Modernising the NHS pay system* (Department of Health, 2000d). This outlines plans to review the NHS pay system and to base it on nationally agreed competencies and a common pay spine for nurses and allied health professions. These reforms will no doubt help to make the development of new professional roles safer for, and more acceptable to, patients and practitioners. However, the government has yet to tackle the crucial question of whether or not the traditional map of the health care professions remains relevant to a modern NHS. Without tackling this question, attempts to reconfigure or modernise the workforce can only ever be partially successful.

References

Audit Commission (1998) *A Life in the Fast Lane: value for money in emergency ambulance services*, London: Audit Commission.

Audit Commission (2001) *Accident and Emergency*, London: Audit Commission.

Balle, M. (1994) *Managing with Systems Thinking: making dynamics work for you in business decision making*, London: McGraw-Hill.

Calman–Hine Report (1995) *A Policy Framework for Commissioning Cancer Services: a report by the Expert Advisory Group on Cancer to the Chief Medical Officers of England and Wales*, London: Department of Health.

Cameron, A. (2000) 'New Role Development in Context', in D. Humphris and A. Masterson (eds) *Developing New Clinical Roles: a guide for health professionals*, Edinburgh: Harcourt Health Sciences.

Cameron, A. and Masterson, A. (2000) 'Managing the Unmanageable? Nurse Executive Directors and new role development', *Journal of Advanced Nursing*, 31, 5, 1081–8.

Department of Health (1991) *Hours of Work of Doctors in Training: the new deal. Executive Letter (91)82*, London: Department of Health.

Department of Health (1997) *The New NHS: modern, dependable*, London: The Stationery Office.

Department of Health (1999) *Making a Difference: strengthening the nursing, midwifery and health visiting contribution to health and healthcare*, London: The Stationery Office.

Department of Health (2000a) *The NHS Plan: a plan for investment, a plan for reform*, London: The Stationery Office.

Department of Health (2000b) *A Health Service of all the Talents: report on the review of workforce planning*, London: The Stationery Office.

Department of Health (2000c) *Meeting the Challenge: a strategy for the allied health professionals*, London: The Stationery Office.

Department of Health (2000d) *Agenda for Change: modernising the NHS pay system*, London: Department of Health.

Department of Health (2001) *Reforming Emergency Care*, London: The Stationery Office.

Department of Health (2002) *Changing Workforce Programme: new ways of working in health care*, London: Department of Health.

Dowling, S., Martin, R., Skidmore, P., Doyal, L., Cameron, A. and Lloyd, S. (1996) 'Nurses Taking on Junior Doctors Work: a confusion of accountability' *British Medical Journal*, 312, 1211–14.

Dowling, S., Doyal, L. and Cameron, A. (1998) *Challenging Practice*, Bristol: Policy Press.

Doyal, L. and Cameron, A. (2000) 'Reshaping the NHS Workforce', *British Medical Journal*, 320, 1023–4.

Fulop, N., Allen, P., Clarke, A. and Black, N. (2001) 'Issues in Studying the Organisation and Delivery of Health Services', in N. Fulop, P. Allen, A. Clarke and N. Black (eds) *Studying the Organisation and Delivery of Health Services: research methods*, London: Routledge, 1–23.

Geldman, A. (2002) 'NHS Staff: the issue explained', *Guardian*, 26 June.

Humphris, D. and Masterson, A. (2001) 'Regulating Role Development', *Professional Nurse*, 16, 4, 1016–17.

Humphris, D., Crouch, R., Masterson, A. and Davey, N. (2002) *New Roles in Immediate Care: a feasibility study of the potential for a new form of emergency care practitioner within Surrey and the Isle of Wight*, Southampton: University of Southampton.

Irvine, B. and Green, D. G. (2002) 'For: Social insurance – the right way forward for health care in the United Kingdom?', *British Medical Journal*, 325, 488–90.

Jessopp, L. and Boyle, S. (2001) 'Developing Whole-systems Learning', in L. Ashburner (ed.) *Organisational Behaviour and Organisational Studies in Health Care: reflections on the future*, Basingstoke: Palgrave – now Palgrave Macmillan, 232–55.

Joint Royal Colleges Ambulance Liaison Committee (2000) *The Future Role and Education of Paramedic Ambulance Service Personnel (emerging concepts)*, London: Joint Royal Colleges Ambulance Liaison Committee.

McKee, M., Dixon, A. and Mossialos, E. (2002) 'Against: Social insurance – the right way forward for health care in the United Kingdom?', *British Medical Journal*, 325, 488–90.

Masterson, A. (2002) 'Cross-boundary Working: a macro-political analysis of the impact on professional roles', *Journal of Clinical Nursing*, 11, 3, 331–9.

Read, S. and Graves, K. (1994) *Reduction of Junior Doctors Hours in the Trent Region: the nursing contribution, Report to the Trent Taskforce*, Sheffield: Sheffield Centre for Health and Related Research.

Read, S. *et al.* (2001) *Exploring New Roles in Practice: final report*, Sheffield: ScHARR.

United Kingdom Central Council for Nursing, Midwifery and Health Visiting (1992) *The Scope of Professional Practice*, London: United Kingdom Central Council for Nursing, Midwifery and Health Visiting.

United Kingdom Central Council for Nursing, Midwifery and Health Visiting (2001) *Report of the Higher Level of Practice Pilot and Project*, London: United Kingdom Central Council for Nursing, Midwifery and Health Visiting.

Walsh, M. and Little, S. (2001) 'Study of a Nurse Practitioner Working in a Paramedic Role', *Emergency Nurse*, 9, 6, 11–14.

5
Challenging Identities: Working Together Differently in Primary Care[1]
Anne Williams

Introduction

The UK NHS faces two central problems: it is under funded and it needs to work differently (Wanless, 2001 and 2002). Derek Wanless' assessment of the NHS as we move into the twenty-first century is qualified by recognition that finance alone will not achieve modernisation, but rather the challenge is to change working practices in order to meet aspirations for a patient centred, effective and efficient health service. Aspirations for modernisation in this sense are reflected in official policy documents where patients are presented as partners in the planning and delivery of services (Department of Health, 1997 and 2001a; Welsh Office, 1998). Patients are taking greater responsibility for their health (Department of Health, 2001b) and demanding more influence over what happens to them (Wanless, 2001; Coulter, Chapter 2). Arguably, this is shaping new patient identities, and where patients are beginning to understand themselves differently, then health professionals will need to adapt.

This chapter focuses on how doctors' and, most especially, nurses' identities are being challenged and shaped on the boundary between the two professions in the context of primary care. On this boundary, as previous work has shown, the substitution of nurses for doctors and the creation of new roles form part of a workforce reconfiguration strategy – used here in the UK and internationally to meet patient expectations, rising costs and skills shortages (Sibbald, McBride and Shen, 2003).[2] The implementation of this strategy is not uniform, as Sibbald and her colleagues note, and it is the implications of its variation for how identities are challenged and reconstructed that I consider here.

The chapter opens with an appraisal of some of the legacies of traditional nursing work and how policy pressures have, over a period of years, begun to challenge these. Then follows a discussion of ways in which nurses might agree to work differently, together with other professionals, at the boundary with primary care medicine. Discussion draws in part on interviews undertaken during 1996–97 for the study 'Cultural differences between medicine and nursing and implications for primary care'[3] in which the substitution of nurses for doctors provided a focus for debating issues related to future working. Two particular themes which emerged were: the possible benefits of re-thinking the current conception of primary care as a GP-led, first contact service, and, linked to this, the issue of continuity of care. In this chapter, I reconsider these themes, treating them as discourses that not only reflect new ways of working but also provide the medium through which changing identities are played out. The chapter concludes by underlining the significance of identity for changing working practices and the challenges that it will bring for professionals.

Beginning to work differently

In this section, a sketch of the key policy initiatives driving changes in working practices is offered. The context within which change is occurring is a complex one, given the variety of nursing roles and associated relationships that contribute to the shape of contemporary primary care, and these are briefly outlined. The section ends with a brief note on the challenges facing nurses as well as general practitioners in respect of their orientation to specialist- and generalist-based health care.

Over a period of some 25 years, policy initiatives designed to improve patient care within the NHS have provided the impetus for changes in the working practices of nurses. Key factors in this process have been the reduction of junior hospital doctors' hours, increased retirement rates in primary care medicine and a move towards part-time working favoured by an increasing proportion of women in medicine (Richardson and Maynard, 1995; Carlisle and Johnstone, 1996; Taylor and Leese, 1997). These factors are linked to concerns expressed in White Papers and subsequent documents about rebuilding public confidence in the NHS (Department of Health, 1997; Welsh Office, 1998). A raised awareness of advanced and specialist practice within the nursing profession has also been an important factor in changing skill-mix, as nurses increasingly begin to undertake roles formerly performed by medical practitioners (United Kingdom Central Council for Nursing, Midwifery and Health Visiting, 1999; Nursing and Midwifery Council, 2002).

The pressure to change has created a situation where long established roles, for example health visiting, district nursing and practice nursing, share the same healthcare territory as new roles encouraged by the policy drive for modernisation of services. These latter include, for example, primary care nurse practitioners employed by general practices across the UK. In England, for example, there are both independent nurse practitioners and nurses who work in the Personal Medical Services (PMS) walk-in centres. Nurses also work for new front line organisations, including NHS Direct. In Scotland, a key new role is the family practice nurse. In the field of midwifery, midwife-led birthing centres are now in evidence right across the UK. Thus, it is apparent that nurses work in a wide range of new ways in and around primary care, and that there is considerable role variation.

Job titles in primary care can cause confusion. 'Practice nurses' and those designated 'nurse practitioners' (Royal College of Nursing, 1997) can be distinguished insofar as practice nurses have traditionally been associated with delegated work supervised by general practitioners, while nurse practitioners have been associated with role substitution, where work and responsibilities pass from doctor to nurse. However, a degree of ambiguity around ideas about delegation and nurse–doctor substitution is apparent (Williams, 2000).

Both practice nurses and nurse practitioners share a particular relationship with general practitioners by whom typically they are employed. The rise of nurse practitioner-led personal medical services, however, is an important further development. There are distinctions to be made between nurses typically employed by general practices on the one hand and, on the other, health visitors and district nurses who while they may be attached to practices, are employed by NHS Trusts. These latter groups have sometimes been referred to as community nurses (Hiscock and Pearson, 1996). However, the term 'community nurse' is not settled and the emergence of primary care Trusts (England), local health boards (Wales) and their equivalents across the UK are likely to have an impact on current distinctions across the nursing workforce. Indeed, increasing cross sector care in relation to specific groups (for example, older people) or diseases (for example, cancer, osteoporosis) means that traditional titles and assumptions about nursing in either 'primary' or 'secondary' care, 'community' or 'hospital' have to be questioned.

Both district nurses and health visitors share a history of working with patients and clients in their homes as well as in health centres and practices (Robertson, 1991). Nevertheless, there are significant differences between the two groups. The former work mainly with an ill population whereas the latter work with a well population and are strongly influenced by the idea of public health.[4] District nurses have tended to be subject to direction from general practitioners whereas health visitors have had their own caseloads. It is also possible for a 'community nurse' to be a nurse practitioner, for example a health visitor may also work as a nurse practitioner having obtained the appropriate training and education at either undergraduate or post-graduate degree level.

These complex contractual and historical differences in respect of all categories of primary care and community nurses affect their relationships with each other and with general practitioners, especially when new roles are created (Williams, 2000: 6). Hiscock and Pearson have noted how the internal market of the 1990s and the purchase of community health services by fund-holding general practitioners had the effect of eroding or abolishing established professional networks among community nurses (Hiscock and Pearson, 1996: 23). These authors' research also revealed anxiety amongst community nurses that practice nurses were eroding their responsibilities. The demise of the National Health Service internal market marked the end of general practice fund holding and heralded a new impetus for partnership. Even so, the market culture has left a legacy of competition, which will inevitably take time to eradicate entirely. This uncertain situation, together with a shift towards services which integrate health and social care, will undoubtedly affect the roles and identities of those involved, particularly in respect of orientation towards specialist and generalist health care.

Primary care means generalist-based health care to the majority of people. In respect of nursing roles and professional identity at the boundary with medicine, career pathways for nurses have tended towards specialist care, so that ideas about holism and compassion take shape in relation to specific areas of care, for example in relation to chronic disease such as asthma and diabetes. Care related to women's reproductive lives, nurses' specialisation in the care of older people and other areas have been identified. However, in certain circumstances, and especially where patients are consulting with nurses about undifferentiated problems (as is increasingly the case with nurse practitioners), then nurses, like general practitioners, must be generalist in their approach – a point noted by some who provide education and training for nurse practitioners (Barton, Thome and Hoptroff, 1999). Equally, specialist approaches to care are not entirely outside the scope of general practice medicine. General practitioners who may have specialist qualifications themselves have a duty to address the epidemiology of need in relation to specialist services (Boyd, 1996: 23–4). Established boundaries between 'general practitioner as generalist' and 'nurse as specialist' are being contested in the UK as they are elsewhere, for example in the USA (Pew Health Professions Commission, 1995), and fears in respect of a perceived threat to generalist medicine have been voiced (Primary Care Network, 1998: 1; see also Lissauer, Chapter 1, Gillam, Chapter 10).

Struggling with practice and identity

Interviews undertaken with a range of practitioners in primary care[5] indicated that substitution was felt, in broad terms, to be a positive force for change. However, as the following discussion shows, in making a case for rethinking primary care, a number of competing ideas are marshalled reflecting different models of working. The interviews show, for example, how ideas about generalist and specialist modes of working are enlisted to make a case for how things should proceed. They suggest that ideas about prevention jostle with ideas about treatment, and multi-professional and multi-agency working collide with issues around professional autonomy. Inevitably perhaps, there are reservations about substitution as a strategy for improving patient outcomes and these are reflected in particular in discussion about threats to continuity of care.

Rethinking primary care

Study respondents' comments and observations by and large, anticipated aspects of the policy development prompted by the change in government in May 1997: the incorporation of a public health perspective, multi-agency working, and user focused services (Williams, 2000). They also anticipated more recent commentary on changes in population morbidity. As noted by Wanless (2001), research suggests that while severe disability may decline, in future years the number of minor health problems may increase as many more of us live longer. The potential role of primary care nurses in dealing with minor illness is by now well documented in relation to cost, quality and acceptability to patients (Venning *et al.*, 2000; Kinnersley *et al.*, 2000; Horrocks,

Anderson and Salisbury, 2002) and there is a place for nurses as well as GPs to react to 'what comes in through the door'.

One respondent involved in nursing policy was very critical of the lack of emphasis on prevention in primary care, and stressed the importance of the linkages between prevention, public health and working collaboratively. She was concerned that 'a lot of primary care nurses ... have lost a lot of their understanding of primary prevention' and emphasised the need for a public health perspective – a perspective, which could be best fulfilled through 'multi-agency working'. She explained:

> Part of it is also recognising that you don't do it on your own either, and that primary care is about recognising the incredible importance of multi-agency working and that as a primary care practitioner you can achieve nothing unless you are co-operating with housing, social services, and social security and benefits – because if you're talking about prevention then that's what it's all about – prevention and not just about giving pills ...

Others within the study broadly shared this respondent's views on the necessity of prevention and a public health role, although not all felt that nurses had lost their understanding of primary prevention entirely. One nurse ventured that 'where nurses manage chronic disease, they do tend to embrace a preventative perspective'. Another felt that prevention of disease could not be taken for granted and that, indeed, nurses had much to offer. She elaborated:

> My thesis is that with the resurgence of infectious diseases and antibiotic resistance, nursing care – true nursing care – is going to come back into its own, and basically nurses have forgotten how to do it, and they are going to have to relearn. Yesterday I taught our child branch students about the major international issues in health care for children – and how they were war, the exploitation of child labour in the work force, the fate of girls, the missing women, and the resurgence of infectious diseases.

She continued:

> I said: 'in your lifetime as nurses, you will encounter diseases that have only just emerged and diseases that have re-emerged, which we thought had been conquered'. I asked them if they knew what

polio was and not one of them was able to tell me. Now I think that, for me, our education for nurses should not just be about the skills based stuff – can you do a venepuncture or whatever. It is 'do you know enough of the basic sciences and how to apply them in order to be innovative and original?' So when you're confronted with something you know how to deal with it.

References to a public health perspective and to recognition of the value of multi-agency working can be read as anticipating changes in policy direction. There is a clear call not to take diseases and their history for granted. The reference to a past 'true nursing care', suggests that the shape, identity and direction of future nursing may not have to stray too far from a once well-trodden way. And it is interesting to note how this past 'true nursing care' is framed as knowing about the context within which nurses practice, as reflected in the reference to major international issues in health care for children, 'war, exploitation of child labour in the work force, the fate of girls, missing women, and the resurgence of infectious diseases'. The need to be knowledgeable and to apply knowledge is also mentioned. These words can be read as a purposeful statement about the direction of travel of nursing work and identity, signalling at least one way in which nursing might reappraise and reshape its identity in the face of changes.

Antibiotic resistance, and the need to be able to react to this innovatively, was a point taken up by general practitioners in the study who were concerned that minor illnesses are not managed well by doctors, and who felt nurses might provide a better outcome for patients through the use of alternative strategies to medication. The notion of alternative strategies was often invoked. A respondent involved in general practitioner training and education commented on the prescribing practices of colleagues saying, 'one of the things we see with doctors during their training for general practice, and even at the end of it, is that they have a very limited repertoire of alternative strategies'. Another general practitioner commented:

I'm not all that convinced that general practitioners manage patients with minor self-limiting illness well, and in terms of minor self-limiting illness nurses might manage it better, because they are perhaps more reluctant to prescribe – or I should say seek a prescription. I think general practitioners over-prescribe in self-limiting conditions whereas there is very little evidence that patients benefit.

He went on to suggest that:

> If nurses could actually offer something better than a prescription to somebody who comes in with, say, a sore throat – a consultation that might involve something like reassurance, explanation of the natural history, what sorts of things will help and what won't work, what the patient can do – then the outcome could be better. What is done during the consultation is important. It's not that difficult to diagnose a cold and it's not all that difficult to find out if there's more than a cold going on ... so with a little more training ... [for a nurse] ... the outcome for patients could be better. Yes I know there's the meningitis that comes in. That may fool any of us.

Another general practitioner recalled how a colleague had 'a nurse and a physio [physiotherapist] looking after patients with arthritis', emphasising that no doctor was involved in the initiative. She commented that the nurse–physiotherapist team was 'actually reducing the prescriptions of analgesia' noting that, 'the nurse and the physio have to look at alternative ways of managing the disease other than prescribing'. From her perspective, nurses had developed a repertoire of care in the face of constraints imposed upon them as a profession, for example, constraints on prescribing. Her comments were made in the context of a discussion with the interviewer about what nurses stand to lose as their role expands, particularly in respect of prescribing medicines, a key element of the process of modernisation. She was concerned that nurses might lose their capacity to 'work holistically'. She noted how 'Macmillan nurses work very holistically – and there's a danger that if they get into the therapeutic prescribing area that they will lose some of their skills looking for management strategies that involve things other then prescriptions.'[6]

There are a number of ways of interpreting general practitioner comments on 'alternative' strategies to prescribing. One is to say that the words they use are an expression of their concern to provide a better service to patients. From this perspective, their comments can be read as part of the wider debate about finding a fit between doctors' and nurses' work and responsibilities in order to provide better outcomes for patients. General practitioners, like nurses, recognise the value of rethinking approaches to primary care that draw for their justification on ideas about public health and collaboration. However, although these particular doctors' identities were not simply tied to the idea of curing (as noted later in this chapter), there is nevertheless a hint of professional boundary marking in the words they use to comment on the contribution of nursing and what counts as nursing care. The words reflect their concern to protect a key element of their practice – therapeutic prescribing – and they appear to appeal to ideas that have become part of the mythology of health care – namely that doctors cure and nurses care.

Continuity of care

Analysis of views on continuity of care provides another focus for exploring the struggles people are experiencing in coming to terms with the implications of working differently. The suggestion that nurses are eminently suited to providing continuity of care, particularly in certain areas, came from general practitioners, nurses and the consumer spokesperson within the study. However, continuity of care was not seen unproblematically as the domain of nursing. Indeed, there were concerns that the substitution for doctors by nurses had disrupted continuity of care – in relation to both general practitioners' and nurses' work – and that it might undermine the two professions' relationships with patients.

One study finding was that the process of substitution had for some GPs eroded their capacity to care for families holistically. Where nurses are now undertaking the care of certain family members – for example, a child who has asthma or an older member with diabetes – the general practitioner's view of the whole family is disrupted. One respondent suggested that GPs are worried that practice nurses are actually taking away from them their role of continuing care management of the chronically ill – asthmatics, diabetics and that they are only seeing people when there is a crisis. She added 'GPs say they don't actually like working in that way because they lose the sense of continuity'. She explained:

> Our work is defined by relationships ... If you say [referring to a patient] well actually she's got this disease, she should go to that clinic [run by practice nurse], then that cuts across our whole approach, which is about relationships and people [as well as] about working with disease ... If the practice nurse is, say, dealing with all the asthma [in the practice] then she is not seeing the whole – the mother, perhaps going through a divorce or an affair or something that – might affect the asthma. Equally you don't have an opportunity as a GP to see the mother alongside the child, when she is apparently well. So you are losing opportunities.

These words are interesting in that they link ideas about disease and pathology with family events and processes (cf. Richardson and Maynard, 1995). The words also suggest a connection between ideas about taking into account the whole situation and, importantly, connecting an understanding of disease to an understanding of relationships. Also conveyed is a hint of concern for the potential loss to patients should a holistic generalist perspective be compromised by work undertaken by nurses who provide specialist care such as given in the asthma clinic. This said, general practitioners recognised the value of nurses' specialist work. 'As far as chronic diseases are concerned', said one GP, 'I honestly think that nurses probably do a better job.' She added:

> I wouldn't have told you that five years ago but the evidence now is that nurses are looking after the asthmatics better and looking after the diabetics and the hypertensives, providing they're routine. The routine stuff can be handled extremely well by practice nurses – immunisation programmes are run by practice nurses. Practice nurses are better than doctors at doing routine audits – certainly carrying them out, and also in terms of planning what audit needs to be done.

As well as reading how holism is shaped within a generalist perspective we can read in the above account how the general practitioner differentiates between medicine and nursing by appeal to nurses' adeptness at 'routine stuff'. From this perspective, it is possible to interpret the words as highlighting a boundary constructed between 'us' and 'them' in a context where the management of what could be perceived variously as a crisis in the UK general practice workforce (Young, Leese and Sibbald, 2001), or an increasingly demanding public, has become critical. The day-to-day encounter with patients whose collective expectations are higher than they have ever been requires ways of working differently, which, in turn, fundamentally challenge the ways in which health care professionals perceive themselves. The general practitioner's words display how she is quite explicitly struggling to make sense of herself and, indeed, her very sense of professional identity. In part she does this through placing the 'other' – in this case the practice nurse – within the particular category of managers of 'routine stuff'. In doing this she engages in a process described by Celia Davies (2002) as creating identity through 'othering', which is reminiscent of Clifford's much earlier (1986) observation that every version of an 'other' is also the construction of a 'self'. However, Davies takes us further by emphasising the ways in which 'othering' 'sets a boundary between people by involving binary thinking that simultaneously values the self and devalues the other'. In the context of the present discussion, it is possible to interpret the general practitioner's reference to 'routine stuff' as doing precisely this, which is not say that the specialist skills of the nurse go unrecognised. As with the deployment of the word 'alternative', 'routine stuff' is part of a complex narrative, which is recounted at the boundary of 'us' and 'them' and where, as Southerton (2002: 173) suggests, group similarities end and differences begin.

Nurses, like general practitioners, struggled with making sense of their roles and responsibilities. Within the study, the substitution of a nurse for a doctor was also seen to disrupt aspects of work seen by many to be central to a nursing role and identity: namely the everyday, basic continuity of what matters to patients. One nurse respondent expressed great concern that there are people who are starving to death and nobody is feeding them because trained nurses no longer feel that feeding patients is part of their role. She added 'primary care nurses at the moment – a lot of them have lost an understanding of primary care as prevention, continuity and attending to basic needs'.

This observation notwithstanding, the point was made by another nurse that 'nurses do have a feel for something much broader in terms of what the delivery of humane care is about'. She said: 'I think this is because they are the people who spend most time with patients. The nurse has to sort of live part of her life with that patient's consciousness.' Another nurse's words throw some light on ideas about continuity of care, meeting basic needs and 'living with the patient's consciousness'. She referred to what she called 'the cup of tea issue' in relation to district nurses. In her words:

> I feel very strongly that there's a lot of therapeutic skill that's involved – which is talked about in a dismissive way as basic nursing care. You know, bed-bathing, helping people to get dressed. I think it's the bringing together of those basic sorts of tasks which actually counts as something much more than that. It might include spending half an hour with someone, unpacking a lot of other issues and anxiety, worries, health issues or family. I think it's that rounded role which is difficult to articulate and difficult to defend when managers are asking for outputs. So I think there's a danger that nurses might lose that aspect of care with the move to substitution ... this is care that is, I think, valued by patients and it is what makes the work rewarding.

The respondent's words can be read as indicative of the way in which nurses can provide continuity to individual patients' lives. In this sense, they underline the view put forward generally by study respondents that, for nurses, holistic care is about caring for the whole person (cf. May, 1991 and 1992). At the same time, as the respondent recognises, the 'rounded role' involved in holistic care of this sort is difficult to articulate and defend when managers are asking for outputs, a reflection of Davies' (1995) assessment of the predicament of nursing, when justifying values that do not easily fit with the world of rational, instrumental action.

Conclusion: identity challenges

These nurses' and general practitioners' accounts bring into sharp focus ways in which identities are being challenged. There are, as suggested, a number of readings to be made. One reading might be that there is evidence of purposeful statements of the direction of travel of nursing work and identity. Another reading might be that there is a degree of uncertainty about orientations to work. Who should care and who should cure? What counts as specialist and what counts as generalist care? Yet another reading might be about the structural and power differences between medicine and nursing and how these impact on the extent to which new identities will be recognised and accepted.

All readings bear on the future of primary care and are intimately related to how the key players identify themselves and their contribution. For example, it is possible to argue from respondents' accounts that some categories of nurses working in primary care define their domain of work more widely than the reactive, first contact service traditionally led by GPs. Nurses tend to prefer the term 'primary health care' to 'primary care', drawing on ideas about public health and community. In this respect, they are shaping their contribution in line with policy steering the incorporation of public health into primary care and the integration of health and social care (Department of Health, 2001a; National Assembly for Wales, 2001a and 2001b). We could say that nurses are distinguishing their practice from that of general practitioners. However, it is also the case that some nurses, particularly primary care nurse practitioners, see themselves as generalist in their approach and therefore there is some convergence between nurses and general practitioners. Similarly, general practitioners differentiate themselves from nurses, for example, by appeal to the idea of nurses' 'alternative' strategies in relation to infection and pain control. At the same time, there is also appeal in the accounts to ideas often associated with nursing – such as 'caring', as opposed to curing, and taking a holistic approach.

In common with the rest of society, nurses and doctors draw on a broad range of ideas and shared values in order to justify their various practices. The ideas and values which influence contemporary life are divergent and seemingly contradictory. Thus, while doctors and nurses value compassion and the holistic dimension of their engagement with patients, they will at the same time value the sense of detachment associated with a spirit of scientific and critical enquiry. Doctors and nurses firmly believe in the centrality of the patient to all their endeavours, and a respect for the integrity of patients is paramount. At the same time, both have attended to the promotion of professional interests (Williams, 2000).

What, therefore, are the challenges around emerging identities that need to be addressed in order to secure changes in practice in support of an effective, efficient patient centred service? As noted, nurses and doctors are involved in a process of constructing and reconstructing identities, and it appears that they are doing this on the same territory and with reference to similar sets of ideas. The process echoes in some respects the reflexive modernisation thesis which contests taken for granted links between identity and the authoritative norms of social institutions. Sociologists including Baumann (1988) Beck (1992, 1994 and 2000) and Giddens (1991) have suggested that in a post-Fordist market place individuals are now free to construct their own identities from a number of lifestyles, albeit with associated responsibilities and risk. The thesis has its critics, notably those who have observed how it ignores gender differences, especially in relation to the interface between work and family life (Wajcman and Martin, 2002). This criticism has potential relevance for the future healthcare workforce. On one level, the changing workforce profile in primary care medicine means that new ways of working, for example salaried appointments, once anathema to a broadly male general practice, are now a possibility because they may be preferred by the increasing number of women who want greater flexibility around work and family. On another level, as noted by Davies (1995: 38), women in nursing and medicine have been called on 'either to renounce a female cultural identity, or ... find themselves defined as female and silenced ... misunderstood when they try to articulate and uphold values that do not fit with the masculine world of rational instrumental action'. General practice medicine continues to be the taken for granted leader in primary care (Williams, 2000: 96) – a powerful identity. Structural inequality between nursing and medicine exacerbates the situation and there is little substantial evidence to suggest that the historical relationship between the two professions is being seriously challenged.

A further criticism of the reflexive modernisation thesis is that it underplays the significance of the need for 'tribal' affiliation or the need to belong (Southerton, 2002). Certainly this critique has relevance for the present discussion, insofar as in drawing boundaries between 'us' and 'them', doctors and nurses indicate affiliation. However, in considering how identities are established, it is useful to bear in mind anthropologist Judith Okely's words 'boundaries may be constructed in unusually elusive ways. Differences can be disguised by similarities and lost in the commonplace' (Okely, 1996: 4). When analysing doctors' and nurses' needs to belong, it is tempting to assume that affiliation lies in relation to profession only. However, it is also important to take account of ideas, values and beliefs that unite people across professional boundaries. One of the wider findings of the study discussed here was that of a tension between allegiances to *profession* on the one hand and to *place of work* on the other. So that, in one instance when a Trust manager was asked about community nurses employed by the Trust but attached to and working in general practices, she said: 'I hate to say it, but I've seen a change in staff loyalties – first to the GPs and to us second' (Williams, 2000: 56). Could it become the case that affiliation to place of work will take precedence over affiliation to profession in the changing context of primary care?

In order for working practices to change, retreat into traditional forms of professional identity must somehow be dislodged. There is also a need for revision of the balance of power between the various stakeholders in primary care – one that might encourage new collective forms of identity. Some might suppose that the competitive legacy of the internal market of the 1990s enterprise culture set in motion the means by which this might be achieved. The argument rests in part on the view that market culture has, at least theoretically, made a difference to the health professional–client relationship, so that once passive users of health services are becoming more skilful in expressing their demands for the health service they want. While forces which serve towards equalising the relationship between medicine and the public may not immediately affect the status of nursing in relation to medicine, the consumer challenge could pave the way for more flexible working practices. Realisation of this would go some way towards meeting aspirations for a patient centred, effective and efficient health service.

Notes

1. I would like to thank the Open University Press, Buckingham for their generosity in allowing me to draw on the book *Nursing, Medicine and Primary Care*.
2. The evidence base supporting the substitution of nurses for doctors in primary care for routine management of chronic disease, management of minor illness and health promotion is by now extensive (Sibbald, McBride and Shen, 2003). Recent findings from randomised controlled trials (Kinnersley *et al.*, 2000; Venning *et al.*, 2000) suggest that nurses will not necessarily save money since, although it is relatively cheaper to train nurses as compared with doctors, longer consultation times, recall of patients at a higher rate together with the fact that nurses tend to have a lower life time workforce participation eliminates any net savings in salary (Sibbald, McBride and Shen, 2003).
3. Interviews were conducted during 1996–97 for this study, based at the National Primary Care Research and Development Centre, University of Manchester. This empirical work provided a foundation for the subsequent publication, *Nursing, Medicine and Primary Care* (Williams, 2000).
4. During the 1980s and 1990s, health policy documents (Department of Health and Social Security, 1987; Department of Health, 1991 and 1992) emphasised the role of disease prevention and health promotion. The Royal College of General Practitioners produced a series of reports on this (Nettleton, 1995: 230). The 1990 and 1993 GP contracts offered specific financial incentives to establish health promotion clinics and programmes. Nurses in practices were seen as essential to moving forward these agendas.
5. The sample of 15 interviews included nurses working in primary care, nurses in senior administrative and academic posts, and general practitioners.
6. Subsequent to the 1996–7 study, the extension of independent nurse prescribing in England has been initiated, see Department of Health (2002).

References

Barton, T. D., Thome, R. and Hoptroff, M. (1999) 'The Nurse Practitioner: redefining occupational boundaries', *International Journal of Nursing Studies*, 36, 1, 57–63.

Baumann, Z. (1988) *Freedom*, Buckingham: Open University Press.

Beck, U. (1992) *Risk Society: towards a new modernity*, London: Sage.

Beck, U. (1994) 'The Reinvention of Politics: towards a theory of reflexive modernisation' in U. Beck, A Giddens and S. Lash (eds) *Reflexive Modernisation: politics, tradition and aesthetics in the modern social order*, Cambridge: Polity Press.

Beck, U. (2000) *The Brave New World of Work*, Cambridge: Polity Press.

Boyd, R. (1996) 'Challenges to a Primary Care-Led NHS: a medical specialist's view', in National Primary Care Research Development Centre (ed.) *What is the Future for a Primary Care-Led NHS?*, Oxford: Radcliffe Medical Press.

Carlisle, R. D. and Johnstone, S. (1996) 'Factors Influencing the Response to Advertisements for General Practice Vacancies', *British Medical Journal*, 313, 468–71.

Clifford, J. (1986) 'Introduction: partial truths', in J. Clifford and G. Marcus (eds) *Writing Culture*, San Francisco: University of California Press.

Davies, C. (1995) *Gender and the Professional Predicament in Nursing*, Buckingham, Open University Press.

Davies, C. (2002) 'Workers, Professions and Identities', in J. Henderson and D. Atkinson (eds) *Managing Care in Context*, London: Routledge.

Department of Health (1991) *The Health of the Nation*, CM 1523, London: Her Majesty's Stationery Office.

Department of health (1992) *The Health of the nation: a strategy for health in England*, CM 1986, London: Her Majesty's Stationery Office.

Department of Health (1997) *The New NHS: modern dependable*, London: Her Majesty's Stationery Office.

Department of Health (2001a) *The NHS Plan: A plan for investment. A plan for reform* [online], Department of Health. Available from: *http://www.nhs.uk/ nationalplan* [Accessed: 23 June 2003].

Department of Health (2001b) *The Expert Patient: a new approach to chronic disease management for the 21st century*, London: The Stationery Office.

Department of Health (2002) *Extending Independent Nurse Prescribing within the HNS in England*, London: The Stationery Office.

Department of Health and Social Security (1987) *Promoting Better Health: the government's programme of improving primary health care*, London: Her Majesty's Stationery Office.

Giddens, A. (1991) *Modernity and Self Identity*, Cambridge: Polity Press.

Hiscock, J. and Pearson, M. (1996) 'Professional Costs and Invisible Value in the Community Nursing Market', *Journal of Interprofessional Care*, 10, 1, 23–31.

Horrocks, S., Anderson, E. and Salisbury, C. (2002) 'Systematic Review of whether Nurse Practitioners Working in Primary Care can provide Equivalent Care to Doctors', *British Medical Journal*, 324, 819–23.

Kinnersley, P., Anderson, E., Parry, K., Clement, J., Archard, L., Turton, P., Stainthorpe, A., Fraser, A., Butler, C. and Rogers, C. (2000) 'Randomised Controlled Trial of the Nurse Practitioner versus General Practitioner Care for Patients Requesting "Same Day" Consultations in Primary Care', *British Medical Journal*, 320, 1043–8.

May, C. (1991) 'Affective Neutrality and Involvement in Nurse–Patient Relationships: perceptions of appropriate behaviour among nurses in acute medical and surgical wards', *Journal of Advanced Nursing*, 16, 552–8.

May, C. (1992) 'Nursing Work, Nurses' Knowledge, and the Subjectificaton of the Patient', *Sociology of Health and Illness*, 14, 4, 472–87.

National Assembly for Wales (2001a) *Improving Health in Wales: the future of primary care*, Cardiff: National Assembly for Wales.

National Assembly for Wales (2001b) *Improving Health in Wales: a plan for the NHS with its partners*, Cardiff: National Assembly for Wales.

Nettleton, S. (1995) *The Sociology of Health and Illness*, Oxford: Policy Press.

Nursing and Midwifery Council (2002) *The Code of Professional Conduct*, London: Nursing and Midwifery Council.

Okely, J. (1996) *Own or Other Culture*, London: Routledge.

Pew Health Professions Commission (1995) *Critical Challenges: revitalising the health professions for the twenty first century*, San Francisco: Centre for the Health Professions, University of California.

Primary Care Network (1998) 'PCGs are Off and Rolling', *Primary Care Network: an information resource service*, 2, 2, 1.

Richardson, G. and Maynard, A. (1995) *Fewer Doctors? More Nurses? A Review of the Knowledge Base of Nurse–Doctor substitution, Discussion Paper 135*, York: Centre for Health Economics, University of York.

Robertson, C. (1991) *Health Visiting in Practice*, Edinburgh: Churchill Livingstone, Second Edition.

Royal College of Nursing (1997) *Nurse Practitioners: your questions answered*, London: Royal College of Nursing.

Sibbald, B., McBride, A. and Shen, J. (2003) *Skill Mix and Substitution*, Paper presented to the SDO Conference 'Delivering Research for Better Health Services', 19 March, London.

Southerton, D. (2002) 'Boundaries of "Us" and "Them": Class, Mobility and Identification in a New Town', *Sociology*, 36, 1, 171–193.

Taylor, D. and Leese, B. (1997) 'Recruitment, Retention and Time Commitment Change of General Practitioners in England and Wales 1990–1994: a retrospective study', *British Medical Journal*, 314, 1806–10.

United Kingdom Central Council for Nursing, Midwifery and Health Visiting (1999) *A Higher Level of Practice*, London: United Kingdom Central Council for Nursing, Midwifery and Health Visiting.

Venning, P., Durie, A., Roland, M., Roberts, C. and Leese, B. (2000) 'Randomised Controlled Trial Comparing Cost Effectiveness of General Practitioners in Primary Care', *British Medical Journal*, 320, 1048–53.

Wajcman, J. and Martin, B. (2002) 'Narratives of Identity in Modern Management: the corrosion of gender difference?', *Sociology*, 36, 4, 985–1002.

Wanless, D. (2001) *Securing our Future Health: taking a long-term view, interim report*, London: HM Treasury.

Wanless, D. (2002) *Securing our Future Health: taking a long-term view, final report*, London: HM Treasury.

Welsh Office (1998) *NHS Wales: putting patients first*, London: The Stationery Office.

Williams, A. (2000) *Nursing, Medicine and Primary Care*, Buckingham: Open University Press.

Young, R., Leese, B. and Sibbald, B. (2001) 'Inbalances in the GP Labour Market in the UK: evidence from a postal survey and interviews with GP leavers', *Work, Employment and Society*, 15, 4, 699–719.

6
Specialties in Transition: the Case of Oral and Maxillofacial Surgery[1]
Jenny Gallagher

Introduction

Consultants, the most highly and thus expensively trained section of the health workforce, and the most specialised, have traditionally occupied a privileged position at the top of the medical and dental professions and the National Health Service (NHS) workforce. Together with their academic counterparts holding honorary consultant appointments they have been the teachers, trainers, researchers and innovators within hospitals since the late nineteenth-century (Peterson, 1978; Abel-Smith, 1964). Their leadership and policies have had a major impact on overall health care (McKee and Healy, 2002). However, specialist services are now facing a range of pressures for change, which will impact on the nature of care, how it is provided, where and by whom (Allen, 2000; Black, 2002). What will be the long-term impact? Will consultants retain their position at the top of the system?

This chapter examines the future of one area of specialist care, oral and maxillofacial surgery (OMFS). OMFS is a recognised surgical specialty in Europe and the lead dentally-based specialty in the UK (British Association of Oral and Maxillofacial Surgeons, 2002). It is best described as a medical specialty with its roots in dentistry, having emerged as the first dental specialty within the NHS and become a recognised surgical specialty of the medical profession. All recently qualified consultants in OMFS are dually qualified in medicine and dentistry. Consideration of this specialty involves examination of its reported overlap in skills and interests with four other groups. These are the two surgical specialties of otorhinolaryngology (ENT) and plastic surgery with which OMFS shares a medical qualification

(Clinical Standards Advisory Group, 1998; Edwards, Johnson, Cooper and Warnakulasuriya, 1998), and the two dental specialties of oral surgery and surgical dentistry.

The chapter opens with some background on the development of these five specialties and their relative size. A health futures study undertaken with specialists is briefly described before moving on to present some of its key findings.[2] A third section considers findings in the light of sociological theorising about professional development and possible future implications are then explored.

Background and study design

At the outset, it is important to distinguish between the terms 'specialist' and 'consultant'. These terms were generally synonymous at the start of the NHS in 1948. However, since the creation of formal specialist lists in the late 1990s, they are no longer one and the same. A 'consultant' is an NHS appointment, traditionally held by doctors or dentists, and one which indicates an established status in the social and economic order of hospital care. A 'specialist' is someone whose name is held on a Specialist Register, held by the General Medical Council (GMC) and the General Dental Council (GDC) respectively.

The numbers of specialists exceed those of consultants because the newly created specialist lists were not limited to those in consultant posts. Applicants who could demonstrate equivalent competencies to those expected of a specialist, as well as all existing consultants, were permitted entry to the requisite GMC and GDC lists. All consultants must now be on a relevant specialist list; but all specialists do not necessarily hold an NHS consultant post. They may be trainees who have completed their specialist training but not yet been appointed as a consultant, or, more importantly, individuals who hold a more junior post within the NHS or work privately.[3]

The NHS dictionary of terms and standards suggests the following definition of specialties, with the rider that only titles recognised by the Royal Colleges and Faculties should be used:

> Specialties are divisions of clinical work which may be defined by body systems (dermatology), age (paediatrics), clinical technology (nuclear medicine), clinical function (rheumatology), group of diseases (oncology) or combination of these factors (NHS Information Authority, 2002).[4]

Of the five specialties considered in this study, ENT is the oldest. It formed in the early part of the twentieth century, prior to the creation of the NHS, from two distinct groups: laryngologists and otologists, these forerunners having been amongst the earliest surgical specialties, with the nose forming an anatomical bridge between the two territories (Stevenson and Guthrie, 1949). During the twentieth century, the two World Wars provided the opportunity for rapid development of skills and knowledge, which were transferable to civilian life. Specialist groups, such as orthopaedics, anaesthetics, plastic surgery and dental/maxillofacial surgery, tentatively established in war, were formalised in the creation of the NHS in the post-war years with consultant appointments (Seward, 1998).

From the creation of the NHS up until the late 1990s, the pace of change was relatively steady with the emergence of new specialties, often from an academic base (Rivett, 1998), and the formalisation of training programmes. However, the current pace of change appears much more swift and the consequences more far-reaching. In the process of implementing European Union (EU) legislation to support the freedom of movement of the workforce and in preparing for the introduction of specialist lists, the Chief Dental Officer took the option to formalise a range of dental specialties considered appropriate to the UK NHS (NHS Executive, 1995).[5] A new non-consultant specialty of surgical dentistry was created in what was essentially a top down, rather than a professionally driven process. Oral surgery, a recognised specialty in Europe, also formally re-emerged[6] in the UK following the introduction of specialist lists. Three specialties thus provide dental surgery under the umbrella of OMFS: OMFS itself, oral surgery and surgical dentistry. Their respective roles are matters of research and keen debate (Shepherd, 1999; Coulthard, 2000b).

ENT and surgical dentistry are the largest of the five specialties to be considered (Figure 6.1). Surgical dentists, as already noted, are a special case. All members of this new specialty joined the list within the last five years on the basis of their experience. Over half will not have had any formal specialist training. Many work under the umbrella of OMFS within hospitals. It is possible for individuals to be on more than one specialist register on the basis of their ability to demonstrate competence in that specialty and, not surprisingly, most OMFS surgeons are on both the oral surgery and surgical dentistry lists. The number of singly qualified oral surgeons is small but the volume of specialists registered for surgical dentistry alone is more than equivalent to OMFS.

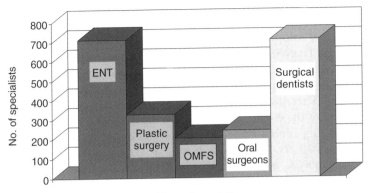

Figure 6.1: Number of UK registered specialists in five inter-related specialties

Note: There is overlap between specialties with a dental base, in that the majority of OMF surgeons are also on the oral surgery and surgical dentistry lists.

Sources: GMC, 1999; GDC, Nov, 2001.

The following sections report on a study of the future of OMFS in London (see Gallagher, 2002). This is the first study of its kind to examine a surgical specialty in the UK. It uses a multi-method health futures approach, advocated by the World Health Organisation (Garrett, 1999) and commonly used in the Netherlands (Schreuder, 1995). Although the focus of the study was largely on London, the surgical caseload is similar to the national picture and the issues arising from this study are applicable nationally and across specialisms (British Association of Oral and Maxillofacial Surgeons, 2002; Dhariwal, Goodey and Shepherd, 2002).

Study findings

Three main methods were used to produce the findings described in this section. A baseline analysis of in patient and day surgery admissions was conducted. It covered all five specialties and used Hospital Episode Statistics for London. Over an eight-year period, this yielded a total of 807,619 episodes of care.[7] In-depth interviews were conducted with experts both nationally and in London. A questionnaire was also administered to London's key players, including all specialists in the five groups, public health directors and primary care leaders, including chairs of local dental committees (Gallagher, 2002).

Overlaps in service provision

Analysis of the baseline data revealed that over half of the cases involved low complexity procedures and that these were different for each group. There was no overlap between the three specialties shown in Figure 6.2 on the core of work of each. The overlap came in the less common fields of facial trauma repair and head and neck cancer, and the overall percentage of overlap rose over the study period from 7 to 12 per cent of the combined caseload during the 1990s. Against a backdrop of falling admissions, OMFS involvement has increased its caseload by over 70 per cent in both areas of activity.

Further analysis revealed that each of the three specialties had a distinct contribution to make within the areas of overlap. In the field of facial trauma repair, ENT and plastic surgery involvement focused almost exclusively on nasal and soft tissue trauma repair respectively, whereas OMFS performed all aspects of repair. OMFS repaired nine per cent of nasal bone fracture cases, 97 per cent of the other facial bone fractures and 43 per cent of soft tissue cases. Altogether, OMFS treated the highest volume of cases (48 per cent), the majority of which required more than one surgical procedure (79 per cent). Figure 6.3 offers a graphic representation of the 'contests for care' between these three specialties around facial trauma repair.

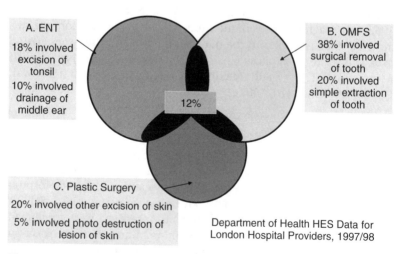

A. ENT
18% involved excision of tonsil
10% involved drainage of middle ear

12%

B. OMFS
38% involved surgical removal of tooth
20% involved simple extraction of tooth

C. Plastic Surgery
20% involved other excision of skin
5% involved photo destruction of lesion of skin

Department of Health HES Data for London Hospital Providers, 1997/98

Figure 6.2: Overlapping activity of three surgical specialties

Note: The two most common operation groups are shown for each specialty.

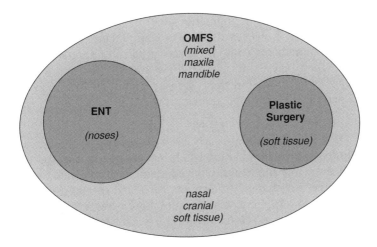

Figure 6.3: OMFS monopoly in facial trauma repair, 1997–8

Notes: This figure relates to skill-base of specialties rather than the volume of care and thus is not a scale drawing. It is also important to note that the volume of cases is small. It represents 3 per cent of total caseload and 5 per cent of OMFS caseload.

The picture for head and neck cancer was slightly different. Here, ENT was the main player by volume, with plastic surgery leading on skin cancer. Over the eight-year period, OMFS had also expanded its activity in the field, focusing on lip and oral cavity, skin, salivary glands and neck dissections. However, by the end of the study period, cancer surgery only represented 4 per cent of OMFS caseload, one-quarter of which related to skin cancer. The most plausible explanation for the increasing role of OMFS in these fields of activity would appear to lie with its formal surgical training.

Further indication of the importance of considering the centrality of OMFS in bridging the surgical and dental spectrum emerged from a calculation based on the percentage of its core workload (see Circle B in Figure 6.2) which could be undertaken by oral surgeons and surgical dentists. The calculation was based on the surgical procedures covered by training programmes in which specialists are expected to be competent (Joint Committee for Specialist Training in Dentistry, 2000a and 2000b). This showed that 96 per cent of OMFS caseloads in 1997–98 fell within the scope of oral surgeons and almost two-thirds of the caseload involved routine operations within the recognised remit of surgical dentists. However, all of this work is currently undertaken under the umbrella of OMFS, as the recognised NHS specialty.

In all, then, each one of the three surgical specialties had its common core of work, but there were clear contests for care in which OMFS played an increasingly dominant role.

Perceived drivers of change

The in-depth interviews among national leaders in the specialties, colleges, academia and health services, identified a wide range of inter-related forces for change. Informants perceived specialist services as being forced to respond to many external pressures, the main impact of which rationalised service organisation and delivery, with major implications for the future nature and range of specialties. In the ques-tionnaire, London's specialists were asked to score a list of the forces for change according to their perceived impact on their own specialty, and if necessary to add to the list (see Table 6.1). There was a strong consensus that 'specialisation' and 'NHS funding' were the main drivers for change. The broad notion of 'health policy', together with specific policy issues such as clinical governance, more formalised training and so on were also seen as important by over three-quarters of the sample. 'Demanding patients' also figured highly. It is important to note that respondents did not raise any issues as of specific relevance for London.

Comparisons between the groups are not shown in the table, but there was one significant difference between the responses of OMFS and surgical dentistry. Whereas only 43 per cent of OMFS perceived that 'specialists' need for fulfilment' was a driver for change, this rose to 82 per cent for the new speciality of surgical dentistry.[8]

Alternative futures?

The questionnaire asked London's key players to judge who would provide various aspects of surgery in 2020. They were given a series of options, derived from the interviews, where each of the main areas of overlapping surgical interest had been addressed. For each category of care, they were asked to identify who they perceived would provide most care in future. The results in Table 6.2 suggest that OMFS, fol-lowed closely by a multidisciplinary team, was the main candidate for facial trauma surgery. For cancer surgery, there was a strong consensus

Table 6.1: Top 10 forces for change identified by specialists in London across the five specialties (n = 112[a])

Forces for change	Mean score	Strongly agree or agree: No. (%)	Uncertain No. (%)	Disagree or strongly disagree: No. (%)	N
Specialisation	4.3	96 (90%)	10 (9%)	1 (1%)	107
Funding of NHS	4.3	90 (82%)	18 (16%)	2 (2%)	110
Health policy [b]	4.1	82 (77%)	21 (20%)	3 (3%)	106
Clinical governance	4.0	83 (76%)	21 (19%)	5 (5%)	109
Evidence-based care	3.9	84 (77%)	18 (17%)	7 (7%)	109
Formalised higher specialist training	3.9	82 (76%)	17 (16%)	9 (8%)	108
Public demands	3.9	81 (74%)	24 (22%)	4 (4%)	109
National service frameworks	3.9	76 (71%)	24 (22%)	7 (7%)	107
Demanding patients	3.8	76 (70%)	24 (22%)	9 (8%)	109
Revalidation	3.7	69 (64%)	29 (27%)	10 (9%)	108

Note: a. The overall response rate was 50 per cent, and there were no significant differences between specialties on the main drivers for change.
b. The survey was undertaken just after publication of the NHS Plan in 2000.

around provision in future by a multidisciplinary team, followed by the notion of a new super-specialty of head and neck cancer surgery. A high proportion of respondents felt that routine surgical dentistry, currently within the scope of OMFS, would be the province of surgical dentists in future.

Additional questions explored the relationship and future roles of the new specialty of surgical dentistry and the established consultant-led specialty of OMFS (Table 6.3), recognising that many surgical dentists work within OMFS teams currently. Surgical dentists were significantly more likely to perceive that working independently from OMFS in future was desirable, whilst consultants in OMFS perceived that surgical dentists would continue to work as part of their hospital teams. In addition, surgical dentists were significantly more likely to

Table 6.2:   London's key players' views on who would provide most care in 2020, by category of care

Categories of care	N	Predicted provider in 2020		
		High support	*Medium support*	*Low support* [c]
Facial trauma repair	93	OMFS (46%; n = 43)	Multidisciplinary facial trauma teams (43%; n = 40)	Head and neck trauma surgeons (10%; n = 9)
Head and neck cancer	96	Multidisciplinary head and neck cancer teams (64%; n = 61)	Head and neck cancer surgeons (20%; n = 19)	Existing individual specialties [b] (16%; n = 16)
Routine dental surgery [a]	58	Surgical dentists (72%; n = 43)	OMFS (23%; n = 14)	

Note: a. This question was restricted to OMFS, oral surgeons and surgical dentists all of whom are currently involved in the provision of this care.
b. ENT or OMFS or plastic surgery were supported as individual providers of care.
c. Scenarios with very low support are not reported.

perceive that higher specialist training in a primary care setting was desirable. In sum, it is clear that both experts and key players were alert to many forces driving change. Among themselves, however, they had different preferred outcomes to the current contests for care.

Table 6.3:   Key players' views on future relationships of dentally-based specialties and future training arrangements (n = 50)

Specialty	Category	Specialists response on desirability of future scenarios[a]		
		Surgical dentists independent of OMFS	*Surgical dentists in a team under OMFS*	*Specialist training in a primary care setting*
OMFS	Mean	1.9[b]	8.5[b]	3.1[b]
	N	20	21	21
	Std Deviation	2.7	1.4	3.1
Surgical dentistry	Mean	7.7	5.2	6.7
	N	20	17	18
	Std Deviation	2.5	3.4	2.7

Notes: a. Responses were scored on a scale of 0–10 with 10 being very desirable.
b. Denotes a significant difference between the two specialities $p < 0.001$ (Mann Whitney).

1. Starting point	Creation of a professional group
2. Overall objective	Achieving:
	Monopoly in the market for services based on their expertise
	Status in the social and economic order
3. Sub-goals	Jurisdiction carved out
	Producing the producers
	Definition, development and monopolisation of professional knowledge
	Achieving respectability
4. Negotiation with other actors	State
	Other occupations
	Educational institutions
	Public
	Clientele/potential patients
5. Context	Social
	Political
	Cultural

Figure 6.4: The professional project

Source: Based on Macdonald, 1995: 187–9.

Exploring a changing professional project

In examining further the inter-relationships between specialties and processes of change, it is helpful to draw on aspects of the sociological analysis of professions which focus on how professional groups achieve and maintain their status. Macdonald (1995), building on Larson's (1997) concept of a 'professional project' provides a theoretical framework for considering the trajectory of the five specialties and analysing their dynamic nature. While Macdonald's arguments were originally designed to apply to professions as a whole, their application as here to specialties, as groups within medicine and dentistry, is revealing. Five elements of Macdonald's account of the professional project are summarised in Figure 6.4. They will be examined in turn.

All five specialties in this study have clearly reached the starting point of creation of a professional group. Macdonald suggests that they must go further to achieve a legitimate monopoly over a demarcated set of activities in the marketplace and a position of status in the social order. The findings have shown that OMFS, ENT and plastic surgery currently have a monopoly on some areas (Figure 6.2). In contrast, surgical dentistry does not currently have anything like such a monopoly (Coulthard, 2000a and 2000b), neither does it have the traditional markers of achievement, namely, consultant status and equivalent salary. However, surgical dentists are clearly seeking fulfilment, a point further demonstrated by their perception that the future would bring separation from OMFS and the development of higher specialist training in a primary care setting, rather than in a hospital as currently occurs (Joint Committee for Specialist Training in Dentistry, 2000b).

Achieving sub-goals

The main sub-goal for a professional group involves achieving clarity over its 'jurisdiction' or 'scope'. This is where contests for care develop between specialists. The findings presented here suggest that OMF Surgery typifies a specialist group that has been very successful indeed in expanding its jurisdiction in dental, facial and head and neck surgery. Macdonald underlines the importance of a proactive approach as a marker of a successful professional group (Macdonald, 1995: 204). In a later, particularly influential, study of professions in the USA, Abbott (1988: 2) underlines that 'jurisdictional disputes are the essence of professional groups'. It will be argued below, however, that shifts in health policy in the British context are also relevant, as they are likely to force specialties to address overlaps in care in a formal manner, rather than allowing individual specialists to do so in a more traditional *ad hoc* approach.

OMFS specialist perceive that facial trauma repair is a core part of their jurisdiction (British Association of Oral and Maxillofacial Surgeons, 2002), a view which is supported by the study findings. However, the future role of multidisciplinary teams could present a challenge to their clear supremacy in this field and force them to share care. Turning to cancer surgery, key players perceived that multidisciplinary teams would have the most likely future here, followed by new super-specialists (Table 6.2). Minority support for the emergence of 'super-specialists' in cancer and trauma surgery, although small, should also not be ignored. These are small volume areas of care.[9] Thus it will only require a small number of super-specialists to completely take over such fields. Interested specialists may thus present an 'internal challenge' to the jurisdiction of their existing specialty.

Will the jurisdiction in high volume dental surgery be yielded to surgical dentists? Surgical dentists themselves certainly think so, however, some in OMFS perceived that they would retain activity in and control over routine dental surgery. Much would seem to depend on the power of other actors, in particular, the influence of the state.

Negotiation with other actors

Both Macdonald (1995) and Abbott (1988) highlight the importance of negotiation with other actors as part of the dynamic process of maintaining a professional group and their jurisdiction. Key players certainly affirmed this and negotiation with the state is now pivotal in several key respects.[10]

First, it would appear that the tensions at the complex end of care, involving the three medical specialties, are being fuelled by new commissioning patterns. These have moved away from traditional disease groups to focus on specific conditions and patient groups through the development of central health policy including National Service Frameworks. This is true for head and neck cancer, cleft lip and/or palate surgery and emergency/trauma care (Calman and Hine, 1995; Clinical Standards Advisory Group, 1998; Department of Health, 2000b and 2000c). While individual specialists working with policy makers have encouraged such policy changes, a state-driven shift towards client and disease-based commissioning provides serious challenges for anatomical and skill-based specialties to reform or justify their existence.

Secondly, at the routine end of care, the implementation of EU legislation on specialisation has enabled the state swiftly to create a formal challenge to the expensively trained specialty of OMFS through the direct introduction of surgical dentistry as a new specialty. This is further and strong evidence of the state involvement fuelling contests for care between specialties through its health policy initiatives. State involvement in the creation of this specialty in a top-down manner has something in common with psychiatry (Johnson, 1995) and communicable disease control (Acheson, 1988), both associated with state intervention in response to a crisis. In this case, it was not a crisis, but a consideration of access to specialist care in high street surgeries which was reportedly an issue (NHS Executive, 1995). However, the decision may or may not have been related to the high cost of OMFS training and of hospital care. Funding was highlighted as a leading driver of change by key players in this study. It is also perceived as a key issue in futures research and health policy analysis (Saltman, Figueras and Sakellarides, 1998; Dargie, 2000; Foresight Health Care Panel, 2001; Wanless, 2002; Mossialos and Dixon, 2002). It could well be financially advantageous to the state if more care were to be provided in high street surgeries – funded, wholly or in part, by patients. Evolving state-led proposals for local commissioning of dental services bring explicit opportunities for the development of specialist services in high street surgeries in contract with Primary Care Trusts (House of Commons, 2003).

Thirdly, the past decade has seen a major change with doctors in training no longer forming a significant arm of the workforce (Rivett, 1998). This represents yet another initiative driven by the state and led by the Chief Medical and Chief Dental Officers (Calman, 1993; NHS Executive, 1995). Furthermore, higher specialist training programmes have been formalised and monitored with consultants increasingly having to serve the needs of their trainees in providing approved training programmes organised through the Royal Colleges. The demands of formalised higher specialist training again emerged in this study and are also highlighted by Allen (1999) in her work with consultants. Will the unit for planning in future be the traditional consultants or the (cheaper) specialists?

Fourthly, the role of patients and the public in health care is also increasing at local and national level. Macdonald identifies the public and potential patients as an important consideration in facilitating or inhibiting the creation and maintenance of professional groups.

Johnson (1995: 7), writing in the mid-1990s, suggested that health professions were already in transition, as 'governments throughout the world are increasingly concerned with the costs and quality of health care'. The findings of this study provide evidence that that proposition is becoming a reality within the UK for surgical specialities.

Challenges from the context

The importance of the context is well recognised in professional group literature, historical and sociological (Peterson, 1978; Grenshaw, 1989; Macdonald, 1995; Smith and Cottell, 1997). It is clear that the way in which professional groups are judged by the public is changing. Knowledge and status are no longer sufficient for public credibility. Surgeons' performance will increasingly be under scrutiny following the Kennedy Report on the Bristol enquiry (Department of Health, 2001d). This provides further support for a proposition that professional groups are losing their status, are increasingly controlled by organisations and the state, and judged on outcomes – an approach that has more in common with traditional blue-collar working than professional groups.

The NHS is an important political issue within the UK; however, more global changes, influenced by geo-political developments, are also important. Greater specialisation was perceived by all five specialties as one of the leading forces for change. The necessity to implement

EU workforce legislation on specialisation has prompted an additional tier in the workforce, as already noted. What then does this study suggest about the future – not only of the specialties analysed here, but of clinical specialisation more broadly? The whole basis of specialisation is changing as the state become increasingly involved in the detail of what clinicians do. The relationships of professions and state needs to be re-examined in the current climate and this makes 'uncertainty' a key element in the picture for the future.

Implications for the future

This case study has demonstrated the pressures which consultants and specialties are facing in the scope and organisation of their work. Specialists perceive that they are under pressure from the wider environment (Gallagher, Gelbier and Sheiham, 2000).The findings support the arguments of Larson (1997) and Macdonald (1995) that specialisation is a dynamic process, shaped by the wider context and involving negotiation, but also suggest that state control has greatly increased. Whereas the negotiation of jurisdictional disputes between specialties may be considered a normal feature of specialist life (Abbott, 1988), the findings would suggest that state involvement in specialist care is fuelling contests for care between and within specialties, a pressure which is common in Europe (Johnson, 1995). Change is occurring through three main routes. First, the policy of specialisation and involvement of the state in regulating the training and registration of specialists is important. Secondly, creation of new specialties presents a challenge to the jurisdiction of traditional specialties. Thirdly, the introduction of client group and disease-based commissioning cuts across the activity of traditional specialties at the complex end of care and begins to restrict such care to designated specialists, reducing clinical freedom.

Lack of flexibility

In a move to prevent 'dabbling', protect patients and improve surgical outcomes through initiatives such as the creation of specialist lists, designated surgeons, teams and centres, the work of specialists is being influenced by the state at various levels. This brings state organisations into a decision-making process that was traditionally negotiated between professional groups. Proposals for 'super-specialisation' will result in specialties losing their broader base and thus their inherent flexibility to shift direction where necessary. In this respect, state initiatives to improve quality of care through restricting the range of activities of consultants are in conflict with their advice on the establishment of new specialties which identify the need for specialties to have a sufficiently broad base to cope with changing needs for care (Department of Health, 2001a).

Access

Should the move towards disease and client group commissioning of services lead to super-specialisation, it will require services to be planned and provided on a large population basis. Such an approach requires further state involvement to avoid gaps in the system or the production of narrowly trained super specialists for whom there is no work. This has several implications, the first being for planners/commissioners to work in a rational and co-ordinated manner. Secondly, specialists may need to undertake additional travelling so that where possible care is provided locally to the patient, but where care needs to be provided in a designated unit, the patient will have to travel further. Thirdly, there is a need for clarity in service planning and provision and appropriate referral mechanisms so that patients get swiftly to the right specialist. The trade-off between local access and access to quality surgical care has not been debated publicly, but perhaps should be, particularly as there is no robust evidence on the volume/quality relation (Birkmeyer, 2000).

Into the high street for specialists

There is a blurring of traditional work locations with consultants/specialists working outside hospitals and general practitioners working on hospital sites. This is again driven largely by state policy (Bloor, Barton and Maynard, 2000). The key players in London perceived that this is the future way of working for surgical dentistry, and legislation under the Health and Social Care Bill (House of Commons, 2003), seems set to provide the opportunity for this. It could work positively to liberate the speciality of surgical dentistry to expand its services within the NHS, and enable highly trained OMFS surgeons to utilise their skills in more complex surgery, or it could potentially destabilise the hospital speciality.

Uncertainty

All of this spells uncertainty for the future, particularly as consultants may respond to pressures in a range of ways. Will they shift to the private sector? If so, the NHS may have to consider seriously how the skills of very highly trained surgeons can be retained and utilised creatively within the NHS. Surgeons' caseloads are increasingly under scrutiny, but is there any evidence that the present changes will improve quality? Could it be that the structures and systems to promote and regulate quality militate against an innovative culture, with long-term implications for research and development? Will the combined impact of current reforms on specialists ultimately be destructive, as suggested in the following quotation from an academic oral and maxillofacial surgeon?

> I suspect ... very long-term ... not just structured training, but things like NICE and CHI and all the rest, ... there is a danger of suppressing innovative developments ... you know, the whole atmosphere of clinical governance, litigation, guidelines, and what have you, is against the bright individual who gets an idea and runs with it.

And finally ...

Specialist surgical services face a time of unprecedented change. Surgeons and the state need to tread carefully. The findings here suggest a paradigm shift for professional groups, with the state dictating the jurisdiction of specialties and a resultant reduction in clinical freedom. Specialists, particularly surgeons, increasingly need to demonstrate their productivity and quality, rather than rely on expert knowledge alone. Clearly, specialist surgical skills will be required for the foreseeable future, but will consultants continue to retain their traditional status? Will the raft of state initiatives to promote quality care combine to destabilise existing specialties? What workforce and service planning will be required to provide the appropriate levels of specialism and retain some flexibility in the system to cope with change? It is my hope that there will be foresight, vision, leadership to take the healthcare workforce through this period of change.

Notes

1. I would like to thank the Department of Health for Access to Hospital Episode Statistics Data for London, for the years 1991–2 to 1997–8.
2. For full details of this study see Gallagher (2002).
3. The current arrangements for UK postgraduate specialist registration came into force in 1996 (for doctors) and 1998 (for dentists). As this book went to

press, new legislation was coming into force to create a Postgraduate Medical and Education Training Board. See *http://www.doh.gov.uk/medical-traininginthEuk/pmetborder.htm* [accessed on 23 June 2003].

4. This definition does not recognise the growing usage of the terms 'consultant' and 'specialist' for members of the nursing and allied health professions. It is clear that traditional labels are becoming less clearly defined as the NHS is challenged to use its talents more flexibly (NHS Executive 2000; Department of Health 2000b).

5. This option is available under EU law. The European Primary and Specialist Dental Qualifications Regulations 1998 provide the legal basis.

6. There is a complex history to this. OMFS itself evolved from oral surgery, leaving a few singly-qualified oral surgeons, and academics with restricted practice.

7. It should be noted that the main focus of analysis was on admitted care as there are no case mix data on the outpatient appointments kept in the same year (537,038 in 1997–8) (Department of Health, 2000a and 2001c). Some of the caseload, particularly in-patients, was also uncoded for surgery (17.6 per cent). This may have included cases admitted for observation, but suggests that there may be under-representing complex cases. For more details on this and on precise definitions of categories in the following analysis, see Gallagher (2002).

8. 'Specialists' need for fulfilment' achieved 15th overall ranking by specialists as a driver for change. Surgical dentists had a significantly higher average score ($\bar{x} = 4.2$ +/– 0.15) when independently compared with OMFS ($\bar{x} = 3.1$ +/– 0.23) (p<0.001).

9. The volume of surgical cases does not equate with workload as this measure does not take complexity into account.

10. State influence is in evidence at different levels, from the EU through national government, and health organisational bodies down to provider Trusts within England. There is also increasing variation in policy between the territories of the UK, with devolved government and separate Departmental policies.

References

Abbott, A. (1988) *The System of Professions: an essay on the division of expert labour*, Chicago: University of Chicago Press.

Abel-Smith, B. (1964) *The Hospitals 1800–1948*, London: Heinemann.

Acheson, D. (1988) *The Report of the Committee of Inquiry into the Future Development of the Public Health Function*, London: Her Majesty's Stationery Office.

Allen, I. (1999) *Stress Among Consultants in North Thames*, London: TPMDE and Policy Studies Institute.

Allen, I. (2000) 'Modernising the NHS – Challenges to the Health Services: the professions', *British Medical Journal*, 320, 1533–5.

British Association of Oral and Maxillofacial Surgeons (2002) *The Organisation of Oral and Maxillofacial Surgical Services in the UK*, London: Council of The British Association of Oral and Maxillofacial Surgeons.

Birkmeyer, J. D. (2000) 'Should we Regionalize Major Surgery? Potential benefits and policy considerations', *Journal of the American College of Surgeons*, 190, 3, 341–9.

Black, N. (2002) 'Reconfiguring Health Systems', *British Medical Journal*, 325, 1290–3.

Bloor, K., Barton, G. and Maynard, A. (2000) *The Future of Hospital Services: management updates,* Institute of Healthcare Management, London: The Stationery Office.

Calman, K. (1993) *Hospital Doctors: training for the future. Report of the Working Group on Specialist Medical Training,* London: Department of Health.

Calman, K. and Hine, D. (1995) *A Policy Framework for Commissioning Cancer Services: a report by the expert advisory group on cancer*, London: Department of Health.

Clinical Standards Advisory Group (1998) *Clinical Standards Advisory Group: cleft lip and/or palate*, London: The Stationery Office.

Coulthard, P., Kazakou, I., Koran, R. and Worthington, H.V. (2000a) 'Referral Patterns and the Referral System for Oral Surgery Care. Part 1: General Dental Practitioner referral patterns', *British Dental Journal*, 188, 3, 142–5.

Coulthard, P., Koran, R., Kazakou, I., and Macfarlane, V. (2000b) 'Patterns and Appropriateness of Referral from General Dental Practice to Specialist Oral and Maxillofacial Surgical Services', *British Journal of Oral & Maxillofacial Surgery*, 38, 320–5.

Dargie, C. (2000) *Policy Futures for UK Health 2000 Report from Nuffield Trust and University of Cambridge Judge Institute of Management*, London: The Stationery Office.

Department of Health (2000a) *Hospital Episode Statistics: the book*, London: Department of Health.

Department of Health (2000b) *The NHS Plan: for investment and reform*, London: Department of Health.

Department of Health (2001a) *Developing Specialties in Medicine: protocol for handling applications for new CCST specialties and for decommissioning specialties which are no longer needed*, London: Department of Health.

Department of Health (2001c) *Hospital Episode Statistics: outpatient data* [online], Department of Health. Available from: *http://www.doh.gov.uk/hes* [Accessed on 23 June 2003].

Department of Health (2001d) *The Report of the Public Inquiry into Children's Heart Surgery at the Bristol Royal Infirmary, 1984–1995: learning from Bristol [Cm5207]*, London: Department of Health.

Dhariwal, D. K., Goodey, R. and Shepherd, J. P. (2002) 'Trends in Oral Surgery in England and Wales, 1999–2000', *British Dental Journal*, 192, 11, 639–45.

Edwards, D. M., Johnson, N. W., Cooper, D. and Warnakulasuriya, K. A. (1998) 'A Survey of Consultants Treating Upper Aerodigestive Tract Cancer in the UK', *Annals of the Royal College of Surgeons of England*, 80, 283–7.

Foresight Healthcare Panel (2001) *Health Care 2020; Foresight – making the future work for you* [online], Foresight Healthcare Panel. Available from: *http://www.foresight.gov.uk* [Accessed 23 June 2003].

Gallagher, J. E. (2002) *A Health Futures Study of Facial, Oral and Dental Surgery in London* [PhD Thesis], London: University of London.

Gallagher, J. E., Gelbier, S. and Sheiham, A. (2000) 'NHS Hospital Dental Services in London: forces for change', *Journal of Dental Research*, 79, 5, 1178.

Garrett, M. J. (1999) *Health Futures Handbook*, Geneva: World Health Organisation.

General Dental Council (2001) *Specialist Dental Lists: December 2001. Specialist lists – information* [online], General Dental Council. Available from: *http://www.gdc-uk.org* [Accessed 23 June 2003].

General Medical Council (2001) 'Specialisation and Specialist list in Oral and Maxillofacial Surgery: numbers on list', [personal communication].

Grenshaw, L. (1989) 'Specialists', in L. Grenshaw and R. Porter (eds) (1989) *The Hospital in History*, London: Routledge.

House of Commons (2003) *Health and Social Care (Community Health and Standards) Bill as introduced in the House of Commons on 12 March 2003 [Bill 70]*, London: Her Majesty's Stationery Office.

Joint Committee for Specialist Training in Dentistry (2000a) *Curriculum for Oral Surgery: October 2000* [online], Joint Committee for Specialist Training in Dentistry. Available from: *http://www.rcseng.ac.uk/dental/fds/docs_and_pubs/ documents_higher_html* [Accessed 23 June 2003].

Joint Committee for Specialist Training in Dentistry (2000b) *Curriculum for Surgical Dentistry* [online], Joint Committee for Specialist Training in Dentistry. Available from: *http://www.rcseng.ac.uk/dental/fds/docs_and_pubs/ documents_higher_html* [Accessed 23 June 2003].

Johnson, T. (1995) 'Governmentality and the Institutionalisation of Expertise', in T. Johnson, G. Larkin and M. Saks (eds), *Health Professions and the State in Europe*, London: Routledge, 7–24.

Larson, M. S. (1997) *The Rise of Professionalism; a sociological analysis*, London: University of California Press.

Macdonald, K. M. (1995) *The Sociology of the Professions*, London: Sage.

McKee, M. and Healy, J. (2002) 'The Significance of Hospitals: an introduction', in M. McKee and J. Healy (eds), *Hospitals in a Changing Europe*, Buckingham: Open University Press, 3–13.

Mossialos, E. and Dixon, A. (2002) 'Chapter 1. Funding health care: an introduction', in E. Mossialos, A. Dixon, J. Figueras and J. Kutzin, J. (eds) *Funding Health Care: options for Europe*, Buckingham: Open University Press, 1–30.

NHS Executive (1995) *UK Specialist Dental Training: report from the Chief Dental Officer [R. B. Mouatt]*, Leeds: NHS Executive.

NHS Executive (2000) *A Health Service of all the Talents: developing the NHS workforce. A consultation document on the review of workforce planning*, London: NHS Executive.

NHS Information Authority (2002) *NHS Data Dictionary and Manual* [online], NHS Information Authority. Available from: *http://www.nhsia.nhs.uk/datastandards/pages/present_user.asp* [Accessed 23 June 2003].

Peterson, J. M. (1978) *The Medical Profession in Mid-Victorian London*, London: University of California Press.

Rivett, G. (1998) *From the Cradle to the Grave*, London: King's Fund.

Saltman, R., Figueras, J. and Sakellarides, C. (eds) (1998) *Critical Challenges for Health Care Reform in Europe*, Buckingham: Open University Press.

Schreuder, R. F. (1995) 'Health Scenarios and Policy Making – lessons from the Netherlands', *Futures*, 27, 953–8.

Seward, M. (1998) 'The Changing Role of Specialist Care in NHS Dentistry', *British Dental Journal*, 185, 34–5.

Shepherd, J. (1999) 'Oral and Maxillofacial Surgery, Oral Surgery and Surgical Dentistry', *British Dental Journal*, 186, 366–7.

Smith, E. and Cottell, B. (1997) *A History of the Royal Dental Hospital of London and School of Dental Surgery*, London: Athlone Press.

Stevenson, S. and Guthrie, D. (1949) *History of Otolaryngology*, Edinburgh: Livingstone.

Wanless, D. (2002) *Securing our Future Health: taking a long-term view [final report]*, London: HM Treasury.

7
A New Push for Public Health?

Stephen Peckham and Erica Wirrmann

Introduction

The roles of people working in public health, as in other areas of the health service, are rapidly changing. Central to these changing roles are the current developments in public health policy which place a renewed emphasis on tackling the causes of ill health. Whilst these developments are well underway, it is apparent that they are being forged through a conceptual minefield in which the meaning and scope of 'public health' is poorly specified. Despite widely adopted formal definitions of public health, different professionals, organisations and the public tend to perceive public health in quite different ways. One of the problems is that such definitions tend to be so broad that their application to practice does not necessarily help us to understand what the public health role is. The World Health Organisation (WHO), for instance, defines public health as the science and art of preventing disease, prolonging life and promoting health through organised efforts of society. This definition, endorsed in recent UK policy (Acheson, 1988; Department of Health, 1998) and by the profession, makes the analysis of public health developments, and the mapping of the role of the future public health worker, very difficult.

Public health definitions and policies reflect a change in attitudes and the development of knowledge over the decades (Baggott, 2000). Public health activities do not operate in a social vacuum, and various powerful interests, as well as unexpected events, will contribute to shape both the definition of public health problems, and the policies and programmes which respond to them (Levenson, 1998). Thus, predicting public health in the future requires an element of crystal ball gazing. This chapter aims to speculate on the future public health workforce in the UK by exploring current developments in public health, showing how they affect the development of the public health workforce, and discussing the ways in which they are likely to unfold in the future. It begins by discussing what is happening to the organisation and delivery of public health services in the UK. It then explores current changes in the public health workforce, discusses how these changes are likely to develop over the next ten years, and finally considers the extent to which such developments provide an appropriate basis for public health practice in the future.

The changing organisational structure of public health

Since the election of the Labour Government in 1997, there has been a greater emphasis on improving the health of the population and addressing health inequalities. The government's strategy, which aims to cut across all departments, includes action at the national, local and individual levels. Targets have been set and frameworks established to encourage public health activities around specific issues, such as coronary heart disease and mental health, and in specific settings, such as schools, workplaces and local communities (Department of Health, 1999a). Whilst the overall strategy is a national one, political devolution to the four UK territories since 1997, and the proposed devolution to the English regions, offers new potential for variation and innovation in policy formation. England, Northern Ireland, Scotland and Wales, while sharing some common themes, have already taken different routes towards the organisation of public health, as will be discussed below.

The organisational history of public health is complex (Lewis, 1986; Baggott, 2000). Originally, the responsibility for public health rested with local authorities, where public health services (community medicine, health visiting and so on), were located. In a major reorganisation in 1974, medical public health and nursing were transferred to new structures within the NHS, while environmental health services remained in local authorities alongside housing, social services, leisure, education and others. This not only fragmented the public health workforce, but also split public health activity in the NHS between the new district health authorities and health boards in Scotland (later to become purchasers and commissioners of health care post 1991) and community health services, increasingly linked with general practice.

The new political focus on health improvement and the reduction of health inequalities has led to a number of organisational developments, with a much greater emphasis on partnership approaches with local authorities through health action zones, local strategic partnerships, healthy living centres, and urban and neighbourhood renewal. There is also an increased emphasis on the role of primary care and, in England, the development of a public health function within primary care trusts (PCTs), which now have a key responsibility for the delivery of public health services to their local communities. Alongside this, attempts are being made to broaden the public health workforce, shifting the focus away from public health medicine. The strong emphasis placed on public health by the National Assembly for Wales and the Scottish Parliament has also added a new political dimension to tackling public health in these countries.

The emphasis on health protection (fuelled by the increasing threat of global terrorism and new disease outbreaks like Severe Acute Respiratory Syndrome in 2003), has recently led to the establishment of a new Health Protection Agency for England and Wales, with responsibilities for protecting people's health and reducing the impact of infectious diseases, chemical hazards, poisons and radiation hazards. In Scotland a similar organisation – the Scottish Centre for Infection and Environmental Health – already existed, but in England and Wales this has involved a major reorganisation of communicable disease control, public health laboratory and scientific services. Whilst all these changes are still in their early stages, they will have a significant impact on the nature and organisation of the future public health workforce. The next section looks more closely at the public health workforce now, in the context of these organisational changes, before taking a speculative look at the future.

Public health workforce developments

The lack of clarity and enormity in scope of the public health function, and the organisational diversity of public health practice, makes the notion of 'a public health workforce' extremely complex. The Chief Medical Officer (CMO), in his report on the project to strengthen the public health function in England (Department of Health, 2001a: 6), considers that people 'from a range of disciplines and at all levels of seniority' contribute to the public health workforce in their daily work. Although many of these people may not have a 'public health' label, or even recognise that they have a public health role, they will, to a greater or lesser extent, be working to promote, protect and improve the health of populations and communities. The CMO describes such people as falling into three categories:

- Public health professionals: consultants and specialists working at a strategic or senior management level or at a senior level of scientific expertise, such as in public health statistics;
- Public health practitioners: professionals who spend a major part, or all of their time, in public health practice; and
- 'The wider workforce': all those who, even if they do not at present recognise it, have a role in health improvement and reducing inequalities (for example teachers, local business leaders, social workers, transport engineers, housing officers, as well as other local government staff and health care professionals) (Department of Health, 2001a: 6–7).

Each of these three categories has been further divided into two: strategic and operational/technical (Burke, Meyrick and Speller, 2001). Any attempt to 'map' a workforce using these distinctions will soon encounter ambiguity (Sim, Walters and Schiller, 2003). Whilst Walters, Schiller and Sim (2002) developed an algorithm in order to help the classification of workers in London into each of the three groups, distinctions are difficult to make when there is so little clarity around what constitutes the roles, or potential roles, of each of the three groups.

Public health professionals

This group, dominated by public health medicine, has received most attention in recent years. It can be traced back to Medical Officers of Health – whose appointment became compulsory for every local district following the 1872 Public Health Act. These early public health professionals took on the responsibility for tracking, dealing with and preventing disease epidemics through social/environmental interventions. Over time, their focus became more medical, concentrating first on immunisation/vaccination and personal preventive approaches, and later widening to include the responsibility for promoting the health of specific groups within the community (Cornish and Knight, 2003). They worked alongside other professional groups such as environmental health officers, community midwives, health visitors and social workers up until 1974, at which point they were replaced by the new speciality of Community Medicine and, together with community midwives and health visitors, were moved into the expanded NHS.

The founding of the Faculty of Community Medicine (later to become the Faculty of Public Health Medicine) in 1972, ensured the professionalisation of this new workforce and the securing of its domain as a medical specialism. Membership of the Faculty, until very recently, was limited to registered medical practitioners who had either attained an appropriate academic standard by passing an examination or, at the discretion of the Council, were deemed to have made distinguished contributions to community medicine (Warren, 2000). Public health professionals then, until 2001, largely consisted of medical directors of public health and their teams of public health consultants and specialists based within health authorities.

Saving Lives: our healthier nation (Department of Health, 1999a) initiated some important changes for the public health profession. It registered that a modern public health workforce must be made up of people from a wider range of professional backgrounds, and it recognised the absence of a true multi-disciplinary basis to the public health profession. The effects of the profession's medical leaning were particularly cautioned against in Scotland where concerns were raised about the ability to develop joint working (Scottish Executive, 2000).

To rectify this situation, *Saving Lives* announced the creation of the post of Specialist in Public Health (Department of Health, 1999a). The doors of the Faculty were subsequently unlocked and a tripartite group (comprising the Faculty of Public Health Medicine, the Royal Institute of Public Health and the Multidisciplinary Public Health Forum) began the process of clarifying the boundaries of the specialist in public health in 1999. Since then, it has developed national standards for specialist public health practice and designed structures and processes for the continuing professional development, appraisal and revalidation of public health specialists (Faculty of Public Health Medicine, 2001a; Donnan, 1999; Doyle, 2002). The Group launched a new system of recognition for multidisciplinary specialists in public health – in the form of a Voluntary Specialist Register (Tripartite Group, 2003; see also Lessof, Dumelow and McPherson, 1998). This opening up of the profession is an important step towards multidisciplinary public health practice. It will, however, take time to counter the historical dominance of the medical profession.

The redesign of the structures of the NHS at local level has brought further challenges. This is most notable in England, where health authorities (formerly the seat of well-developed public health and health promotion departments) have been abolished to make way for smaller, more local PCTs and fewer, more remote, Strategic Health

Authorities (StHAs) (Department of Health, 2001b). Thus, public health teams have largely been relocated to a greater number of PCTs, where they are expected to lead the work on improving health and reducing inequalities in local neighbourhoods by integrating public health into primary care and by working in partnership with local authorities and other agencies. Each of these teams will have a director of public health who can be either medical or non-medical – although the majority of appointments to the new PCTs have so far been doctors (personal communication, M. Tingle, Department of Health, 2003). Appointees will be overseen and co-ordinated by a small, high level team in each StHA, and a regional public health group located in the nine regional offices of government (Department of Health, 2001b). These health authority and regional office teams are each led by a medical director of public health. This contrasts with Scotland, where (medical) directors of public health remain in the Health Boards – the Scottish equivalent of the old English health authorities.

The new cadre of public health experts is expected to be able to work effectively in the community-oriented setting of PCTs, across new organisational boundaries and with new populations. This is a particular challenge given the time it will take to offset the still overwhelmingly medical focus within the profession. As well as the obvious need to develop and nurture new skills that this change entails, there are also concerns that valuable expertise could be lost if specialist skills are dispersed around the health economy in an uncoordinated fashion (Faculty of Public Health Medicine, 2001b). Added to this is the fear of professional isolation of staff who are being moved to smaller teams within smaller organisations. The development of public health networks is seen as an important step in countering these concerns (Department of Health, 2002a).

Public health practitioners

Efforts to clarify the membership and roles of the 'public health practitioners' category are much further behind. The potential scope of this group is huge, and much will depend on how 'public health practice' is defined, and what is deemed to constitute a 'major part' of a practitioner's time. The Tripartite Group, as part of its national standards programme, has defined public health practice as that which:

- takes a population perspective;
- mobilises the organised efforts of society and acts as an advocate for the public's health;

- enables people and communities to increase control over their own health and wellbeing;
- acts on the social, economic, environmental and biological determinants of health and wellbeing;
- protects from and minimises the impact of health risks to the population;
- ensures that preventive, treatment and care services are of high quality, based on evidence and are of best value, (Royal Institute of Public Health, 2001: 1).

The Group has recently extended its programme in order to establish standards for public health practitioners, based on this definition of public health practice.

Within the NHS, the focus has tended to be on selected disciplines – notably health visitors, community nurses, school nurses and midwives – with much discussion around the potential for enhancing public health roles (Department of Health, 1999b; National Assembly for Wales, 1999; Scottish Executive, 2001 and 2003; Poulton *et al.*, 2000). However, the exact roles – as opposed to the rhetoric surrounding them – remain to be demonstrated (House of Commons Select Committee on Health, 2001). Whilst public health is increasingly being incorporated into training programmes and competency frameworks (Quality Assurance Agency for Higher Education, 2001; Department of Health, 2002b and 2003), in practice, the application of public health knowledge and skills is too often viewed as the role of specialist practitioners. This leaves the potential public health roles of other practitioners underdeveloped and unsupported.

The situation, however, varies in the different regions of the UK. Scotland, for instance, has developed a new public health practitioner post, based in local health care co-operatives (LHCCs) (Scottish Executive, 2001). This new role is open to people from a variety of backgrounds, including nursing and health visiting, community education, health promotion and dentistry (Scottish Executive, 2003). The post holders, who undertake a new training programme, act as a catalyst for change. The aim is that they work inside and outside the LHCC to develop public health practice and improve the health and wellbeing of the local population. As yet, there are no plans to develop a similar post in England, although the efforts being made within the health visitor and school nurse development programme (Department of Health, 2001c), might see these disciplines emerging as more generic public health practitioners in the future.

Outside of the NHS, there are many practitioners who spend time contributing towards public health. These include: community development workers, environmental health officers, youth workers, urban renewal officers, social workers, project officers (for instance in any one of a plethora of new projects and programmes including New Deal for Communities, Education Action Zones, Health Action Zones, Healthy Living Centres, and so on), and many paid and unpaid workers in the voluntary sector. Here the difficulties of talking about public health practitioners as an occupational group become obvious. Whilst one social worker might spend a major part of his/her time practising public health, another might have a much lesser role in health improvement. Even within the NHS and within the disciplines with more 'traditional' public health roles, such as health visiting, examples of good public health practice are often a result not of mainstream activity, but rather of *ad hoc*, isolated projects without formal recognition (Taylor, Peckham and Turton, 1998; Billingham and Perkins, 1997).

A concerted effort is being made in some disciplines to develop strategically within the new public health agenda. Within environmental health, for example, a strategic vision has been produced which explores the projected growth of environmental health officers' roles in improving the public's health and reducing health inequalities over the next ten years (Burke, Gray, Paterson and Meyrick, 2002). Within other disciplines, though, most notably within the voluntary sector, much public health work goes unrecognised and undervalued. Much is still to be done to harness the potential of this diverse workforce, and to develop and co-ordinate roles.

'The wider workforce'

The final category mentioned by the CMO is the most ambiguous and least helpful and, despite having the widest scope, is the last to receive attention in efforts to strengthen the public health workforce. This category includes a great range and number of people whose public health roles are seldom appreciated at all. At the very top, in terms of strategic policy making at a local, national or international level, are people engaged in assessing the health impacts of policies. At a community level, people from all sectors work towards making their community a safe and healthy place to live – whether that involves a company initiating a stress reduction project, or a tenants' association working to improve green spaces. Finally, at an individual or family level, people are (often unwittingly) engaging with public health issues on an everyday basis – putting the rubbish out for elderly neighbours, or campaigning for traffic-calming measures to be introduced.

The increased attention given to public health and health inequalities in recent years has started to reinforce and legitimise the roles played by members of the wider workforce. The new duties placed upon local authorities to improve the economic, social and environmental wellbeing of their areas, have opened the field up to the very great range of workers in this sector (Department of the Environment Transport and the Regions, 2001a and 2001b). Local authorities are also responsible for developing local strategic partnerships with an emphasis on tackling health inequalities (Department of the Environment Transport and the Regions, 2001a; Department of Health, 2001a). These new powers and duties place a public health remit on local authority departments such as social services, housing, transportation, and highways for example, broadening the more traditional health roles of local authorities invested in environmental health and in some places health promotion. Similarly, health practitioners who might traditionally have concentrated on their clinical roles, are increasingly being expected to participate in planning services according to local needs and gearing these towards improving health and reducing inequalities.

The part played by patients and the public is becoming more important, too, as the Commission for Patient and Public Involvement in Health (CPPIH, established January 2003) takes shape. The pivotal role of lay knowledge in generating understanding about causes and remedies is firmly supported in the literature (Popay and Williams, 1994; Williams and Popay, 1994; Gabe, 1995; Popay, Williams, Thomas and Gatrell, 1998). The Health and Social Care Act 2001 places a new duty on the NHS to involve and consult patients and the public, not just when a major change is proposed, but in the on-going planning of services. The potential role of the public in planning and delivering the public health function requires careful development and support, which will depend on the currently emerging structures locally (through patient fora for example) and nationally within the CPPIH.

To be really effective, it is essential that people and organisations develop and strengthen a shared public health mindset that will influence the way they approach their day to day work. It is vital, too, that their work is recognised, rewarded, and, crucially, co-ordinated, so that the public health function can be a truly collaborative one.

Diverse approaches in future

Given the current developments in the public health workforce, it is likely that over the next few years the focus will be on the public health specialist rather than on developing a broader range of public health practitioners. This specialist group will remain largely medical. In England, for example, it will probably be many years before real change in the balance between medical and non-medical directors of public health occurs. The directors of public health in the new local structures – English PCTs and Welsh Local Health Boards – need to be prepared to face the challenges of developing local public health capacity following the fragmentation of previously established public health specialist teams. Of increasing importance will be the distinct differences that are emerging in the organisation and shape of the public health workforce in England, Northern Ireland, Scotland and Wales.

The Welsh Assembly has prioritised public health and the coterminosity between local authorities and local health boards, with their broad memberships, provide opportunities for close co-operation and co-ordinated activity. Moreover, the founding of the National Public Health Services in Wales, which brings the public health resources of the five former health authorities together under one national organisation, promises strong national leadership in public health to support multi-disciplinary action that cuts across policy and organisational boundaries.

In Northern Ireland, where a second hiatus in devolution (from October 2002) has meant a period of relative inaction, future developments are less clear. The suspension of the Assembly has hindered the implementation of decisions arising from consultation on the future of primary care. Within the existing health and social care workforce, however, it is nurses who have received most attention, and their existing and potential contribution to the public health agenda has been both recognised and supported (Poulton *et al.*, 2000; Mason and Clarke, 2001).

In England, the Minister for Public Health is perhaps more politically remote from the delivery of public health than in Scotland and Wales. The structure of the public health function will be determined by the way regional government offices and StHAs, with their medical directors of public health, direct and performance manage the wider public health workforce in PCTs and local authorities. Meanwhile, on the ground, public health activity is likely to remain largely locked into funding structures which are influenced by political demands for reduced waiting lists, and which stress quick, 'measurable' outputs. Even in new quasi-autonomous structures, such as health action zones, which aim to encourage bottom-up, locally sensitive, innovative activity, the reality is somewhat less than inspiring. In practice, they face the same political imperatives to secure tangible improvements and to meet performance targets as statutory agencies (Painter and Clarence, 2001). Pressure from the centre for quick results is likely to continue to undermine the conditions needed to build a sustainable collaborative infrastructure, and to develop meaningful partnerships with the local community.

In Scotland, the role of the Scottish Parliament is likely to become particularly significant and it may well take a more multi-sectoral approach to public health (Scottish Executive, 2001). In addition, early assessment of the new public health practitioner posts indicates good progress in developing local public health skills and identifying and supporting 'champions' (Scottish Executive, 2003). The rest of the UK should be watching these developments carefully. Meanwhile, the public health practitioner workforce across the UK is being strengthened by an incorporation of public health skills and values into the training and practice of existing practitioners, most notably in health visiting and community nursing. A public health component is now embedded in all nursing curricula, and specialist practitioner programmes currently prepare nurses for the variety of roles in which they function in the community (Latter and Westwood, 2001).

National and regional public health skills audits and training needs analyses, though, have identified many deficits in qualified practitioners, particularly in community development and leadership (Burke, Meyrick and Speller, 2001). The lack of a shared public health mindset is a key challenge. Where there remains confusion around the meaning and scope of public health, it is hard to imagine how this will develop. A further fundamental challenge is the gap between theory and practice. The emerging public health workforce needs not only an education/training imbued with public health values, but also good role models of empowerment, participation, political acumen and working collaboratively with others (Clark and Maben, 1999). Exposure to public health practice for students on placements remains limited (Latter and Westwood, 2001). Many teachers lack confidence in educating practitioners for a public health role (Clark and Maben, 1999), and organisational and structural barriers (such as lack of time, staff and other resources) often prevent public health theory from being put into practice (Burke, Meyrick and Speller, 2001).

In England, where the idea of generic public health practitioners has not yet been progressed, the focus has tended to be on health visitors, despite the frequent assertions that all health practitioners have an important part to play. There is a danger, if public health is considered to be the role of just one discipline, that others will not realise their potential. This will be likely to hinder partnership working and participation in innovative public health practice. Thus it is likely that, as now, those who have always been involved in public health (environmental health, social workers, community health workers, and so on), and those who are new to the game through new types of programmes (Health Action Zones, Healthy Living Centres, Sure Start, urban renewal, and so on) will carry on. However, where locally-led projects are incompatible with strategic (politically determined) priorities, and are unable to deliver on short term targets, they are likely to remain at the mercy of short term funding, and will have to fight hard to receive the support and recognition they deserve. Those involved in public health on the periphery are likely to learn the necessary skills 'on the job', rather than being equipped and prepared to initiate and influence public health activities.

There is still much unexplored potential in developing the wider role of the communities whose health is to be improved. Again, the rhetoric is evident in policy, but true community involvement remains a rare sight. In England, for example, PCTs need to demonstrate that the public have been involved in the development of plans for local action in public health, and that these plans are sensitive to local need as well as meeting government targets (Department of Health, 2002a). However, whilst the public health activity of PCTs is located in the community, primary care professionals do not necessarily engage with the community about public health issues and about the relevance of their activity to the community's priorities (Taylor, Peckham and Turton, 1998). Generally, the structures and cultures of primary care organisations reflect the dominant medical model, which inhibits the development of community perspectives on health (Taylor, Peckham and Turton, 1998). Professionals who do engage with the community on wider public health issues, go beyond their formal role (Taylor, Peckham and Turton, 1998; Abbott, Florin, Fulop and Gillam, 2001; Wilkin, Gillam and Leese, 2000; Anderson and Florin, 2000; Gillam, Abbot and Banks-Smith, 2001). Until community development and community involvement in public health is positively and formally sanctioned at PCT level, such activity will remain marginal.

In the immediate future, we suggest that two main issues will influence the development of the public health workforce – and that ultimately, these will create tensions for policy and practice in the long term. The first is the continued professionalisation agenda dominating public health, with its focus on developing the specialist register and defining core competencies. This will lead to the exclusivity of roles, thus maintaining the profession's stranglehold on public health. The second contextual issue will be the increasing diversification in public health practice. Organisations outside of the NHS, such as local authorities and voluntary groups, are becoming increasingly engaged with the public health agenda through local strategic partnerships (Department of the Environment Transport and the Regions, 2001b), neighbourhood renewal, healthy living centres and a range of partnership activities (Peckham, 2003). These developments are underpinned by the growth in multi-disciplinary public health training which, in the long term, is likely to alter attitudes and challenge the clinical dominance of public health. In addition, there is growing diversification between the four countries of the UK.

Looking further into the future, we will need to think more broadly about how the roles of future public health workers will be shaped by the tensions described above. The most recent and comprehensive assessment of future scenarios for health care was undertaken by Derek Wanless (2002, see also Sausman, Chapter 12). While the focus of his report is on health care, Wanless highlights the importance of a public health approach. Two elements are essential if either his *solid progress* or *fully engaged* scenario is to be achieved. The first is progress towards achieving public health goals on reductions in smoking, obesity, tackling poverty, and inequalities in health; the second is the extent of public engagement, supported by greater access, improved information and more involvement in health care. The report concludes that the continuing development of the National Service Frameworks (NSFs) across the whole of the NHS is central to improving the quality of services over the next 20 years. Public health, and the emphasis on developing the public health responsibilities of all staff, are key elements of the existing NSFs – an emphasis that is likely to continue.

The concept of public engagement also reflects the findings of the 'future patient' project (Kendall, 2001). Kendall has argued that patients want quick and convenient access to healthcare, to receive services more attuned to their needs, to improve their access to information, and to develop relationships with practitioners that allow them to participate as active and equal partners in their own care. While these relate to healthcare, it is possible to take these same principles and apply them to public health. In fact, since communities and individuals contribute so much to their own health, there may be even more relevance to notions of shared information, access to health resources and partnerships with practitioners in public health.

So, if the NHS is to strive with *solid progress* towards Wanless' vision of the future, what implications are there for the public health workforce? The challenges of meeting current public health targets are already evident. PCTs are concerned that they are to be performance managed on public health targets over which they can only have a partial impact, given the close association between deprivation and health inequalities or teenage pregnancy rates (Clews, 2003). The road to solid progress is based on an assumption that health promotion activity, and actions to address health inequalities contained in the NSFs, are fully developed. There is a danger that the focus will remain on meeting current disease based targets through a predominantly medicalised approach.

Attaining the *fully engaged* scenario will require further effort. In this scenario, public health targets are exceeded, resulting in greater reductions in hospital visits and GP admissions, and higher expenditure on health promotion. Achieving all this involves tackling socio-economic problems, reducing inequalities in socio-economic status, decreasing levels of smoking and obesity and increasing levels of physical activity. There is also a particular emphasis on the role of individuals in taking active ownership of their own health. Clearly, such a scenario requires political action both to address wider inequalities in society, and to facilitate actions by individuals, families and community groups. This will involve breaking the stranglehold of the public health profession, with greater emphasis on the multi-disciplinary nature of public health roles at all levels, and in all sections, of society. The development of the public health function, therefore, will require the integration of the wider public health workforce (and the recognition of their role), within local communities (Peckham, 2003).

So, is everyone to be a public health worker? We need to look more carefully at how different public health roles are undertaken, and by whom. It may be more appropriate to argue that everyone should share a public health *mindset*, but that different people should undertake different roles. The key difficulty here is the lack of agreed definitions and perceptions of public health, and a tendency to retreat into professionally defined roles and responsibilities. Such an approach also tends to diminish the important role played by a whole range of non-health professionals in local government and the voluntary sector, not to mention the role of people in their own communities. The key to developing public health in the future is to address the tension between increasing professional specialisation in public health and growing diversification in practice.

Five conditions for change

Rather than thinking about the future public health worker, we should be focusing on the conditions that are required to allow public health to flourish. These need to be identified at all levels in society.

Public health leadership – this must transcend organisational, professional, historical and political issues, and the single hierarchical structures that tend to dominate the NHS. Existing public health professionals will need to work in partnership with other public health leaders. If this is to be possible, the notion of leadership needs to move away from its association with authority, to embrace more than just management competencies. Such leadership will foster the development of complementary skills amongst a multi-disciplinary cadre of public health professionals and practitioners with a wide range of experience and backgrounds.

A strong value base for developing public health – this requires recognition by the NHS of the importance of shifting the focus from health improvement to tackling health inequalities. Furthermore, there needs to be a shift from a focus on health inequalities to inequalities in general. A greater emphasis on, and commitment to, tackling social injustices will include measures to tackle social deprivation, poor housing, food poverty and so on. Ultimately these are likely to have important impacts on health.

Public health perspectives in policy – this moves on from the (important) practice of considering the health impacts of all policies to include a proactive commitment to developing, implementing and evaluating policy with a public health approach. Notions of equity, collaboration and participation would therefore underpin all policies at local, national and international level.

Greater integration and prioritisation of public health action – organisationally, public health needs to be integrated into all national, regional and local organisational structures and to be central to regional and local development. Public health as a function needs to operate inter-organisationally and intra-organisationally with clear identification of distinct opportunities for public health action to occur.

Greater recognition of the important public health roles played by communities, individuals and families – public health is not achieved by just delivering a public health service to people. It requires real collaboration and involvement, working with local communities, drawing on their experience, knowledge and skills. In addition, a lay perspective:

- gives insights into patterns of behaviour and lifestyles;
- helps understand factors that underpin and create health inequalities;
- suggests new factors that influence people's health and their ability to use existing resources; and
- helps understand how people live and manage their lives.

Such an approach will also encourage people's interest and achieve their active involvement in maintaining their health. This will require mechanisms for dialogue and debate, as well as the successful implementation and monitoring of programmes of health improvement with the ownership of the people they aim to help (Taylor, 2003).

These conditions are achievable, and indeed, important developments are already taking place. Within Wales, for instance, the Assembly has made its political commitment to public health clear. The Welsh Assembly has also developed complete coterminosity between its new local health boards and local authorities in order to improve co-ordination between them. In England, whilst political leadership remains more remote, there is a concerted effort towards opening up the public health profession to multi-disciplinary specialists. These are likely to have a significant impact on the extent to which public health is prioritised and supported within their patch. Also, there is the potential for local strategic partnerships to drive forward an inter-sectoral approach to public health by developing strategies, setting clear local objectives, co-ordinating activity, and providing local political leadership through local authorities. Finally, in Scotland, the strong emphasis on developing public health practitioners in LHCCs provides an opportunity for local public health leaders to be supported and developed. These leaders will be likely to integrate public health into regional and local organisations and structures, and identify opportunities for public health action to occur and for public health 'champions' to flourish.

For any of these developments to have a major impact on the public health function as a whole, however, the stranglehold of public health professionalism must be challenged. Shared leadership in public health must support a clear value base which prioritises social justice and encourages public health specialists, practitioners, the wider workforce and local communities to think and act in new ways. We need to develop an approach to public health that combines elements of all these approaches, providing stronger national and local political leadership, and new public health leaders located outside of the NHS and statutory sector, with strong links between these and public health specialists.

References

Abbott, S., Florin, D., Fulop, N. and Gillam, S. (2001) *Primary Care Groups and Trusts: improving health*, London: King's Fund.

Acheson, D. (1988) *The Report of the Committee of Inquiry into the Future Development of the Public Health Function*, London: Her Majesty's Stationery Office.

Anderson, W. and Florin, D. (2000) *Involving the Public – one of many priorities*, London: King's Fund.

Baggott, R. (2000) *Public Health: policy and politics*, London: Macmillan, now Palgrave Macmillan.

Billingham, K. and Perkins, E. (1997) 'A Public Health Approach to Nursing in the Community', *Nursing Standard*, 11, 43–6.

Burke, S., Gray, I., Paterson, K. and Meyrick, J. (2002) *Environmental Health 2012: a key partner in delivering the public health agenda*, London: Health Development Agency.

Burke, S., Meyrick, J. and Speller, V. (2001) *Public Health Skills Audit 2001 – research report*, London: Health Development Agency.

Clark, J. M. and Maben, J. (1999) *Health Promotion and Public Health: challenges for nurse education*, Southampton: University of Southampton.

Clews, G. (2003) 'PCT Chief Executives Concerned over New Targets', *Health Service Journal*, 113, 29 May, 6–7.

Cornish, Y. and Knight, T. (2003) *Exploring Public Health Career Paths: an overview of career opportunities in public health and health improvement in England*, London: National Health Service Executive, Birmingham University and South East Institute of Public Health.

Department of Health (1998) *Independent Inquiry into Inequalities in Health Report. Chairman Sir Donald Acheson*, London: The Stationery Office.

Department of Health (1999a) *Saving Lives: our healthier nation*, London: The Stationery Office.

Department of Health (1999b) *Making a Difference: strengthening the nursing midwifery and health visiting contribution to healthcare*, London: The Stationery Office.

Department of Health (2001a) *The Report of the Chief Medical Officer's Project to Strengthen the Public Health Function*, London: The Stationery Office.

Department of Health (2001b) *Shifting the Balance of Power within the NHS: securing delivery*, London: Department of Health.

Department of Health (2001c) *Health Visitor Practice Development Resource Pack*, London: Department of Health.

Department of Health (2002a) *Shifting the Balance of Power: the next steps*, London: Department of Health.

Department of Health (2002b) *Liberating the Talents: helping Primary Care Trusts and nurses to deliver the NHS Plan*, London: Department of Health.

Department of Health (2003) *The NHS Knowledge and Skills Framework (NHS KSF) and Development Review Guidance – working draft*, London: Department of Health.

Department of the Environment Transport and the Regions (DETR) (2001a) *Power to Promote or Improve Economic, Social or Environmental Well-being*, London: Department of the Environment Transport and the Regions.

Department of the Environment Transport and the Regions (DETR) (2001b) *Local Strategic Partnerships: government guidance*, London: Department of the Environment Transport and the Regions.

Donnan, S. (1999) *Revalidation in Public Health Medicine (draft)*, London: Faculty of Public Health Medicine.

Doyle, Y. (2002) *A New CPD System for Public Health*, London: Faculty of Public Health Medicine.

Faculty of Public Health Medicine (FPHM) (2001a) *Good Public Health Practice – general professional expectations of public health physicians & specialists in public health* [online], Faculty of Public Health Medicine. Available from: *http://www.fphm.org.uk/standards/standards.shtml* [Accessed 23 June 2003].

Faculty of Public Health Medicine (FPHM) (2001b) *Developing Public Health in Primary Care Trusts – a framework for discussion*, London: Faculty of Public Health Medicine.

Gabe, J. (ed.) (1995) *Medicine, Health and Risk* (Sociology of Health and Illness monograph), Oxford: Blackwells.

Gillam, S., Abbott, S. and Banks-Smith, J. (2001) 'Can Primary Care Groups and Trusts Improve Health?', *British Medical Journal*, 323, 89–92.

House of Commons Select Committee on Health (2001) *Public Health, 2nd Report*, London: House of Commons.

Kendall, L. (2001) *The Future Patient*, London: Institute for Public Policy Research.

Latter, S. and Westwood, G. (2001) *Public Health Capacity in the Nursing Workforce. Phase 1: a pilot project to identify current practice in educational preparation*, Southampton: School of Nursing and Midwifery, University of Southampton.

Lessof, S., Dumelow, C. and McPherson, K. (1998) *Feasibility Study of the Case for National Standards for Specialist Practice in Public Health*, London: London School of Hygiene and Tropical Medicine.

Levenson, R. (1998) 'Issues at the Interface of Medical Sociology and Public Health', in G. Scambler and P. Higgs (eds) *Modernity, Medicine and Health*, London: Routledge.

Lewis, J. (1986) *What Price Community Medicine? The philosophy, practice and politics of public health since 1919*, Sussex: Wheatsheaf Books.

Mason, C. and Clarke, J. (2001) *A Nursing Vision of Public Health: all Ireland statement on public health and nursing*, Belfast/Dublin: Department of Health, Social Services and Public Safety and Department of Health and Children.

National Assembly for Wales (1999) *Realising the Potential*, Cardiff: National Assembly for Wales.

Painter, C. and Clarence, E. (2001) 'UK Local Action Zones and Changing Urban Governance', *Urban Studies*, 38, 1215–32.

Peckham, S. (2003) 'Who are the Partners in Public Health?', in J. Orme, J. Powell, P. Taylor, M. Grey and T. Harrison (eds) *Multi-disciplinary Public Health: policy and practice*, Buckingham: Open University Press.

Popay, J. and Williams, G. (eds) (1994) *Researching the People's Health*, London: Routledge.

Popay, J., Williams, G., Thomas, C. and Gatrell, A. (1998) 'Theorising Inequalities in Health: the place of lay knowledge', *Sociology of Health and Illness*, 20, 5, 619–44.

Poulton, B., Mason, C., McKenna, H., Lynch, C. and Keeney, S. (2000) *The Contribution of Nurses, Midwives and Health Visitors to the Public Health Agenda*, Belfast: Department of Health, Social Services and Public Safety.

Quality Assurance Agency for Higher Education (2001) *Benchmarking Academic and Practitioner Standards in Health Care Subjects* [online], Quality Assurance Agency for Higher Education. Available from: *http://www.qaa.ac.uk/crntwork/benchmark/nhsbenchmark/benchmarking.htm* [Accessed 23 June 2003].

Royal Institute of Public Health (RIPH) (2001) *National Standards for Specialist Practice in Public Health: an overview* [online], Royal Institute of Public Health. Available from: *http://www.riph.org.uk/nationalstand.html* [Accessed 23 June 2003].

Scottish Executive (2000) *Review of the Public Health Function in Scotland*, Edinburgh: Scottish Executive.

Scottish Executive (2001) *Nursing for Health: a review of the contribution of nurses, midwives and health visitors to improving the public's health in Scotland*, Edinburgh: Scottish Executive.

Scottish Executive (2003) *Nursing for Health: two years on*, Edinburgh: Scottish Executive.

Sim, F., Walters, R. and Schiller, G. (2003) *A Diversity of Talents: public health people in London*, UK Public Health Association Annual Conference, Cardiff.

Taylor, P. (2003) 'The Lay Contribution to Public Health', in J. Orme, J. Powell, P. Taylor, M. Grey and T. Harrison (eds) *Multi-disciplinary Public Health: policy and practice*, Buckingham: Open University Press.

Taylor, P., Peckham, S. and Turton, P. (1998) *A Public Health Model of Primary Care: from concept to reality*, Birmingham: Public Health Alliance.

Tripartite Group (2003) *Communications Bulletin 1: UK voluntary register for public health specialists* [online], Tripartite Group. Available from: *http://www.education-brokering.org.uk/vol__spec__register.htm* [Accessed 23 June 2003].

Walters, R., Schiller, G. and Sim, F. (2002) 'Mapping the Public Health Workforce 1: a tool for classifying the public health workforce', *Public Health*, 116, 6, 388.

Wanless, D. (2002) *Securing our Future Health: taking a long-term view*, London: HM Treasury.

Warren, M. D. (2000) *The Origins of the Faculty of Public Health Medicine*, London: Faculty of Public Health Medicine.

Wilkin, D., Gillam, S. and Leese, B. (2000) *The National Tracker Survey of Primary Care Groups Progress and Challenges, 1999/2000*, Manchester: National Primary Care Research and Development Centre.

Williams, G. and Popay, J. (1994) 'Lay Knowledge and the Privilege of Experience', in J. Gabe, D. Kelleher and G. Williams (eds) *Challenging Medicine*, London: Routledge.

8
What Future for Health Care Assistants: High Road or Low Road?[1]

Carole Thornley

Introduction

One of the major recommendations in Derek Wanless's hugely influential final report to the Treasury on the longer-term future of the health service concerned the 'considerable scope' which greatly increased numbers of 'health care assistants' (HCAs) might make to changes in the 'skill-mix' in the health care labour force (Wanless, 2002: 57). It was argued that in future health care assistants could 'undertake a large part of the routine work which nurses currently undertake in primary and secondary care' (ibid: 58). In one scenario,[2] around 144,000 additional HCAs would need to be recruited, one of the largest projected increases of any staff group – although Wanless acknowledged that 'it might be difficult to recruit this many' (ibid: 91). This is noteworthy for two reasons, which are explored in this chapter. First, it assumes a clear and easy current distinction between HCAs and 'nurses'. Second, it points to a clear strategy of substitution, as if this were a new idea with no prior history in this sector.

The motives for the recommended increase in HCA numbers in Wanless can easily be understood from an economist's perspective. As the report notes, two-thirds of the NHS budget is spent on pay,[3] and the 'pay and productivity of the health service workforce will be an important driver of the financial resources required to deliver a high quality service over the next 20 years' (ibid: 57). The nursing workforce is a key target for any savings or cost restraint policies because of its sheer size, both in terms of employment and percentage of the overall paybill (see Thornley, 2001a: 88–9). At the same time, there are limited methods for controlling cost, and labour substitution or 'grade dilution' – in which grades and grade boundaries are redefined to substitute cheaper labour for more expensive[4] – represents a relatively subtle way of restraining the paybill (ibid). As is shown below, historically this has meant making use of the on-the-job experience and accumulated skills of HCAs, without translating this into a formal recognition of value, with associated improvements in status, pay and career progression. It remains to be seen if the Wanless recommendation will fall into this category. The same is true for the NHS Plan, which claims to challenge 'traditional professional boundaries', 'demarcations' and 'old hierarchical ways of working' (Department of Health, 2000a).

This chapter aims to cast light upon the debate over HCAs, and the implications for policy intended to shape the future healthcare worker. A distinction is drawn between policies which take the 'high road' to reform, with due recognition of worker contributions and appropriate rewards and progression, and policies which take the 'low road' of short-term cost-restraint through suppression of employee aspirations.[5]

The lack of clarity in the Wanless report about what is actually meant by a 'health care assistant', and even about current numbers and the work currently performed, is consistent with past policy and academic neglect of this 'invisible' group of workers. This chapter will rectify this neglect by building on a series of national surveys, case studies and interviews commissioned by UNISON and conducted between 1996 and 2001 (Thornley, 1996b; 1997; 1998a; 1999 and 2001b). These research projects, taken jointly, constitute the most extensive independent study yet made of health care assistants (and nursing auxiliaries/assistants), and their findings have formed part of UNISON's evidence to the Review Body for Nurses, Midwives, Health Visitors and Professions Allied to Medicine in successive years. Firstly, it will be argued that internal debates on the 'appropriate' division of labour in nursing, and associated labour substitution strategies, are as old as formal nursing itself: in the past, policy options chosen have certainly produced some 'low road' outcomes. Secondly, the chapter draws upon the body of original research mentioned above to address and clarify the issues of who HCAs are and what they do. Finally, the chapter explores the challenges posed by an historical-empirical approach to healthcare delivery, focusing on the key contemporary debate about what 'nursing' is, or should be, and the formulation of pragmatic policies that take the 'high road' to reform. Potential constraints on alternative futures are noted in the concluding section.

Context

The early formalisation of 'nursing' in the nineteenth-century, and its location in the wider health service labour force, was deeply influenced by existing gender and class divisions in the wider economy and society. With women excluded from the emerging medical professions, nursing and auxiliary/ancillary roles were in turn divided internally on the basis of class and gender, in ways which reflected the class-based provision of health care itself as well as wider class and gender stereotypes and constraints.[6] By the latter part of the nineteenth century, upper- and middle-class women were attempting to redefine nursing as a respectable occupation for themselves and for some working-class women. The model of nursing that emerged was deeply patriarchal, hierarchical and class conscious (Abel-Smith, 1960), with an ethos stressing 'vocation, selflessness and dedication' (Stacey, 1991: 109).

These gender- and class-based divisions were still apparent in the divergent approaches taken by health workers to issues of 'professionalisation' and representation in the late nineteenth and twentieth centuries. Within nursing a wide variety of professional associations arose, located mainly in the upper echelons of the voluntary sector. These associations sought professional 'closure' through exclusionary practices. Successive attempts were made via national standards of training and examination to 'draw a firm line between those who were fitted to practice as nurses and those who were not' (Abel-Smith, 1960: 61). Following formal registration of nurses in the 1919 Act, the College of Nursing (later the Royal College of Nursing) emerged as the dominant association. 'Unqualified' nurses were excluded from membership by definition. Trade unions formed in part as a reaction to the conservatism and the exclusive nature of the professional associations, with a core membership located in the poor law and asylum sectors. They represented in particular the interests of working-class workers lower down the health hierarchy and those excluded by the professional associations (including student nurses and male nurses). With a primary focus on obtaining material improvements in pay and conditions, rather than professional status *per se*, the unions increasingly recruited 'qualified' nursing staff alongside other staff (Carpenter, 1988; Abel-Smith op. cit.).

State and employer strategies tended from an early stage to foster and exploit the division of labour and representational forms within nursing, through manipulation of pay systems and outcomes. However, as pay remained poor and public concern crystallised around resulting nursing shortages, successive policies of labour substitution were followed. Prior to the establishment of the NHS in 1948, 'unqualified' nurses were prevalent on hospital wards. Labour substitution practices continued in the new state system, with the introduction of enrolled nurses (ENs) in 1943, and the formal recognition and expansion of the nursing auxiliary (NA) role in 1955. Both grades drew on married women, part-timers, the less educationally advantaged and more working class. They also drew on ex-colonial and commonwealth recruitment, reinforcing ethnic divisions alongside those of class and gender. Such policies were predicated on the fluidity of nursing boundaries, particularly at the 'lower' end of the hierarchy. In practice, the associations had failed to achieve closure with the 1919 Act (Witz, 1992), and many 'unqualified' people continued to engage in duties that could be defined as nursing, while, conversely, many registered nurses engaged in duties that could be defined as auxiliary or ancillary. The delineation and ownership of skills remained a contested terrain, and one in which class-based advantage played a leading role. At the same time, the role of experience versus formal training were continuing points of contention, and the 'intellectual' requirements and real 'content' of nursing remained unresolved issues (Thornley, 1996a).

In the second half of the twentieth century employer strategies continued to represent an approach which could be described as 'low road', and which also entailed some important contradictions. A cycle arose in which relatively poor pay, shortages and increases in workers at the lower end of the hierarchy all contributed to rising discontent, a growth in trade union membership, and a more militant approach by health service workers, underpinned by public concern about health service provision and sympathy for health service workers. Membership of the TUC-affiliated unions greatly expanded. By the early 1980s, their combined nursing membership actually exceeded that of the RCN, which had itself adopted trade union status in 1977, in part to enable it to compete. Industrial unrest erupted in the early 1980s. Driving this cycle were employer strategies which continued to seek nursing services on the cheap, and to build inequalities into the system. Perhaps predictably, the response to unrest in the 1980s was a new round of labour substitution strategies, alongside traditional attempts to change pay determination mechanisms.[7] These strategies coalesced with the introduction of a 'new' and locally-paid grade of health service worker, the Health Care Assistant (HCA) (or support worker), in the 1990 NHS and Community Care Act. Here, the government built on proposals for changes in the nurse education system which became known as Project 2000,[8] while concurrently pushing ahead with proposals for National Council for Vocational Qualifications (NCVQ) certificates for the 'new' grade of HCA and intensifying a series of initiatives around so-called skill-mix and reprofiling.

Casting some light: research on non-registered nurses

Negligible academic and policy attention had been paid to the long-standing, nationally-paid, grade of nursing auxiliary/assistant at this point, despite the fact that much direct care was carried out by them. As Salvage noted, NAs were 'a neglected group of people' with 'virtually no serious, extended discussion of the role [they] play in caring for patients, despite its importance' (Salvage, 1985: 88; see also Davies 1995: 95).[9] The introduction of locally-paid HCAs, while clearly conceptually founded as a policy to address nursing shortages at low cost, threatened to add to the relative invisibility of workers and work at the lower end of the nursing hierarchy.

An early national study on the decentralisation of pay arrangements in the mid 1990s (Thornley, 1996b; 1998b) pointed to the growing significance of the locally paid grade of HCA, and to the fact that HCA numbers and duties appeared to be rapidly outstripping official accounts. This study was subsequently augmented by a series of national surveys of managers, trade unionists, nursing auxiliaries and HCAs, together with case studies and focus group interviews, also commissioned by UNISON (Thornley, 1997; 1998a; 1999; 2001b; see also Thornley, 2000; 2001a). The following commentary draws on these findings as a means of analysing current policy proposals and debates over nursing 'content'.

Profile and characteristics

Official recognition of the full extent of workers now involved in nursing tasks and the scope and range of their involvement is sorely deficient. Department of Health statistics continue to muddle the categories of HCAs and support workers (SWs) working in hotel and property areas, and remain ambiguous over whether or not HCAs/SWs are considered part of the non-registered nursing workforce (see, for example, Department of Health, 2000b). This in turn makes it very difficult to gauge the precise extent of the growth in the non-registered nursing workforce, and causes problems of definition and interpretation of Trust returns on the number of workers employed in nursing capacities, whether listed as 'HCAs/SWs', 'NAs', or under one of many alternative job titles. HCAs and SWs also continue to be excluded from direct consideration by the Review Body for Nursing Staff, Midwives, Health Visitors and Professions Allied to Medicine,[10] and have typically been employed on generally inferior local terms and conditions of employment.

A detailed consideration of the profile of both NAs and HCAs (Thornley, 1997; 1998a; 1999)[11] helps explain why such confusions in official counts, and in the treatment of non-registered nurses, arise. Firstly, the non-registered workforce profile has been changing dramatically, with a proliferation of the HCA grade and a corresponding decline in the numbers employed in the NA grade. The percentage of Trusts now employing HCAs may be as high as 70–80 per cent. Significant numbers of NAs have now been incorporated into the HCA workforce: nearly a fifth of Trusts have incorporated all NAs in this way, and no longer employ this nationally-paid 'Whitley' grade at all. A further impediment to official data gathering, and an issue in itself, is to be found in the wide range of titles in use for HCAs, as shown in Figure 8.1.

This is compounded by a widespread official ignorance about whether these workers are engaged in 'nursing' or direct patient care or clinical duties, or solely on 'ancillary' duties. However, despite a wide range of titles, the rationale driving the introduction of the 'new' grade of HCA is clear: from a ranking of eight main reasons for having introduced the grade, 'cost-effectiveness' emerges as the first-ranked criterion for managers, followed by 'flexible hours and deployment'. Written comments on questionnaires and interviews with managers typically elicit references to cheapness, flexibility,

---

- Generic support worker
- Clinical support worker
- Healthcare support worker
- Care team assistant
- Nursing assistant
- Ward assistant
- Theatre assistant
- Community care worker
- Home carer
- Scientific helper
- Doctors' assistant
- 'Bedmaker'

Figure 8.1:   Range of titles in use for HCAs

and, even, multi-skilling, demonstrating that grade dilution is a primary factor. They explain that the introduction of HCAs has been viewed as a necessary response to resource constraints, and to the declining availability of enrolled, student and registered nursing staff on the wards or in the community.

The particular workforce characteristics (and striking similarities) of NAs and HCAs clarify how such labour substitution is enabled, and also call into question more hierarchical views of nursing content and career progression. As is shown in Thornley (1997; 1998a), over four-fifths of both HCAs and NAs are female – with around two-fifths to a half working part-time – with the usual implications for undervaluation of 'women's work'. The outstanding characteristic of these workers is their maturity and experience. The great majority of HCAs and NAs are aged over 30, with nearly half of all HCAs and 60 per cent of NAs aged over 40. Fully a third of NAs are aged 50 and over. In line with this mature age profile, there is overwhelming evidence on the part of each group of workers of both formal and informal experience of caring, prior to taking up current roles. In the case of HCAs, almost two-fifths have direct prior experience as an NHS NA, with a further two-fifths having prior caring experience in the NHS and/or local government: 12 per cent have prior experience in the voluntary caring sector. Many also recognise their 'informal' caring experience at home (care of children, older people and people with disabilities, for example) as an important part of their ability to cope with the role of HCA. NAs similarly come into their current role with a wide range of prior formal and informal caring experience. Length of service and experience in current, or, in the case of HCAs, associated, roles is also striking. For HCAs coming from an NHS caring background, around half have over five years of experience and nearly a third have between 10 and 28 years of experience. The average length of employment as an NA is over 12 years, and more than a quarter have worked between 19 and 31 or more years in the job. In line with this degree of experience, both HCAs and NAs tend to undertake self-teaching during their employment: over three-quarters of NAs read nursing practice textbooks and journals in their own time, and interviews demonstrate that many also read medical textbooks and specialist journals, reading up on techniques and conditions as necessary throughout their jobs, as well as asking other staff around them for instruction and explanation.

The prevalent notion in the literature, and a popular misconception, that HCAs and NAs are 'unskilled', 'untrained', or 'unqualified' workers, is also flawed from the perspective of formal accreditation and training, and the introduction of NVQs has really begun to challenge such stereotypes. The key point is that NVQs are primarily designed to give recognition and accreditation for existing competencies/skills following occupational standards and norms (for a detailed review of NVQs and levels, see Hoskins, 1999: 2–4). Such competencies and skills may be acquired either through experiential learning or specific on- or off-job training, and are subsequently verified by internal and external assessors from the nursing and educational professions. Despite a substantial minority of laggard Trusts, NVQ attainment is gradually becoming an expectation for both HCAs and, more surprisingly given original official pronouncements, for NAs. Although managers report that in two-fifths of Trusts training is not explicitly linked to NVQ attainment, just under a third of HCAs in the national sample have managed to acquire an NVQ (usually at level 2), and many more are working towards it. Similar results are obtained for NAs, although here even more (almost two-fifths) had acquired an NVQ (8 per cent having achieved level 3) at the point of survey.[12] There are therefore few remaining justifications for generalised references to these staff as either 'unqualified', 'untrained' or 'unskilled'. This point is amplified by the fact that both HCAs and NAs also demonstrate a high degree of interest in acquiring NVQs and the potential recognition such qualifications may provide. Many have had to fight, either individually or collectively through their union, UNISON, to get access to NVQ accreditation, and are fiercely critical of managerial limitations in providing access to NVQs, necessary training and appropriate reward for qualifications. Some note that they paid to put themselves through NVQ training as their Trust would not or could not, and substantial numbers feel that not enough training is provided or that they would like more off-the-job training. Problems with assessment/assessor availability are frequently noted. Interestingly, of those who have achieved NVQ2, many feel they are being prevented by lack of resources or management disinclination from accessing NVQ3.

It is also necessary to understand why HCAs and NAs have not chosen, or did not originally choose, to enter registered nurse training. The body of research included an extended questionnaire for NAs which explored this issue, but given a high degree of overlap the findings are also relevant for HCAs. There is very considerable interest in registered nurse training, with just over half all NAs keen to undertake this. This figure is actually an underestimate, as many of those who respond that they are 'not interested' explain that they cannot afford to take the drop in income or are now 'past the age limit'. Of those who are interested in registered nurse training, the main factors preventing them from undertaking this are 'domestic commitments' or 'prior educational requirements'. If most training were conducted on the job, and salaries could be maintained, substantially more would be interested. Finances are a particularly important factor for many (along with domestic caring commitments), with the bursary level for registered nurse training viewed as prohibitively low, and the seconded level also inadequate.[13] Nearly all HCAs and NAs are low-paid under official definitions and earnings are vital: many are thus trapped in this situation and prevented from undertaking further formal training.

These findings fundamentally challenge preconceived ideas about 'commitment' and 'competency'. Most HCAs and NAs demonstrate a maturity and level of caring experience which means that *experiential learning and self-teaching* has to be taken fully into account in any evaluation of 'skills' and 'competency'. The basis for both *de facto* substitution and formal accreditation is clearly illustrated, and it may readily be envisaged that higher levels of NVQ (NVQ3 and NVQ4) are realistic propositions for HCAs and NAs, given their years of on- and off-job caring experience.

Work

The evidence about work actually performed is striking, and can be better understood in the light of the above discussion of profile and characteristics. There is a high degree of agreement between managers, HCAs and NAs on work performed, and conclusive evidence that the boundaries between so-called auxiliary/ancillary work and nursing work continue to be highly blurred and fluid: both the traditional grade of NA and the 'new' grade of HCA engage widely in 'nursing' duties, and job titles are used almost interchangeably in most Trusts. Managers report that the great majority of HCAs (as with NAs) engage in nursing/clinical duties and direct patient care as part of their overall responsibilities, and the detailed sample surveys of HCAs/SWs and NAs themselves overwhelmingly confirm this view. Definitions of work as 'non-clinical' or 'clinical' will remain contentious. However, while many of these workers are expected to engage in certain aspects of 'non-clinical' work (such as clerical, cleaning, cooking/making drinks, portering, transport, messenger work, and, in a few cases, laundry), the very great majority are also employed in the performance of 'clinical/nursing' duties. Comparisons between the two groups of workers demonstrate that work content is almost identical, that it clearly constitutes 'nursing work', and that substantial minorities of both grades also engage extensively in more 'technical and advanced' tasks such as drug administration, invasive procedures and taking blood. Figure 8.2, listing some of the clinical duties described by HCAs and NAs, underlines these points. The extent to which some of these duties are undertaken is clear from the fact that over a third of NAs (in the more extended study of work tasks conducted for NAs in 1998: Thornley, 1998a) report that they liaise with doctors, and just under a third that they have performed cardiac massage in cases of arrest and/or helped train student/newly-qualified nurses.

Interviews suggest that HCAs and NAs are more likely to under-report than over-report the extent of their work roles: many note that some of the work tasks they perform in practice are done 'unofficially' or 'informally', and for this reason they did not report them. There is a strong suggestion that involvement in nursing and extended nursing duties has actually been increasing over the period of the field research (see especially Thornley, 2001b), with participants also noting that over recent years they have been expected to pick up more and more nursing tasks, especially where NVQs have been acquired. The evidence is strongly suggestive of a process of further job enlargement or, alternatively viewed, a more extensive labour substitution process.

This research has provided the first detailed aggregate evidence of a significant overlap in duties between non-registered and registered nursing staff, a point which is further emphasised by detail on the extent to which HCAs and NAs are supervised by registered nurses and the extent to which they substitute for them. The majority experience is that both grades 'undertake the same or similar work as a registered nurse' frequently or sometimes, with only a minority reporting that they 'rarely or never' substitute for registered staff. With respect to supervision, over half of all HCAs and NAs report that 'little' or 'none' of their work is supervised, and only a small minority report that 'all' or 'most' of their work is supervised. In the extended NA questionnaire (Thornley, 1998a), respondents also note that they and HCAs now perform the great bulk of direct patient care: only 15 per cent report that the majority of direct patient care is carried out by registered staff. These findings clearly provide a cumulative challenge to conventional thinking, and raise a number of important issues.

Undervaluation: the limits to 'vocation'

One such issue concerns the double bind experienced by non-registered nurses, in the sense of relative task invisibility and hence undervaluation. Thornley (2001b) in particular demonstrates that

- Giving drugs without supervision*
- Running clinics single-handed
- Phlebotomy
- Running therapeutic groups
- Organising and chairing client review meetings
- Training agency staff on nights
- Giving advice on the phone
- Setting up all instruments for theatre
- Making up instrument trolleys for doctors
- Computer evaluations
- Acting as scrub nurse
- Tracheostomy emergency suction
- Writing care plans and keeping them up to date
- Initiating admissions and discharges
- Speech therapy assessment
- Venepuncture
- Plastering
- ECGs
- Massage in cardiac arrest cases
- Preparing patients for suturing
- Being in charge of a shift
- Assisting mothers with breast feeding
- Dealing with doctors
- Infection control
- Going on ward rounds with doctors and being asked for views
- Restraining aggressive patients
- Setting up diagnostic machines and feeds
- Looking after student nurses and newly-qualified nurses

Figure 8.2:   Some clinical duties described by health care assistants and NAs

*It can be noted that giving drugs without supervision is sometimes noted as a source of concern, especially by younger staff, and others concerned about potential legal implications.

NAs and HCAs are caught in the wider problem associated with nursing more generally, of whether to emphasise 'technical' skills, which receive a high social valuation, or 'soft, holistic' skills, which are typically undervalued (along with other skills associated with 'women's work' more generally[14]). When interviewees describe the 'soft' skills aspects of their jobs it is apparent that these are at least as professionally demanding as the 'technical' skills, and often also a source of particular personal stress for these healthcare workers, who 'care' deeply for their patients:

> You learn the art of dealing with people – a big part of my job is as a counsellor. If someone dies, I'm a widow ... so I go and sit at home and cry – who can we really talk to about it?

At the same time, despite experiencing job enlargement with respect to more advanced, clinical tasks, the unclear status of the NA/HCA/SW within the 'clinical team' means that these workers fail to receive recognition and reward for more 'technical' work actually performed, and are often therefore also placed in an extremely difficult position. Interviews illustrated time and again the frustration these healthcare workers feel over the perceived failure of others in the healthcare team to acknowledge their input to a holistic model of healthcare, and to recognise the value of their hands-on experience with patients, encompassing both 'soft' and 'technical' skills.

This neglect is all the more pertinent as NAs and HCAs exhibit strong vocational characteristics: many interviewees give deeply personal reasons for choosing to work in the health service and demonstrate an enormous commitment to caring for others:

> I wanted to care for patients – I had had a blind and handicapped relative, had looked after my nan and grandad, and nursed my mother before she died. I worked in a private nursing home first and then got this job.

However, 'career' in the sense of adequate recognition and remuneration is a vital consideration and a necessary adjunct to any 'vocational' instincts: the lack of appropriate remuneration and career progression is a source of real financial hardship, deep frustration and poor morale. Pay remains extremely poor for NAs,[15] and even worse for HCAs. Both groups have seen their relative pay decline compared with registered nurses, and the great majority remain on Whitley Nursing Grade A or an equivalent. At the same time, pay is an important issue for all, with many the sole or main earner in their household and earnings in all cases an important source of household income. Lack of adequate mechanisms and resources for accreditation and training, and an apparent unwillingness on the part of Trusts to recognise work actually performed and accreditation achieved, or to employ the full range of nursing grades for these workers, exacerbates income problems through lack of progression routes.

To sum up, this body of evidence clearly shows that policy routes to date have tended to be 'low road' approaches: inequalities have been intensified in recent years and the nursing 'hierarchy' widened through the exploitation of workers who have demonstrated large amounts of commitment and ability. Putting to one side issues of justice and equity, there are two key reasons to question such low road approaches. Firstly, and returning to the proposals in Wanless and the NHS Plan, there is a wastage of potential productive efficiency here[16] and of a source of potential recruitment to registered nurse training. Secondly, there are increasing problems of recruitment and retention among NAs and HCAs themselves (see especially Thornley, 1999 and 2001b; see also Review Body, 2001): it is therefore unclear how these grades can be expanded to resolve shortages elsewhere without due attention to their specific problems. Perhaps paradoxically, however, current policy proposals and the realities of non-registered nursing employment do offer the potential for a 'high(er) road' policy approach. We explore some of the associated challenges in the next, concluding, section.

Discussion and conclusions: alternative futures?

These findings about non-registered nurses offer a potential impetus for a wider-ranging discussion of nurse education and content (and, therefore, career entry and progression) than is at present on the health care workforce agenda. This dovetails with an important academic debate which has grown up in particular around registered nursing. This latter debate has notably been carried forward, albeit with differential emphasis, by Celia Davies (1995; 2001) and Ann Bradshaw (2000; 2001a; 2001b). Davies has argued that registered nurses run the risk of losing the value of their caring role because caring carries a strong association with 'women's work' and the nature of the 'soft' skills of nursing work conflicts with professionalising strategies in nursing which emphasise 'male, technical' skills. In reviewing (*inter alia*) the work of Salvage and Stacey, Davies explores concepts of 'professionalism'. She refers to its 'blindness to the skill base which is involved' in care giving, and the 'conflict that such work sets up when incorporated into a regular bureaucratic control system' (2001: 349). For nursing, bringing the 'terms profession and care together' is thus 'more than a step in semantics', and nursing stands to gain in this exercise by 'focusing on unpaid and low paid carework' (ibid: 350–1). Davies concludes that work on the 'rationality of caring' 'offers a real potential to reflect back to nurses their subjective understanding of their work, to legitimise the work that nurses do and to give them a new confidence in policy settings' (ibid). Coming from a very different perspective, Bradshaw has also argued that there is 'confusion and paradox' in the modern nursing identity, with 'urgent debate' needed about the 'current mutation of the nursing role and the increasing loss of its foundational place in the bedside delivery of "total patient care"' (2000: 328). In a wider review of the history of nursing (2001a; 2001b), Bradshaw draws on Thornley's work to argue that, as nurse education becomes more academic, the 'real' work of nursing and 'front-line personal care' is now being conducted by NAs and HCAs: 'Care assistants [are] becoming nurses in all but name' (2001b: 91).

These contributions show the continuing importance of debates on 'core' skills and worth in nursing, and equally demonstrate the impor- tance of including all those who actually nurse (including non- registered nurses) within this debate. They also demonstrate that there is the potential for a very fundamental re-evaluation of nursing, and more holistic approaches to patient care. The present chapter hopefully adds to this debate by demonstrating that there are urgent efficiency and equity arguments for change, and that 'vocation' cannot be a substitute for adequate remuneration and progression (or 'career'), but must be considered alongside it.[17]

These kinds of debates undoubtedly open up the possibilities for high(er) road policy approaches to the future healthcare worker, which are both more egalitarian and more efficient, and, indeed, add impetus to them. However, the challenges are likely to be substantial. Changes may require a significant re-evaluation of what a nursing 'career' is, and the different ways in which training and accreditation of prior learning, career progression, and (possibly) registration and national regulation might be approached. This will almost certainly entail a higher degree of diversity than is currently the case, and some (modest) steps have already been taken (for example, NHS Learning Accounts), or are in the process of negotiation.[18] Progression is likely to be a key issue for the next decade at least, with growing calls for formalised 'national occupational standards of good practice' which can 'provide the bedrock on which role development is built', with 'progression to nursing or other disciplines ... as seamless as possible' (Chapman, 2001: 16). At the same time, the resource implications in the sense of training provision and fairer remuneration are not insub- stantial: governments may be very tempted to avoid the more ambi- tious and radical programmes – with outcomes which would be historically predictable. In this respect, we may see a continuation of 'low road' approaches, with all the attendant longer-term problems discussed above. Negotiations are also still continuing at the time of writing over a new pay system in the NHS, *Agenda for Change* (Department of Health, 2003), which is likely to be based on pay spines with job evaluation and supplements. Depending on the precise shape of the system that emerges, and the development and implementation of standards, skills and training plans, this may provide both the extra stimulus for change and (paradoxically) highlight the potential constraints in realising such change.

Ultimately, alternative futures will hinge on the ways in which resource-based, strategic and social constraints impact upon this picture, and these aspects will require careful research. Strategic constraints may include lack of information – and of imagination – as well as lack of political will. Current and potential initiatives on training, a new skills escalator and pay and grading systems (as they emerge) will need to be evaluated, not least for their impact on pay and progression. The extent to which resource constraints or managerial approaches prevent roll-out of more progressive reforms (where these are formulated) to local levels will require evaluation. The constraints within nursing will also need to be researched. Here, the division, hierarchy and traditions noted in this paper will undoubtedly be stumbling blocks, and there are likely to be major differences of opinion between UNISON and the RCN. UNISON, on the one hand, represents registered nurses as well as the largest number of health service workers in the NHS, including the great majority of non-registered nurses. The RCN, on the other hand, is still exclusively focused on part of the registered nurse workforce, despite recently allowing a very small and clearly defined number of HCAs into 'associate membership'.[19] As this chapter has also shown, changes in nursing (as elsewhere) may also require changes in attitudes towards wider divisions and inequalities on the basis of class, gender and ethnicity – and vice versa. This is a tall order for all concerned. However, research will be needed to investigate the extent to which the highly unequal nursing sector can both influence, and be influenced by, wider concerns for equity.

Notes

1. My thanks, as always, are owed to UNISON, and to around two and a half thousand respondents and interviewees, who made this research possible. My thanks, too, to Professor Celia Davies for suggesting a policy analysis might be of interest. Finally, I am indebted to Dr Dan Coffey, Professor Celia Davies and Paul Chapman for detailed comments on drafts of this chapter.

2. The Report costs a variety of future 'scenarios', but the implications for employment numbers become increasingly vague.

3. This percentage rises if indirect labour (for example, contracted-out labour or labour services provided by the private sector) is also considered.

4. These concepts should be distinguished from the concept of 'deskilling': as should be clear from the detailed content of this paper, a more complex argument is being conducted.

5. For a series of more general discussions of 'high road', and 'low road', strategies in UK government policy, see Coffey and Thornley (2003).

6. For a full review, see Thornley 1993, 1996a, 2001a.

7. For a review of pay determination strategies and outcomes in the last two decades, see Thornley, 1998b, 2001a.

8. A *de facto* bid for professional closure by the nurse professionalisers (see Thornley, 1996a: 168–76).

9. NAs accounted for around one-quarter of the total nursing workforce throughout the 1980s.

10. This is despite an increasingly fluid use of terminology concerning 'health care assistants' and the 'non-registered nursing workforce' (see Review Body for Nursing Staff, Midwives, Health Visitors and Professions Allied to Medicine, 2001).

11. Thornley (1997) draws from 3 national questionnaire surveys conducted in 1997 in the UK with responses from over 1000 HCAs, over 100 staff side lead negotiators, and 80 Trust human resource or personnel managers, as well as case studies and interviews. Thornley (1998a) draws from a national survey conducted in 1998 in the UK, with responses from almost 900 NAs, supplemented by interviews. Thornley (1999) draws from a national questionnaire survey conducted in 1999, with responses from managers in 123 Trusts and from 60 lead negotiators, again supplemented by interviews.

12. It can be noted that the NA survey was conducted a year later than the HCA survey and may reflect a growth in attainment over the intervening period. In line with this, the follow-up research conducted in 2001 (Thornley, 2001b) suggested even higher levels of NVQ attainment for both HCAs and NAs.

13. This is due in part to the lack of inclusion of additions to normal earnings which are often substantial for this group of workers.

14. For an excellent discussion of this issue, see Davies (1995, 2001).

15. Despite the recent 'more generous' settlement under the Review Body for Nurses for 2001.

16. Because of the deficits in recognition, accreditation, training, progression and reward discussed here, NAs and HCAs are 'artificially' constrained from conducting tasks to the full extent of their abilities.

17. Alternatively viewed, it could be argued that a 'premium' should in fact be paid for people employing such a high degree of 'emotional labour' and suffering disproportionate amounts of associated stress.

18. UNISON has been working with NHS employers to secure improvements in education and training, including better access to NVQ assessment, 'fast-tracking' into and through registered nurse programmes, and part-time and work-based courses, amongst other things – a focus reflected to some extent

in the Knowledge and Skills Framework provisions in the proposed agreement *Agenda for Change* (January 2003 version).
19. Currently, only a very tiny percentage of HCAs/NAs have been enabled to obtain NVQ level 3 and few would therefore be eligible for 'partial' and 'restricted' membership.

References

Abel-Smith, B. (1960) *A History of the Nursing Profession*, London: Heinemann.
Bradshaw, A. (2000) 'Competence and British nursing: a view from history', *Journal of Clinical Nursing*, 9, 321–9.
Bradshaw, A. (2001a) *The Nurse Apprentice 1860–1977*, Aldershot: Ashgate.
Bradshaw, A. (2001b) *The Project 2000 Nurse: the remaking of British general nursing 1978–2000*, London: Whurr.
Carpenter, M. (1988) *Working for Health: the history of COHSE*, London: Lawrence & Wishart.
Chapman, P. (2001) 'Should Health Care Assistants be Called Nurses?', *Nursing Times*, 97, 45, 16.
Coffey, D. and Thornley, C. (2003) *Industrial and Labour Market Policy and Performance: issues and perspectives*, London: Routledge (Taylor and Francis).
Davies, C. (1995) *Gender and the Professional Predicament in Nursing*, Buckingham: Open University Press.
Davies, C. (2001) 'Professionalism and the Conundrum of Care', in B. Davey, A. Gray and C. Seale (eds) *Health and Disease: a reader, 3rd edition*, Buckingham: Open University Press.
Department of Health (2000a) *The NHS Plan: a plan for investment*, London: The Stationery Office, Cm 4818.
Department of Health (2000b) *Statistical Bulletin 2000/11, May*, London: The Stationery Office.
Department of Health (2003) *Agenda for Change* [online], available from: *http://www.doh.gov.uk/agendaforchange/* [Accessed 20 May 2003].
Hoskins, C. (1999) 'NVQs: It's time they got the recognition they deserve', *Nursing Times Learning Curve, Nursing Times*, 3, 2–4.
Review Body for Nursing Staff, Midwives, Health Visitors and Professions Allied to Medicine (2001) *Nineteenth Report on Nursing Staff, Midwives and Health Visitors 2001*, London: The Stationery Office, Cm 5345.
Salvage, J. (1985) *The Politics of Nursing*, London: Heinemann.
Stacey, M. (1991) *The Sociology of Health and Healing: a textbook*, London: Routledge.
Thornley, C. (1993) *Pay Determination for Nurses: pay review, grading and training in the 1980s*, unpublished PhD thesis, University of Warwick.
Thornley, C. (1996a) 'Segmentation and Inequality in the Nursing Workforce: re-evaluating the evaluation of skills', in R. Crompton, D. Gallie and K. Purcell (eds) *Changing Forms of Employment: organisations, skills and gender*, London: Routledge.
Thornley, C. (1996b) *Poor Prospects: local pay bargaining in action*, London: UNISON.
Thornley, C. (1997) *The Invisible Workers: an investigation into the pay and employment of health care assistants in the NHS*, London: UNISON.

Thornley, C. (1998a) *Neglected Nurses, Hidden Work: an investigation into the pay and employment of nursing auxiliaries/assistants in the NHS*, London: UNISON.

Thornley, C. (1998b) 'Contesting Local Pay: the decentralisation of collective bargaining in the NHS', *British Journal of Industrial Relations*, 36, 3, 413–34.

Thornley, C. (1999) *Out of Sight, Out of Mind: evidence and perspectives on the recruitment and retention of non-registered nursing staff in the NHS*, London: UNISON.

Thornley, C. (2000) 'A Question of Competence?: re-evaluating the roles of the nursing auxiliary and health care assistant in the NHS', *Journal of Clinical Nursing*, 9, 3, 451–8.

Thornley, C. (2001a) 'Divisions in Health-care Labour', in C. Komaromy (ed.) *Dilemmas in UK Healthcare, 3rd Edition*, Buckingham: Open University Press.

Thornley, C. (2001b) *Still Invisible: non-registered nurses in the NHS*, London: UNISON.

Wanless, D. (2002) *Securing our Future Health: taking a long-term view*, London: HM Treasury.

Witz, A. (1992) *Professions and Patriarchy*, London: Routledge.

9
The Growth of Complementary and Alternative Medicine: Challenges for the Future

Geraldine Lee-Treweek and Sarah Oerton

Introduction

There has been a huge growth of interest in complementary and alternative medicines (CAMs) on the part of both the public and the orthodox medical profession in the last twenty years or so (Rankin-Box, 2001), and this is reflected in the diverse range of therapeutic modalities now on offer. Notwithstanding this, it is almost impossible to obtain reliable figures of how many CAM practitioners there are, since most work from private houses, health and healing centres, clinics, spas and saunas and are thus outwith the NHS. Furthermore, and with the exception of chiropractors and osteopaths, there is to date no national statutory registration of CAM practitioners. Budd and Mills (2000) estimate that there may be as many as 56,000 in the UK, but this figure may under-represent the numbers currently practising. Not only do some not appear on any professional registers – others are NHS staff, qualified in and/or practising various CAMs through their doctoring, nursing, midwifery and health visiting activities. It is safe to say that the numbers are growing.[1] This is not to suggest that there is widespread acceptance of CAMs by NHS staff (or NHS patients for that matter). But there has been a subtle sea change. British Medical Association Reports of 1986 and 1993 are often cited as indicators of the shifting attitudes of the orthodox medical profession, and indeed, whilst still expressing reservations about the efficacy, training and safety of some CAM practitioners, the British Medical Association Report (1993) was much more supportive than its predecessor (British Medical Association, 1986). Generally speaking then, CAMs are increasingly moving out of the sidelines and towards the mainstream of UK health care delivery.

There have been further developments since the early 1990s. In 1997, the Foundation for Integrated Medicine (now the Foundation for Integrated Health) published a report that outlined various issues associated with the integration of CAMs into mainstream health care. The four main issues were research and development, education and training, regulation, and delivery mechanisms (Foundation for Integrated Medicine, 1997). Budd and Mills (2000) have mapped the professional status and standing of CAM therapies in the UK, and their survey provides a comprehensive review of the characteristics and activities of the various CAM professional associations who responded. This work became known as the Exeter Report and was drawn upon by the House of Lords Select Committee Report on Science and Technology (2000), which had as its brief an examination of the state control and licensing arrangements of CAMs. This report divided the various CAM therapies into three groups, based in part upon the degree to which they were likely to achieve self-regulation and to establish national occupational standards. The first group comprised the more formally organised therapies such as acupuncture, chiropractic, homeopathy, osteopathy and medical herbalism (henceforth known as the 'big five'). The second group of therapies included those which had some evidence-base for efficacy, did not make claims to diagnose and had made some progress towards voluntary self-regulation. The third group was defined as those whose alternative beliefs on health and disease could not be integrated within western allopathic frameworks. There has been serious resistance to this taxonomy, not least from Aruyvedic medicine (a traditional Indian healing system) which found itself defined within the third group, despite centuries of formal organisation and recognition for its work in health care within other cultures. Despite and maybe because of all these disputes, professionalisation and integration are now very much live issues for CAMs.

The drive by CAM practitioners to professionalise has been gathering momentum in the twenty-first century. Following government recommendations, the current trend is towards the establishment of single lead bodies for each CAM therapy (House of Lords Select Committee Report on Science and Technology, 2000; Department of Health, 2001a). Even at a cursory glance however, progress on this front has been piecemeal. The UK currently leaves the regulation of CAMs to a plethora of independent professional associations. Such associations vary considerably in terms of what might constitute a professional body. Generally speaking, their role is to promote minimum training requirements, compile national and/or local databases of accredited practitioners, operate codes of ethics, concern themselves with complaints and disciplinary procedures and so on. Most of these associations tend to employ the rhetoric of professionalism, to make claims to expertise, and variously to promote altruistic, ethical and therapeutic orientations to CAM health care. Many have business-like appearances, as manifested in their glossy brochures, newsletters and websites. Behind the scenes however, they are often run from small, sometimes home-based offices. With many of these professional associations currently operating at a pre- or semi-professional level then, it is not surprising that there are serious concerns about when, how and in what form CAMs might be integrated into the NHS. Furthermore, without the clear support of the majority of practitioners of any one particular modality, the state is unlikely to move to recognise a particular association as the single lead body with whom the government, orthodox medical profession and consumer associations can 'do business'.

For many CAMs, attempts at self-regulation have led to bitter disputes, philosophical and political divisions and a failure to begin uniting under a single lead body. Many CAM professional associations are still in the early stages of formulating their core curricula, accreditation mechanisms, complaints and disciplinary procedures. At times, some of this appears to be happening with little systematic reference to the strategic manoeuvres adopted by the first group of CAM therapies undergoing formal regulation (the 'big five'). There is sometimes a sense that other CAMs do not want to take the same road as the 'big five'. At other times, there has been considerable opportunistic and sometimes flagrant borrowing from each other's codes of ethics, political agendas, and publications. The difficulty is that a host of professional associations has proliferated in recent years, with registered members in each case numbering from a few hundred to several thousands (Budd and Mills, 2000). Some of these associations appear to wind down, only to re-constitute under another guise. As such, the situation of professional association membership is often fragmented and difficult for the lay person to decipher. To give just one example, in the case of therapeutic massage, as well as belonging to a wide range of different professional associations, various groups of massage therapists offer distinct massage applications. These different applications include accupressure massage, aromatherapy massage, baby and infant massage, beauty massage, biodynamic massage, floor massage, on-site (seated) massage, Indian Head massage, oriental or Thai massage, no-hands massage, pregnancy massage, remedial and sports massage, Swedish massage, tantric massage, yogic massage and so on. Although it is not the case that each massage application has its own identifiable professional association, nonetheless there are a dozen or more different associations that a massage practitioner may join. At the moment, the General Council for Massage Therapy (GCMT), formed in 1999 and previously known as the British Association for Massage Therapy, is attempting to pull together most of the main associations in order to become the single lead body. However, the field is a tightly packed one, and with all the conflicts involved, it is not surprising that attempts to bring practitioners together under a single umbrella have to date been unsuccessful.

Before going further, it is important to point out that we do not seek to interrogate these issues solely as critical outsiders. Instead, this is an insider account, based upon our different backgrounds and experiences as academic sociologists who have both been directly involved in CAMs for a number of years, both as qualified practitioners (of hypnotherapy and therapeutic massage respectively) and users[2] of a range of different CAMs. We are not unusual in adopting self-reflexive, critical standpoints towards our subject matter and in the CAMs world particularly, awareness and acknowledgement of one's subject position is seen as crucial (Cant and Sharma, 1998). As sociologists with both academic and experiential interests in CAMs, our aim in this chapter is to discuss some key concerns which need addressing if the integration of CAMs into the NHS is to be a successful 'medical marriage' (Featherstone and Forsyth, 1997) rather than a clandestine, fraught and risky affair. These concerns are the education/training of CAM practitioners; research-based evidence for efficacy of CAMs; professional boundary-setting and boundary-maintenance and finally, professional ethics. It is to the last two of these that we give particular attention as they have been relatively underplayed in the official reports referred to earlier. We also argue that this neglect is highly problematic for any future integration project, as these issues go right to the heart of what constitutes professional practice.

Education/training of CAM practitioners

The education and training of CAM practitioners is a volatile business. Demand is high but quality is questionable, as courses vary tremendously in depth, breadth and content. Moreover, it is difficult to obtain a clear picture regarding the provisions offered by privately-owned and run schools, colleges, correspondence courses and so forth, and public sector institutions such as FE colleges and HE institutions. That much said, Rankin-Box (2001) claims that there are now more than 20 universities in the UK offering a range of undergraduate and postgraduate courses in CAMs. Stuttard and Walker (2000) point to a trend towards integrating CAMs into existing curricula for health care professionals, in particular for pre- and post-registration nursing courses. It is claimed that there are elective modules on several undergraduate health degree programmes. Some HE institutions also provide degree programmes with clear career pathways; for example, the three-year degree course in Herbal Medicine offered by the University of Central Lancashire leads to qualification for membership of the National Institute of Medical Herbalists. Such degree courses are designed to train CAM practitioners by integrating practical, theoretical and philosophical concerns to produce practitioners who have a broad awareness of the social and political context of CAM therapies. Other courses are designed for the generalist and focus primarily upon providing a critical awareness of the role of CAM therapies in health care delivery.[3]

On the whole however, developments in education/training within the HE sector have tended to focus on the 'big five' – constituting only a minor part of the available training opportunities in CAMs. Other therapies, which may be less professionally organised but are no less popular, use different methods, ranging from one-to-one training (such as in Reiki master training), to part-time home study, evening classes and weekend courses in privately-owned and run schools, colleges and institutes. Some weekend and short courses are run as introductory tasters, whilst others are promoted as postgraduate or advanced, often with esoteric titles such as 'Aroma Magic', 'Breathing Bodies' and 'Unlocking the Secrets of the Face'. To date, there are no formal requirements for entry onto any of these courses. Most of them are facilitated by attractively packaged 'early bird' discounts, instalment plans and so on. But however well-established such training provisions may appear to be, there is often no systematic socialisation into nationally-agreed sets of working practices, bodies of knowledge, or standards of professional reputation or conduct. Some privately-run establishments offer accredited Independent Therapists Examination Council (ITEC) and/or National Vocational Qualifications (NVQ), diplomas or certificates, but most simply promote the qualifications accredited by their relevant professional associations, none of which have any state-endorsed status.

In encouraging all CAMs to develop single lead bodies, the state may eventually promote and oversee education/training standards. However, in many cases, political wrangling between different associations, aggravated by differences in therapeutic ideology about approaches to treatment or particular techniques, currently makes this an unachievable aim. Therefore, most CAMs face considerable problems in terms of developing an integrated approach to education/training. Not surprisingly, the lay person is in an impossible position when choosing a competent and safe practitioner.

Research-based evidence of efficacy

Another of the major stumbling blocks for CAMs has been the issue of demonstrating the efficacy of treatments. Some CAMs, indeed, have marked themselves out as anti-science or as precursors of a necessary paradigm shift. However, many critics have argued that in terms of integration into the NHS, CAM therapies need to undergo rigorous scrutiny in order to ensure that dogma or faith does not take precedence over balanced, open-ended enquiry. McGourty (1993) has argued that what appears to happen at present is that CAM practitioners claim that their therapies constitute a self-contained and consistent 'whole', even when looked at in terms of the scientific method. This is because they are based on observation over a long period of time; they have been tried, tested and refined; they have their own coherent and consistent theoretical framework and their effects are predictable within those frameworks (McGourty, 1993). Within such parameters, personal observation and apparent patient satisfaction are often deemed enough 'proof' of efficacy. On the other hand, the claim that CAMs do not need to be researched via the principles of the scientific method is strongly contested even within CAMs, on the grounds that scientific standards provide a degree of safety to the public (Ernst, 2002). It is even argued that the rejection of the need for evidence-based research into CAMs is harming the chance of potentially beneficial therapies being properly investigated, and that this does not augur well for the future of CAMs, whether inside or outwith the NHS.

Notwithstanding this, there are lively debates within particular CAMs about what constitutes valid research (see for instance, in relation to osteopathy research, Power, 1994: 7; Burton, Sykes and Bennett, 1994: 8). For some, the randomised control study remains the gold standard for research and this has provided a model for studies of osteopathy, chiropractic, herbalism and acupuncture. Others accept a far wider range of research methods. For instance, the Royal London Homeopathic Hospital lists research questions about the use of homeopathy that cannot be answered purely by the use of 'scientific methods' and advocates a mixed methods approach (Royal London Homeopathic Hospital, 1997). Undoubtedly, randomised controlled trials remain central to demonstrating the efficacy of CAM treatments, but cost effectiveness analysis, case studies, health status measurements, observational studies and qualitative approaches that take into account client/patient perspectives are also essential to answering the broader questions raised by CAM therapy usage (British Medical Association, 2000: 22).

The higher ranks of the 'big five' accept and promote evidence-based research as important. However, resistance operates at other levels. For example, for many osteopaths, working alone or in small groups in private practice, the need to carry out studies of efficacy becomes fairly meaningless to their daily experience of the work. There are plenty of patients to see, with or without formal 'evidence' of efficacy and there are few incentives to carry out more than basic auditing (most likely for external bodies, such as BUPA or PPP). Research costs money (not least in terms of loss of salary) and there is the possibility of undermining long-standing treatments. Even periodic practice audit, which in the osteopathic set of competencies is seen as very important (General Council and Register of Osteopaths, 1993: 2), can easily be neglected in the hectic schedule of consultations. The subtle mixing of modalities by CAM practitioners can also prove a stumbling block to identifying which practices work. For example, some CAM practitioners routinely combine treatments drawn from different CAM modalities, whilst others develop their own esoteric styles. It is hard to see how this could be scrutinised using conventional, evidence-based research approaches.

Even where the need for research is widely accepted, there is still the problem of infrastructure. CAMs are not used to providing structures to support research and often lack the credibility which would put them on a par with orthodox biomedical research. There is a basic lack of training in research methods on CAM education/training courses. Even in the case of established and legally recognised professions such as osteopathy and chiropractic, undergraduate training may not provide practitioners with the full range of research skills. This paucity of research skills impacts upon the ability of practitioners to procure research funds (British Medical Association, 2000: 22). During the period 1995–2000, the Medical Research Council received six applications from CAM practitioners and all but one failed to reach the standard necessary for funding (British Medical Association, 2000: 86). Moreover, despite a Department of Health call in 2002 for universities to bid to host post-doctoral CAMs fellows, the lack of research infrastructure, research incentives and research culture in CAMs is likely to prove prohibitive in terms of developing the high calibre researchers the Department of Health has in mind. The bid seeks to support post-doctoral CAMs fellows, failing to recognise that CAM practitioners trained to doctoral level are few and far between. There also seems to be a cultural insensitivity to the way that CAMs have had to develop outwith traditional education structures, and a lack of career structures for CAMs within orthodox university settings (Research Council for Complementary Medicine, 2002).

Thus the issue of demonstrating efficacy remains a contested area not only between CAM and orthodox biomedicine but also within and between CAMs. For most hands-on CAM practitioners, efficacy is an issue of patient satisfaction and having a healthy livelihood. And even within the NHS, integration and collaboration has tended to proceed without the scientific proof which doubtless will be demanded in future. Pain clinics, for example, have integrated CAM therapists or offered their staff training. CAM has therefore 'informally' moved into areas where there is a need to provide treatment to patients whose conditions currently fail to be relieved by orthodox means. The growing requirement for evidence based practice may prove a stumbling block to the continuance of such practices.

Professional boundary-setting and boundary-maintenance

Unlike the first two concerns discussed above, and with some recent exceptions, the issue of professional boundaries within CAMs has received limited critical attention (Cant and Sharma, 1999; Fournier, 2001). The therapeutic relationship within most CAMs is emphasised as being collaborative and non-hierarchical, where both practitioner and client/patient work together towards heightened well-being (Budd and Sharma, 1994). Hence such therapeutic relationships are often constituted as encounters between near-equals, both of whom are seen to be on a shared healing journey, or at least to have a common agenda for health and healing. Notwithstanding this, the setting and the maintenance of clear and appropriate professional boundaries are important issues (Malin, 2000; Dent and Whitehead, 2002). In more orthodox health care, boundary-setting often takes the form of marking 'professional distance' between staff and patients. The necessity for clarity around personal, emotional and bodily contacts is emphasised, whereas in the case of some of the more hands-on CAMs like therapeutic massage, such issues often become blurred and messy

(Oerton and Phoenix, 2001). NHS professionals are usually keenly conscious of boundary issues but whether, how, and in what ways such concerns have also preoccupied CAM practitioners is another matter.

It is worth noting that for a minority of CAM practitioners, certainly those who are working within modalities such as Reiki, polarity and crystal therapies, the constitution of a different therapeutic relationship has led to increased dissolution of formal boundaries. The role of 'professional expert' is downplayed in favour of an 'interactive partnership' model of healing. Nevertheless, the performance of professionalism is still very important. Practitioners want to be seen as 'professionals' and in this respect, professional personae have to be actively constituted. Many CAM practitioners feel the need to mark themselves out as distinct from what have traditionally been seen as negative stereotypes – the bogus, dangerous and unscrupulous charlatan or quack, the naïve amateur and the 'hippy-dippy brigade'. All of these have traditionally been used to keep CAM practitioners: 'on the margins of the medical marketplace' (Cant and Calnan, 1991). The first British Medical Association (1986) Report into CAMs took a similar approach, likening chiropractic and other CAM therapies to 'old wives tales' and 'home remedies'.

One way to achieve this is to deploy professional personae which act to establish them (and their work) as clean, hygienic, safe and reputable. These personae often draw upon wider discourses of the clinical and/or angelic health care professional. To this end, CAM practitioners dress in white or pastel tunics, use white paper couch rolls, and generally present themselves as clean and uncontaminated. Moreover, the spatial arrangements used for many CAM treatments typically evoke a warm, relaxing atmosphere (sometimes referred to as a 'safe space'). Such informality and comfort is often achieved via the deployment of devices such as thickly padded couches or futons, cushions, towels, oils, candles, flowers, music, and 'soft' décor or lighting. Many CAM practitioners also make regular use of 'soft' imagery (open or praying hands, birds in flight, flowers in bloom) in their advertising, promotional materials and 'how-to' textbooks. As a result, practitioners are often able to present themselves as caring, warm and welcoming. Somewhat paradoxically perhaps, this 'white and shining' professional persona also sits easily with both clinical and holistic/spiritual traditions.

Other professional personae are also routinely deployed which evoke altruism, cleanliness and purity of intent. One such is that of the 'prima donna' custodian or veteran, who is held to safeguard the cultural heritage, traditions and wisdoms of CAMs. In the case of therapeutic massage for example, attractive, white and able-bodied figures such as Clare Maxwell-Hudson (author of six best-selling reference books, training manuals and the owner-director of a large massage training school), are used to promote therapeutic massage as belonging to an honourable lineage of serious (but also glamorous) health care delivery. Witness the way in which the 2001 prospectus for the Clare Maxwell-Hudson School describes her as: 'Britain's sensible and reliable ambassador of massage therapy ... and acknowledges her as pioneer and doyen [*sic*] of massage in Britain' (ibid: 2–3, emphasis added). However, there are problems with the deployment of these particular professional personae. In the case of some hands-on CAMs like therapeutic massage, there are boundary problems because of the need to deal with the slippages between massage and 'sexual services'. Indeed, there are widespread historical, legal and socio-cultural elisions between massage and sex work. Hence practitioners have obvious motives for promoting themselves as clean, hygienic and pure. The boundary-setting devices for so doing are already available and well-recognised within more orthodox health care environments. What seems to be happening is that many hands-on CAM practitioners are adopting them in a wholesale manner in order to avoid any taint or association with dirt, disreputability and the 'sleaze trade'. Indeed, many of them deny that there are any problems at all in this area or claim that they can be easily handled.

Clearly though, there are difficulties. The personae identified above tend to run counter to the holistic commitments of many CAMs, and some lament the loss of what they see as the ethereal and esoteric dimensions of CAM health care delivery. In the case of many CAMs, intuition, empathy and rapport are held to be central. However, if boundaries between practitioners and clients/patients are seen as open, fluctuating and fluid, then this risks imputations of excessive 'merger' and at worst, potentially unethical hands-on sexual encounters. It also perpetuates the dangerous, marginal and 'exotic' status of some CAMs (Saks, 1995). But for CAMs, holism has always been seen as crucial and cannot be abandoned just in order to be seen as 'beyond reproach'. CAM practitioners are walking something of a tightrope here and it is clear that the issue of professional boundaries presents serious difficulties. But simply putting on a white coat does not make anyone a competent or trustworthy health care professional. Whilst some of the boundary-setting devices deployed by CAM practitioners mirror those found within orthodox health care, others run counter to some of the accepted standards found within those environments. The boundaries around informed consent, touch, 'no-go' areas and so on (for example, codes of conduct which delimit the hugging, fondling and kissing of patients) are more vague and less well understood in the case of many CAMs. These issues will need to be addressed if CAMs are to be offered alongside more conventional NHS health care. All this also relates to the fourth and final concern we want to raise in this chapter, that of professional ethics.

Professional ethics

In modern orthodox health care, ethical considerations have become central to training and practice. The emergence of notions of 'patient-as-consumer' and the 'expert patient' (Stone, 2002: 33; Department of Health, 2001b) also indicate a policy shift towards patient participation in health. Such changes in the constitution of therapeutic relationships would appear to be to the benefit of CAM practitioners who, some might argue, already demonstrate patient-centred care. Closer examination, however, reveals that there is a paucity of ethical understanding and debate in the majority of CAMs.[4] We argue that any integration into the NHS would necessarily have to involve a substantial development in ethical awareness/training in CAMs and a greater recognition that some current practices would simply not be acceptable in orthodox healthcare settings.

Traditionally, CAMs have been associated with two sets of assumptions that encapsulate entirely different attitudes towards ethics compared with those found within the NHS. The first set of assumptions is to some extent the product of claims made by some practitioners, that they are providing a much-needed service for which their clients choose to pay. As a result, it is assumed that 'customers' of CAMs have more power in the therapeutic relationship because they are paying. This appears to suggest that a relationship begun and driven by 'consumer choice' is less likely to produce situations that demand a heightened awareness of ethics. The CAMs 'customer' is seen as being in a better position to make their own decisions and defend themselves and their choices than someone who is in danger of losing their life or is critically ill (Stone, 2002: 15). In effect, there is a notion that CAM patients are not as vulnerable as their biomedical counterparts. The perception of CAMs practice as less ethically fraught than allopathic health care also relates to a second set of assumptions, those concerning the holistic values held to be central to most, if not all,

CAM therapies (Semmes, 1991). Whether a central part of most CAM treatments or not, there is a public perception that CAM practitioners are more likely to examine the whole person, that care will be individualised and that altruism is a central motivation for becoming a CAM practitioner. The assumption that all CAM practitioners are 'caring' thus becomes entwined with the professional personae discussed in the last section, and particularly with the assumption that 'caring' equals ethical (Lee-Treweek, 2002: 61).[5] The 'caring' practitioner is automatically assumed to be serving the patient's best interests and to be working in an egalitarian, therapeutic relationship to attain health or wellbeing.

These assumptions do not stand up to scrutiny. Even if we accept that many practitioners have good intentions it does not necessarily follow that they will have a 'natural' understanding of issues such as informed consent, confidentiality and privacy. CAMs often involve the disclosure of highly personal information to a depth one would not necessarily see in a conventional healthcare encounter, and, particularly where individuals are expected to get undressed, also involve intimate physical contact with a practitioner whose qualifications are often unknown or not fully understood by the client. Hence, even if CAMs really are characterised by more egalitarian relationships, the need for ethical knowledge and consideration by the practitioner is not obviated.

We turn now to discuss four ethical problems in greater detail. One issue is how CAM practitioners can make and substantiate claims to being ethical professionals. The 'big five', to demonstrate their claims for standardised ethics, often cite the evidence of their ethical and professional codes and rigorous disciplinary procedures. However, the use of such mechanisms to protect the public from unscrupulous or dangerous practitioners did not, and could not, stop individuals, like Dr Harold Shipman or nurse Beverley Allitt from carrying out crimes against their patients. Moreover, investigations into breaches can only occur after a patient/client considers that they have been injured or upset by a practitioner's treatment/behaviour. Furthermore, as Chaitow (2001) asks: 'What protection exists for the public against misbehaviour by a practitioner or therapist from one of the professions which has no statutory status, or which has not even established effective self-regulated procedures?' (Chaitow, 2001). This comment, made by a CAM practitioner, highlights the danger of weak ethical codes that in practice have little power to chastise the unacceptable, unsafe or unregistered therapist. On the whole, codes of ethics are hardly ever explicated as a crucial issue on CAM education/training courses and merely make up part of the membership information a practitioner is expected to peruse and agree to before joining a professional association. There is, in addition, a growing tendency to recycle codes of ethics developed for other therapies. This downplays differences between various CAMs that demand particular ethical attention. For example, in relation to therapies that require touch, such as massage, one might expect particular attention to be given in codes to ethical handling of the body. Another important issue is whether the practitioner has a history of sexual offences or violence towards other people. Very few CAM codes of ethics (outwith the 'big five') address whether a CAM practitioner has a criminal record.

A second problem is that there are different standards with respect to the dissemination and enforcement of ethical codes. In the case of chiropractic, developing and publicising patient-friendly codes of proficiency (including the ethics of conduct) has been a central task of the regulatory body. (General Chiropractic Council, 2001). Cases against chiropractors are heard on a regular basis by the General Chiropractic Council and practitioners can be struck off, admonished or have restrictions placed upon their practice. However, chiropractors are in the forefront of developing standards in this area and here we use the example of hypnotherapy, to demonstrate issues of ethical concern to the majority of CAMs. Clients attending a hypnotherapist are likely to be given a leaflet explaining the therapy and stating the organisational membership of the therapist. Such leaflets furnish an image of professionalism and terms such as 'registered' can appear to suggest similar professional standards to orthodox registered groups (GPs, dentists and so on). However, memberships and registration on lists of practitioners do not necessarily denote high quality professional practice. Although umbrella bodies for standards are developing in hypnotherapy, they tend to represent clusters of schools or associations which use similar sets of techniques, advocate particular approaches to treatment, or which have similar criteria for admission to training. Judging the standards of practice of a practitioner is almost impossible for the lay person.

As with many CAM therapies, hypnotherapeutic professional organisations have codes of ethics and most of these are available to the public on the web. Despite the public visibility of these documents, procedures for disciplining practitioners are usually weak. Often the process of investigating and disciplining therapists who have broken codes is not clearly explained and the consequences of any action are not readily apparent in information provided to the public. Titles that are not protected in law, such as 'hypnotherapist' or 'masseur' mean that excluded members can leave a register and still practice. Furthermore, CAM professional associations need a critical mass of members to maintain a position of legitimacy and too strict an approach, towards either accepting new members or striking offending members off, could mean loss of status and revenue. Codes of ethics can only protect insofar as a profession is organised in such a way that the public is aware of what constitutes unacceptable behaviour, that there is somewhere to complain to, and that there are real consequences for breaching ethical standards.

A third ethical problem is the growing trend within CAMs towards 'holistic' practitioners whose market strategy and therapeutic approach is based around combining modalities. Although this can benefit the practitioner by providing more clients and the client by providing choice at one point of access, this also raises a set of complex ethical concerns that are less likely to arise in orthodox health care due to the firmer boundaries between specialisms and treatments. It is unlikely for instance that a GP will suddenly, and without warning or explanation, shift into the role of dentist, whereas many CAM therapists combine modalities such as reflexology, aromatherapy, energy-based therapies (such as spiritual healing or Reiki) and massage, often without seeking full informed consent. Integrating these 'holistic practitioners' into NHS settings will need careful monitoring in relation to the rights of the patient to refuse treatment and to demand careful boundary maintenance between modalities.

A fourth problem is that integration into the NHS will demand new ethical considerations relating to referral and the management of professional boundaries between colleagues. In the NHS, the ethics of referral are a well-researched topic (King, Bailey and Newton, 1994; Grembowski, Cook, Patrick and Roussel, 1998; O'Donnell, 2000) whereas within CAMs, referral is not only under-researched but is poorly covered on most education/training courses. CAMs knowledge, as with other health care areas, is subject to sub-specialisms, so that practitioners may find the scope of their competence being challenged (Stone, 2002: 215). One potential positive effect of this could be that referral to more appropriately trained CAM practitioners may become more commonplace, but internal occupational disagreements may prevent this happening. Undoubtedly, greater integration with the NHS will bring to the fore the need for CAM practitioners realistically to evaluate their own scope of expertise and referral practices.

As public interest in CAMs increases, it is essential that high levels of ethics be demanded from professional associations that represent individual CAM therapists. Ethical issues need to become more central themes in all education/training in CAMs (not just the 'big five') so that 'ethical lag' between CAMs and orthodox health care training can be narrowed. All this raises serious questions about where CAMs is heading in the future.

Conclusion: integration for whom and on whose terms?

In this chapter, we have attempted an analysis of the current professional status and standing of complementary and alternative medicines (CAMs). We have raised serious questions about the ways in which CAMs may be falling short in terms of accepted and standard professional practices. It is clear that CAMs have a different heritage from the NHS in terms of education/training, research cultures, boundary-setting, regulation, patterns of working and ethical understandings. The question remains as to whether the CAMs workforce can develop sufficiently in line with the standards of orthodox health care professionals to allow widespread collaboration and integration to become a reality. What implications might all this have for the future of the UK healthcare workforce? Although so far it has been intimated that the current situation with regard to CAMs may be considered a 'revolution from without', it can also be argued that there have been driving forces coming from within the NHS. Primary care, and in particular, the treatment of chronic and recurrent problems, has proved to be one of the key areas in which CAM has made headway into NHS provision. CAMs have also proved popular in a range of areas including cancer and palliative nursing, care of older people and in maternity and childbirth. Hence there are already several projects that successfully bring a range of CAM services to NHS patients and these often serve the dual function of developing models for the integration of CAM and orthodox healthcare as well as being trials of the various CAM therapies available. At the same time as formal integration (often of the 'big five') is occurring, the myriad of other CAM therapies available represents greater challenges for an NHS that makes claim to taking patient choice seriously.

At present, orthodox health practitioners who have undertaken further training in CAMs treat the majority of patients who experience complementary therapy in the NHS. However, the moves towards statutory and non-statutory self-regulation in CAM that are endorsed and expected by the government, will also mean the expectation of continuing professional development in each CAM therapy practised. Such an approach makes the integration of non-NHS practitioners more likely and at the same time demands that CAM practitioners, used to working in a private setting, be trained and prepared for the new challenges of NHS work. Current policy indicators seem to suggest that integration to some extent is seen as positive, as a way of attending to patient demand and dealing with patients whom the NHS have traditionally been unable to help. For example, there is an underlying assumption in the recent Department of Health call for research and development in CAMs that the integration of the latter into the NHS is seen as a 'good thing'. If driven by public demand, more informed choice and patient participation, there could even be major shifts in the future away from 'high tech' bio-medicine and towards much more holistic, person-centred health care approaches which take into account social, emotional and spiritual needs. In short, CAMs might revolutionise health care delivery in the future.

Closer examination, however, would indicate that integration has costs and benefits for both CAMs therapists (within and outwith the NHS) and the NHS itself. 'Successful integration entails a gradual acclimatisation to what is ... a foreign environment, where the CAM practitioner will encounter language difficulties and perspectives quite different from the safe, self-directed world of independent, private-sector CAM practice' (Peters, Chaitow, Harris and Morrison, 2002: 1). We have discussed the shortcomings that CAM experiences in relation to education/training, research, professional boundaries and ethical awareness. For some CAM practitioners, 'acclimatisation' in these areas may not be perceived as positive, integration may not bring the rewards expected and may remove some of the freedoms of direction, philosophy and income-generation available in the private sector (Peters, Chaitow, Harris and Morrison, 2002). For some groups, such as osteopaths and chiropractors, regular NHS work would almost certainly mean lower financial returns. For many CAM practitioners, the constraints placed on their practices by the structures of the NHS, and the different culture of being an 'illness' service, will be good enough reasons not to work in this setting. In addition, it could also be argued that currently there is no career development structure within the NHS for those working in CAMs (for instance, no CAM consultants). This may prove problematic for attracting CAM therapists of the highest calibre (especially when they can command high salaries and high status in the private sector) and may also work against encouraging NHS staff to integrate CAMs into their practice.

In conclusion then, there are many battles to be fought not only within orthodoxy to win over colleagues who still take a sceptical stance towards CAMs, but also to settle the 'turf wars' between CAM practitioners in private practice and those based within NHS medicine, nursing and allied professions. The scope of clinical governance that orthodox health care workers are prepared to hand over to CAM qualified colleagues, or private CAM therapists, also remains to be seen. There is a distinct possibility that CAMs, whilst welcomed in the hospice, maternity suite, pain clinic and in dealing with general stress and/or anxiety, and chronic musculo-skeletal problems, may not be given free reign to develop in other 'higher status' areas. Hence any comprehensive integration is set to involve vested interests, power brokers and blocs, territorial disputes and political wrangling. Investing in CAMs will also mean investing in CAM education/training, in CAM research and in ensuring that all CAM practitioners can practice their skills in such a way that professional and personal advancement is possible. In short, the rise of CAMs has profound implications for the future management of health personnel, the redefinition of health skills and health worker roles. It raises difficult questions not only about how health care should be reconfigured in the twenty-first century but also about what skills are needed to keep an increasingly health-conscious population content and well.

Notes

1. For more detail on the significance of the CAM workforce, see the estimates of Healthworks UK, reprinted in the Appendix to this book.
2. In this chapter, the terms 'user', 'client' and 'patient' are deliberately used interchangeably to indicate members of the general public who make use of CAMs. Our choice of term is made in relation to the terminology that the majority of CAM practitioners use in the specific type of CAM therapy under discussion.
3. For instance, The Open University is currently developing a distance learning course designed to appeal to general interest students from across the University as well as CAM practitioners wishing to integrate a critical perspective into their practice (some as part of continuing professional development).
4. It is noteworthy that popular assumptions made about CAM practitioners as 'caring' are being countered by powerful sections of the media and orthodox medicine, but often in ways that are extreme and seem to miss the key issues. For instance, Beaven (1989: 102) maintains: 'Practitioners

of alternative medicine, unfettered by regulatory standards, or any established code of ethics, take advantage of minors and the credulous. Ethnic minorities, immigrants and younger people are among those who may not understand methods of access to orthodox medicine and are particularly vulnerable.' Fears around the abuse of 'vulnerable' patients are apparent and often take the form of scaremongering. For example, in the United States, a range of websites provide 'evidence' of quackery in CAMs (Chirobase *http://www.chirobase.org/* [Accessed 10 June 2003] and Quackwatch *http://www.quackwatch.org/* [Accessed 10 June 2003]).

5. Despite the differences in levels of professional development and regulation, many CAM professional associations do publish codes of ethics. Some of these focus on core values of the therapy, as in the case of Reiki practitioners (UK Reiki Federation, 2002). Others follow a format that mimics the ethical documents of more orthodox health care professions.

References

Beaven, D. W. (1989) 'Alternative Medicine a Cruel Hoax – your money and your life?', *The New Zealand Medical Journal*, 102, 416.

British Medical Association (1986) *Alternative Therapy: report of the Board of Science and Education*, London: British Medical Association.

British Medical Association (1993) *Complementary Medicine: new approaches to good practice*, Oxford: Oxford University Press.

British Medical Association (2000) *Acupuncture: efficacy, safety and practice*, London: British Medical Association.

Budd, S. and Mills, S. (2000) *Professional Organisation of Complementary and Alternative Medicine in the UK 2000: a second report to the Department of Health*, Exeter: University of Exeter.

Budd, S. and Sharma, U. (eds) (1994) *The Healing Bond: the patient–practitioner relationship and therapeutic responsibility*, London: Routledge.

Burton, K., Sykes, D. and Bennett, G. (1994) 'Osteopathic Research', letter published in response to R. Power, *Journal of Osteopathic Education*, 4.

Cant, S. and Calnan, M. (1991) 'On the Margins of the Medical Marketplace?: an exploratory study of alternative practitioners perspectives', *Sociology of Health and Illness*, 13, 139–57.

Cant, S. and Sharma, U. (1998) 'Reflexivity, Ethnography and the Professions', *Sociological Review*, 46, 2, 244–63.

Cant, S. and Sharma, U. (1999) *A New Medical Pluralism? Alternative medicine, doctors and the state*, London: UCL Press.

Chaitow, L. (2001) *Ethics and Integration (or incarceration)* [online], Positive Health. Available from: *http://www.positivehealth.com/permit/ Articles/Regular/ chaito49.htm* [Accessed 10 June 2003].

Dent, M. and Whitehead, S. (eds) (2002) *Managing Professional Identities; knowledge, performativity and the 'new' professional*, London: Routledge.

Department of Health (2001a) *Government Response to the House of Lords Select Committee on Science and Technology's Report on Complementary and Alternative Medicine*, London: The Stationery Office.

Department of Health (2001b) *A New Approach to Chronic Disease Management for the 21st Century*, London: The Stationery Office.

Ernst, E. (2002) 'What's the Point of Rigorous Research on Complementary/Alternative Medicine?', *Journal of the Royal Society of Medicine*, 95, 4, 211–13.

Featherstone, C. and Forsyth, L. (1997) *Medical Marriage: the new partnership between orthodox and complementary therapies*, Scotland: Findhorn Press.

Foundation for Integrated Medicine (1997) *Integrated Healthcare: a way forward for the next five years: a discussion document*, London: Foundation for Integrated Medicine.

Fournier, V. (2001) 'Amateurism, Quackery and Professional Conduct: the constitution of 'proper' aromatherapy practice', in M. Dent and S. Whitehead (eds) *Managing Professional Identities: knowledge, performativity and the 'new' professional*, London: Routledge.

General Chiropractic Council (2001) *Standard of Proficiency and Code of Practice*, London: General Chiropractic Council.

General Council and Register of Osteopaths (1993) *Competencies Required for Osteopathic Practice*, Reading: General Council and Register of Osteopaths.

Grembowski, D., Cook, K., Patrick, D.L. and Roussel, A. E. (1998) 'Managed Care and Physician Referral', *Medical Care Research and Review*, 55, 1, 3–31.

House of Lords Select Committee Report on Science and Technology (2000) *Complementary and Alternative Medicine*, London: The Stationery Office, HL Paper 123.

King, N., Bailey, J. and Newton, P. (1994) 'Analysing General Practitioners' Referral Decisions I. Developing an analytical framework', *Family Practice*, 11, 1, 3–8

Lee-Treweek, G. (2002) 'Trust in Complementary Medicine: the case of cranial osteopathy', *Sociological Review*, 50, 1, 48–68.

Malin, N. (ed.) (2000) *Professionalism, Boundaries and the Workplace*, London: Routledge.

McGourty, H. (1993) *How to Evaluate Complementary Therapies: a literature review. Observatory report: 13*, Liverpool: Liverpool Public Health Observatory.

Oerton, S. and Phoenix, J. (2001) 'Sex/Bodywork: discourses and practices', *Sexualities: studies in culture and society*, 4, 4, 387–412.

O'Donnell, C. A. (2000) 'Variation in GP Referral Rates: what can we learn from the literature?', *Family Practice*, 17, 6, 462–71.

Peters, D., Chaitow, L., Harris, G. and Morrison, S. (2002) *Integrating Complementary Therapies in Primary Care*, London: Churchill Livingstone.

Power, R. (1994) 'Points of Discussion for Research in Osteopathy', *Journal of Osteopathic Education*, 4.

Rankin-Box, D. (ed.) (2001) *The Nurse's Handbook of Complementary Therapies*, Edinburgh: Bailliere Tindall, published in association with the Royal College of Nursing (2nd Edition).

Research Council for Complementary Medicine (2002) *National Strategy for Research and Development in Complementary Medicine* [online], Research Council for Complementary Medicine. Available from: *http://www.rccm.org.uk/ static/RCCM_national_strategy.asp* [Accessed 10 June 2003].

Royal London Homeopathic Hospital (1997) *The Evidence Base of Complementary Medicine*, London: Royal London Homeopathic Hospital NHS Trust.

Saks, M. (1995) *Professions and the Public Interest: medical power, altruism and alternative medicine*, London: Routledge.

Semmes, C. (1991) 'Developing Trust: patient–practitioner encounters in natural health care', *Journal of Contemporary Ethnography*, 19, 4, 450–70.

Stone, J. (2002) *An Ethical Framework for Complementary and Alternative Therapists*, London: Routledge.

Stuttard, P. and Walker, E. (2000) 'Integrating Complementary Medicine into the Nursing Curriculum', *Complementary Therapies in Nursing and Midwifery*, 6, 2, 87–90.

UK Reiki Federation (2002) *Establishing Codes of Ethics and Standards of Practice for Reiki* [online], UK Reiki Federation. Available from: *http://www.reikifed.co.uk/codes.htm* [Accessed 10 June 2003].

10
The Future of the General Practitioner[1]

Stephen Gillam

Introduction

The key roles of general practice have been described as 'firstly, to serve as interpreter and guardian at the interface between illness and disease and, secondly, to serve as a witness to the patient's experience of illness and disease' (Heath, 1995: 5). This view originates from the psychodynamic school of GP writers and researchers who so influenced the profession in the 1960s. Their platform was Michael Balint's pioneering work in distinguishing the distinctive features of general from specialist medical practice: a wider framework of individual human relationships, and its potential for harnessing energies in support of medical care (Balint, 1964). Forty years on from Balint, doctors feel that, while they retain public respect, they have been steadily losing ground in terms of social status, pay and professional autonomy. In an information-rich society, GPs are struggling to come to terms with a shift in power relations with ever more knowledgeable patients. Day to day, it seems that loss of trust is reflected in rising levels of complaints and increasingly frequent litigation. The public's expectations continue to outstrip the health system's capacity to improve quality and access to care.

The purpose of this chapter is to examine the implications of contemporary policy and organisational change for the future general practitioner. Will the expanded roles and responsibilities afforded primary care by today's new policies and organisations subsume or supersede the individual GP? Conversely, will the underlying philosophy and principles of general practice embrace all parts of our health and social care system? Or will general practice-based primary care simply continue to muddle through, with its customary step-wise approach to strategic change?

Past: the fading vision of 1948

The profession of general practice derived over the course of the nine-teenth century from the trade of apothecaries who dispensed medi-cines. In the growing industrial cities where GPs relied on patients' fees, nobody was seen in the outpatient clinics of charitable hospitals unless referred by a GP. This was the origin of the first of three funda-mental principles of general practice in the UK, that of referral, whereby GPs became the 'gatekeepers' to secondary care (Hannay and Mathers, 2000).

The second principle concerns non-specialisation. Most scientific advances and medical care took place in hospitals. The evolution of the 'expert generalist', able to co-ordinate the management of patients from the centre of a web of health professionals, is seen as a source of NHS efficiency. By the beginning of the twentieth century, GPs were increasingly being paid an insurance fee by patients as members of 'sick clubs'. These foreran the National Insurance Act in 1911, which covered male wage earners. This was extended to the whole population with the creation of the NHS in 1948, which provided the basis of the third principle: that of capitation and a fee to the GP for everyone on a registered list of patients.

Following the foundation of the Royal College of General Practitioners in 1952 (the culmination of a long battle for recognition within the medical establishment), the postgraduate training and pro-fessional development of British general practitioners became increas-ingly sophisticated. Over the same period, many countries saw the status of family practice decline. International comparisons of the extent to which health systems are primary care orientated suggests that those countries with more generalist family doctors acting as gate-keepers with registered lists are more likely to have better health out-comes as well as lower costs and greater satisfaction (Starfield, 1994). Other evidence suggests that the gatekeeper function is a consequence rather than a cause of lower health expenditure (Forrest, 2003). However, the three key principles outlined above are increasingly seen as constraining.

Referral arrangements are now seen as monopolistic and restric-tive. Many of Labour's health policies since 1997 have been designed to increase access to care through other routes. The generalist is under threat. How can any single health professional stay abreast of advances in all branches of medical science? Informally indeed, some are beginning to question whether qualifications in 'general practice' can still be offered with academic integrity. The GP's personal list of patients coupled with doctors' sense of 'womb-to-tomb', round-the-clock responsibility in the traditions of Dr Finlay has provided the bedrock of family practice for generations but can be seen as fostering the paternalism that many are now calling into question (Coulter, 2002).

The second half of the old century had witnessed the continuous rise of the profession. Its individualistic style fitted then with society's stratification and sources of solidarity. By the early 1990s, the term 'general practice' could legitimately be applied not just to the profession and its clinical disciplines, but to its services, staff, buildings and structures as well. The cost efficiency of the NHS had long been attributed in large measure to general practice controlling access to expensive specialist services. However, the tripartite division between hospital, community and family practitioner services had changed little since 1948. This structure contributed to a service criticised as poorly co-ordinated, unresponsive and of varying quality. GPs had long fought to retain an 'independent contractor' status with the NHS. Accordingly, their complex national contract, based on an arcane statement of capitation fees and a complex set of allowances, has been periodically renegotiated with government.

The reforms introduced by the Conservative government in 1990 concentrated on controlling cost and quality through the introduction of an internal market (Department of Health, 1989). A central policy instrument was fundholding, which drew on general practitioners' intimate knowledge of local services (derived from their 'gatekeeping' function), and their financial entrepreneurialism (derived from their autonomy as independent contractors). General practitioners were felt to be best placed, if not best equipped, to act as advocates for their patients and at the same time to bring in the cost and quality checks that government was seeking.

Although the proponents of GP fundholding claimed great benefits from the scheme, the evidence to support these claims was equivocal (Le Grand, Mays and Mulligan, 1998). Fundholding was ultimately rejected for several reasons. It was bureaucratic, involving high transaction costs. It was perceived as unfair, in that successful fundholders generated inequities in access to care (two-tierism). Above all, the internal market failed to deliver anticipated efficiency gains. Yet it did entrench political support for widening the involvement of general practitioners in resource allocation and it empowered those same practitioners with a new sense of their political potency.

New Labour's first White Paper formally announced the demise of GP fundholding and the internal market (Department of Health, 1997). It underlined the role of the NHS in improving health, renewed an ideological commitment to equity in access and provision, and tackled the need to ensure quality through clinical governance and accountability to local communities. Of fundamental importance was the move to loosen the restrictions of the old tripartite structure – hospitals, GPs and local authority services – by moving towards unified budgets for general and specialist medical services. The major structural change introduced to deliver these policy goals was the graduated formation of primary care trusts (PCTs).

As Labour's modernisation strategies took root, concerns for the nature and value of general practice re-emerged. The primary care policies and organisations of the new millennium are geared to a different sort of society, where cohesion depends, for example, on the use of such terms as 'partnership', not to justify GPs' uni-professional legal status but to describe and promote inter-professional alliances (Ashcroft, 2001). People come to surgery for something more than GPs have traditionally offered, and other primary care professionals are often available to provide it. Counsellors may be better listeners; osteopaths, chiropractors and physiotherapists can manage the majority of musculoskeletal problems; and nurses in their new professional guises can now do anything in the realm of community-based care from prescribing and public health to chronic disease management. Paradoxically, as GPs have embraced new roles and as PCTs have developed, the expertise and body of knowledge upon GPs' claims to professional status have rested, have become less distinctive.

Present: tensions in transition

PCTs have been saddled with heavy expectations. Predictably, they are moving at different speeds. Organisational development has consumed much early energy and by 2003, many were only beginning to translate priorities into clear local health strategies, targets and action plans – let alone delivering visible new services. They have made progress in developing and integrating primary and community care, but their commissioning and health improvement functions remain immature (Wilkin, Gillam and Leese, 2000). PCTs have started to develop minimum standards for practice services and agreed plans for redistributing resources. In other words, they are beginning to intrude beyond the front door of their constituents' surgeries. Nevertheless, many practices remain disengaged from the work of PCTs. And they lack the managerial capacity to deliver the local changes their constituents demand, let alone ever-mounting responsibilities as defined centrally. The collectivisation of general practice via these new intermediate organisations was seen as providing an opportunity to address longstanding policy preoccupations. These included the lack of responsiveness of general medical services and their variable quality, particularly in inner cities. The following sections consider a number of key issues impinging on professional practice in turn.

W(h)ither the independent contractor?

General medical services (GMS) and general practice as providers of services were left largely untouched by the internal market. The contract imposed in 1990 provided tools to increase the accountability of GPs but failed to address deep-rooted deficits in primary care and was criticised for its lack of local flexibility. Recruitment and retention of doctors were problematic, and a growing minority of GPs was seeking salaried or alternative employment options (Lewis and Gillam, 1999).

The NHS (Primary Care) Act 1997, passed in the dying days of the Conservative regime, initiated a quiet revolution. Personal Medical Services (PMS) pilots fundamentally changed the relationship between government and general practice.[2] PMS pilots involve local service contracts, negotiated between the provider and primary care trusts. They are subject to local targets, local budgets and local monitoring.[3] PMS thus breaks the monopoly of the independently contracted general practitioner. Now NHS Trusts, PCTs, nurses and, more rarely, companies can contract to provide personal medical services. As a result, the number of salaried general practitioners employed has risen sharply (Lewis and Gillam, 1999). If independent contractors will not deliver local or national targets, for example in relation to national service frameworks, primary care trusts can now call on alternative providers – at least in theory.

PMS pilots are also beginning to address long-standing inequities in primary care. They are increasing access to services and, in particular, serving population groups often poorly served by traditional general practice such as homeless people, refugees and people with severe mental illness. PMS pilots have also led to changes in primary care skill-mix. Nursing roles, in particular, have been extended into new areas. At the most extreme, 'nurse-led' pilots have seen nurses manage the majority of first contact care as well as provide overall leadership within the primary care team.

PMS pilots have made progress in meeting the most obvious deficits of GMS but there have been some disappointments. The new cadre of salaried general practitioners, for example, may do little to increase the numbers of general practitioners overall. Most salaried general practitioners in PMS pilots have simply traded one post for another. Only 15 per cent of first wave salaried general practitioners were new to general practice (Huntingdon, Walsh, Barnes, Rogers and Baines, 2000).

General practice has thus been faced with two potential contractual futures. Ministers have stated that an old-style GMS contract will remain for doctors who want it. The newly configured 'national' contract incorporates elements of PMS and allows more local discretion at the margins. Local contracting through PMS remains and is expanding also into other arenas such as dentistry and pharmacy, but in all this there are significant risks for government. The cost efficiency of the NHS is often attributed to strong general practice with its comprehensive financing mechanism. Whatever its defects, the 'red book' (the Statement of Fees and Allowances) has proved adaptable in directing the development of general practice. Will local contracts prove as flexible or as inexpensive?

Accessible or continuing care?

The raft of post-1997 policy initiatives designed to improve access to primary care initially appeared to be a reflex, populist response to long-standing public concerns. The purpose of NHS Direct, for example, was to provide 'easier and faster advice and information' for local people, supporting them in caring for themselves and their families' (Department of Health, 1998: para 1.11). More specific objectives for NHS Direct included the encouragement of self-care at home and reducing unnecessary use of other NHS services – that is management of demand. NHS Direct was unpopular with most general practitioners, who feared it would add to their workloads. Evaluations confirm that the new service has had little early impact on other emergency services (Munro, Nicholl, O'Cathain and Knowles, 2000).

Walk-in centres were another 1997 initiative, and, already sensitive to threats to their professional monopoly over first contact care, the medical profession was doubly wary. These centres were an explicit response to the apparent success of instant access primary care facilities established by the private sector, for example on railway stations serving time-pressed commuters. GP sensitivity was heightened by an awareness that experience in other countries suggested that multiple access points with poorly co-ordinated record-keeping could result in fragmented care (Jones, 2000). Nevertheless, the new centres did expose the limitations of conventional general practice in providing for groups who have not, for reasons of culture or convenience, gained satisfactory access to primary care in the past.

These innovations nicely crystallise the differences in priority that different players attach to access. Their apparent popularity with users contrasts with their reluctant acceptance by health professionals. Concerns over their cost-effectiveness remain but the trade-off implied between personal continuity and modern care can be exaggerated. Continuity of carer is already a thing of the past in large practices without personal lists. The trade-off is more often between small (more familiar) teams and large (more cost-efficient) ones.[4] PCTs offer the opportunity to separate administrative and clinical functions that work best on different scales (Guthrie and Wykes, 2000).

Other innovations too are changing the ways in which primary care is perceived. Both NHS Direct and the new walk-in centres involve forms of nurse triage. Growing proportions of new entrants to general practice are women seeking to reconcile career aspirations with family responsibilities. Greater 'feminisation' of the primary care workforce in these ways is altering the accessibility, the image – and possibly also the status – of family doctoring.

Quality assurance and the limits to self-regulation

The invention of 'clinical governance' as part of Labour's reforms heralded the latest of many attempts in the NHS to exercise greater managerial control over clinical activities. Governmental concerns over professional self-regulation – heightened in the wake of events at the Bristol Royal Infirmary – were about to be raised still more dramatically by the conviction of GP Harold Shipman. Clinical governance has been described as providing NHS organisations and individual health professionals 'with a framework within which to build a single, coherent, local programme for quality improvement' (Department of Health, 1998: para 3.3). It draws together elements of quality assurance that are often ill co-ordinated. The corporate nature of this new responsibility requires, in the overused phrase, major 'cultural change'. For PCTs, this implies sharing intelligence about quality across professional and practice boundaries, and health professionals seeing themselves as collectively accountable for the clinical and cost-effectiveness of their colleagues' work.

The most pressing challenge remains the management of poor performance. Patients' complaints, colleagues' expressed concerns and financial audit have been the main means of detection in the past. The future is about compulsory annual audit and regular revalidation, with assessment and support centres for failing doctors (National Health Service Executive, 1999a). A package of performance indicators to help identify sub-standard performance remains the Holy Grail. But the easily measurable is rarely useful and most indicators are influenced by factors outside the control of health systems.

PCTs are trying to adopt a non-threatening, facilitative and developmental approach to clinical governance while setting up new local monitoring mechanisms. In the current climate, engendering a 'no blame' culture has not been easy. The threats both to independent contractor status and professional self-regulation have increased doctors' feelings of vulnerability. However, there is growing understanding that reactionary notions of clinical freedom are redundant. Reform of the General Medical Council and the processes of professional self-regulation was long overdue. Ready co-operation with new forms of scrutiny is a mark of professional strength. Future general practitioners will look back disbelievingly on the days before regular revalidation, when information on clinical performance was not freely shared with patients.

Information sources or knowledge managers?

Traditionally, medicine has been based on knowledge acquired during training, topped up from time to time from sources such as scientific journals, conferences and medical libraries. Sources dated quickly, but clinicians nevertheless had more knowledge than their patients who were denied access to such professional sources. However, 'the worldwide web, the dominant medium of the postmodern world, has blown away the doors and walls of the locked library as efficiently as, but much more quietly than, semtex' (Muir Gray, 1999: 1552). Increasingly, patients are more knowledgeable than their doctors about the management of their chronic disease.

The computer screen threatens the interpersonal nature of the consultation but new tools are changing clinicians from being repositories of facts to being managers of knowledge. Some clinicians are nervous about giving patients better information, and not all patients want it. However, most people want to be in charge of decisions about their health – for the default approach to be empowerment rather than paternalism. Giving patients more knowledge or a consultation style that facilitates shared decision-making improves not only patient satisfaction but also clinical outcomes (Florin and Coulter, 2001; Coulter,

Chapter 2). Indeed, as people gain access to information about risk, a higher proportion may choose not to accept the offer of screening or treatment.

Patients' champions or guardians of the public's health?

The last 30 years (following the death of the old medical officers of health posts in the 1974 NHS re-organisation) have been chequered with pleas for closer co-operative working between primary care and public health. Many such pleas envisaged the emergence of new hybrids. The best known was Julian Tudor Hart's 'community general practitioner' – 'a new type of physician engaged in local participatory democracy to maximise the population's health' (Tudor Hart, 1988: 23). While there have always been plenty of GPs who understand the central role of primary care in tackling health inequalities, the majority remains less supportive (Skrabanek, 1994).

GPs like Michael Fitzpatrick, for example, regard the activities of the Social Exclusion Unit around issues such as homelessness and teenage pregnancy as fostering a dependency relationship between the State and recipients of welfare benefits. In his view, programmes such as Sure Start are nothing more than a sophisticated instrument for social regulation. He suggests that the high standing of general practice, which makes it such an attractive base for New Labour's role in engineering projects, is an asset that will be wasted rapidly if GPs continue to assume a social work guise (Fitzpatrick, 2001). His plea is for a form of medical practice that treats illness rather than regulating behaviour, and puts the autonomy of the individual and the privacy of personal life before the imperatives of political correctness. But Fitzpatrick's challenge to the 'tyranny of health' amounts to retrenchment – a withdrawal from a wider social role, a more restricted definition of medical practice. Patterns of behaviour are, after all, socially conditioned rather than pharmacologically determined.

If PCTs are to drive forward public health goals, they need, as they corporatise primary care, to reinforce the culture of support for 'upstream' solutions. They have an important role in helping to redistribute resources within and between their areas. They are already investing in services that will improve access and reduce variations in quality of care. They are beginning to invest in health-promoting initiatives beyond the NHS that address social determinants of health (Gillam, Abbott and Banks-Smith, 2001). Where GPs have neither the time and skills nor the inclination to lead this work, primary care nurses, particularly health visitors, could be equipped to spearhead this role. A renewed emphasis on the development of public health skills across a range of primary care disciplines could further change in support of population health (see Peckham and Wirrmann, Chapter 7).

Overwhelming resistance to reform

The development of effective primary care trusts was always going to take more time than the electoral cycle allowed. The NHS Plan (Department of Health, 2000) was an implicit acknowledgement that Tony Blair's mission to modernise the NHS was foundering (Lewis and Gillam, 2001). Public failures, particularly those of the medical profession, armed the government to challenge entrenched medical interests and strengthened the case for reform. The Plan represented a 'new deal' between the government and the health sector (Figure 10.1). In return for substantial new funding, the government sought to challenge some of the long-established foundations of the NHS and, in particular, to revisit the settlement between organised medicine and the state. Alternative methods of funding health care (private insurance, co-payments, social insurance) were, however, explicitly rejected (Department of Health, 2000). What does all this presage for general practice?

An expansion in hospital beds and consultant numbers with consequent reductions in waiting times should ease the burden of containment in primary care. The expansion by 2000 of GP numbers over four years is less impressive, representing only a modest increase over long-term trends. Even allowing for investment in other community-based services, GPs will not easily be able to improve access to their services or extend consultation lengths.

Increasingly, patients who currently go to hospital will be able to have tests and treatment in one of 500 new primary care centres.

- 500 one-stop health centres by 2004
- 3000 surgeries upgraded by 2004
- 2000 more GPs and 450 more registrars by 2004
- NHS Lift, a new private-public partnership, to develop premises
- 1000 specialist GPs
- Consultants delivering 4 million outpatient appointments in primary care
- 2100 extra acute and general hospital beds
- 5000 extra intermediate care beds
- Outpatient appointments to drop from six to three months

Figure 10.1: The NHS Plan – some key points

Source: Abridged from Gillam and Meads, 2001.

Consultants who previously worked only in hospitals will be seeing outpatients in these settings, while 'GPs with special interests' will be taking referrals from their colleagues in fields such as ophthalmology, orthopaedics and dermatology. The model for these is untested. Similarly, the investment in intermediate care – a bridge between hospital and home – represents a triumph of ideology over evidence.

The consolidation of NHS Direct opens up new approaches to demand management. The vision is of a single phone call to the one-stop gateway to all out-of-hours health care. Many primary care providers will be nurse-led and ostensibly more cost-efficient (see Williams, Chapter 5). The same substitution of less expensive human resources is reflected in new extended roles for pharmacists. GP sub-specialists similarly will take on work previously undertaken by hospital consultants.

After nearly a decade of rhetoric in support of the 'primary care-led NHS', there is little evidence of a shift in the balance of NHS expenditure (Gillam, 2000). In absolute terms, it is the acute sector which continues to attract most new money. In many areas, PCTs begin to resemble the health authorities they replaced and appear to lack the leverage required to move resources from hospitals into community-based services. Furthermore, the introduction of foundation hospital trusts with their greater financial independence may further weaken the hands of the commissioners.

If the Plan signalled a major investment in new staff and facilities, the government expected more than just 'principled motivation' in return. GPs have long bemoaned their terms of employment. Their old contract was highly focused on the individual practitioner and failed to recognise adequately the role of the wider practice team; quality measures were sparse and crudely applied. Perverse incentives often served to reward poor quality services. Surveys exposed high levels of stress, poor morale, and planned early retirement or exit from the profession. The new national contract proposed in the summer of 2002 marked an important departure. As this book went to press (June 2003), GPs had just voted in its favour.

A new funding formula was designed to help recruitment in deprived areas that are already under-doctored. Crucially, the national pricing of the contract will take into account the changing demands on general practice through an annual assessment of doctors' workload. The new contract will be between a primary care trust and a practice (rather than with an individual doctor), and services will be categorised as either essential, additional or enhanced. All GPs must provide 'essential' services, envisaged as a tightly defined core, but can reduce some of their current commitments. In particular, an 'opt out' for out of hours care will be introduced. Conversely, those doctors who wish to will be able to offer 'enhanced' services for extra pay. A new quality and outcomes framework will cover standards to measure clinical and organisational quality as well as patients' experiences.

These proposals offer much to general practice and to patients but, again, there are risks attached for the government. In future, GPs should be better able to control their workload and trade leisure for income. Importantly, the new contract proposes significant changes to the incentives facing GPs. Quality of care is likely to be a more powerful motivator than it has proved in the past. The perverse incentive for GPs to manage large lists with a limited range of services should reduce.

Shifting the contract from individual practitioners to practices introduces new incentives to make greater use of non-medical staff – since under current arrangements, many payments are linked to the existence of a general practitioner. In addition, practices may become larger, with sub-specialisation among general practitioners. The prospect of a practice-based contract may also in future open the door to other contractors, including private limited companies.

Much of the government's modernisation programme for the NHS requires the tacit backing of GPs whom they cannot afford to alienate. Much therefore depends on the manner of implementation of the contract – and its costing – for by clearly specifying general medical services for the first time the government will be paying for additional services it currently receives for free.[5] The new contract seems set, however, to change the face of British general practice in other ways. Patients may receive services from their own registered practice, from another practice, from staff employed by primary care trusts, or from others such as community pharmacists. The linkage between daytime and out of hours services is set to break forever. The traditional family doctor will no longer be the only hub around which first-contact care revolves. Continuity of care based on a long-term relationship between patient and general practitioner is threatened. This may be the ultimate price of the new contract.

Future: a generalist for the twenty-first century

Is structural and contractual change enough to resolve the tensions described above? Can the imperative for personal and pastoral care be re-asserted in a modern context? If the profession's rise over the past two centuries depended upon being so in tune with grass-roots society and class cultures that most people came to accept, without questioning, their GP as a natural phenomenon, what could be the sources of a comparable relationship in future?

The answers lie in the profession of general practice continuing to behave as a profession: building on its scientific knowledge base, self-determining, independently practising but peer-supported and, above all, committed to public service through relationships of direct, reciprocal accountability with local people at an individual level. It means getting rid of the baggage of the past. Figure 10.2 summarises some of the changes discussed that are likely to characterise general practice in future. The forces of modernisation seem threatening but they do provide the means for GPs to mould their own destinies.

In practical terms, primary care organisations look likely to move beyond diversification to deregulation. General practice as an exclusive professional legal partnership is an anachronism. Its ownership and management now require different criteria and forms. A national contract smacks of restrictive practice, of income protection, and, above all, of fearfulness in the face of contemporary changes. Education, housing, transportation and all other sectors of public service are moving down a road to new kinds of partnership, participation and public accountability. General practice needs to do the same. In the contemporary context, the personal and pastoral care GPs offer merits not crude, centrally administered contracts but the consolidation of co-ownership arrangements with community representatives, the commercial integrity of a (social) market, and the endorsement of patient-citizens (Lewis, Dixon and Gillam, 2003). New mechanisms for framing personal health care include individualised accounts, covenants and electronic health records. Some practices have already experimented with forms of personal contract (Gillam and Meads, 2001). Gift-aid is not new to practices that enjoy close links with the communities they serve. More practices are engaging with groups of patient participants or 'critical friends'. PMS has spawned new types of primary care organisation. The more innovative PMS practices are supporting new forms of practice-based community development in areas of high need (Pietroni, 1996).

The primacy of personal care

Patients consistently attach highest priority to three particular facets of general practice (Carter *et al.*, 2000). They want a personal relationship with someone who communicates well and who understands them.

Present	Future
• nationally government administered and negotiated GMS contract • patient registration/local lists	• individually covenanted according to personal needs and services offered • individual enrolment/membership bodies
• uni-professional, legal partnership monopolies • independent sector status	• multi- and non-professional organisation partnerships • multiple status, including voluntary/ independent sector providers
• NHS exclusive commissioning (e.g. primary care trust)	• range of approved commissioners, including health care companies, professional consortia, and corporate agencies (e.g. charities, employers) without geographic constraints
• local medical committees • micro-medical services and expenses	• local societies for primary care • long-term, reviewable and renewable outcome/output-based franchises
• distinct medical education and end-point certification • sole secondary care gatekeeper/ commissioner • access to doctor or nurse	• continuing professional development and re-accreditation • multiple primary care access points with referral rights • plurality of provider disciplines integrating front line
• doctor as generalist for life	• portfolio careers, increasing role diversification and sub-specialisation
• GP as lead primary medical care organisational manager • separation from social care	• GP as co-ordinator of integrated health and social care team • local combinations of resource sharing and service development across public/independent and social services

Figure 10.2: The fall and rise of general practice

Source: Based on Gillam and Meads, 2001.

Second, they need to know that their doctor is technically sound in clinical terms. Third, they want to be able to rely on their general practitioner as a source of information, as someone with whom they can share decision-making. Personal care and continuity are not necessarily the same thing but the latter provides the doctor with the contextual knowledge required for the former (Roland, Holden and Campbell, 1998). There is plenty of evidence to suggest that levels of satisfaction with general practice remain high. But surveys also reveal consistent generational differences with people aged over 65 years broadly more satisfied than younger people (National Health Service Executive, 1999b). This may in part be a 'cohort effect', with greater support for the NHS evinced among those old enough to remember what preceded it. It is more likely to relate to changing needs. With age and the onset of chronic conditions, instant access may become less important than personal care. In other words, much of what both server and served value is shared – and enduring.

Continuous personal care remains the guiding principle, but the rigidities of individual GP-only registered lists, with their associated automatic rights of closure and fixed local limits, are no longer appropriate to mobile populations. Most people would be astonished if they knew how general practitioners are still paid: the extraordinary microeconomics of fees and allowances, taxable income, non-taxable grants and differential capitation scales. Even if they could understand the financial system, they could scarcely recognise any reflection of their current service needs. In vain would they search for the profession's monetary incentives to tackle back pain or stress management, long-term disabilities or mental health. They would see that consumerism has scarcely scratched the surface of UK primary care. Simply as service users and payers the modern public and its patients require different ways of sourcing and resourcing their kind of general practice. The parallels with social care and housing are obvious. The growth in domiciliary, respite and residential care has been unprecedented over the past 15 years. Charities, companies, community groups (both local and national), clients and collaborative ventures should in future play their part. The personal and comprehensive care offered by general practice in this new context for future resource investment carries a premium. In all kinds of ways, people should be able to show their support – as shareholders, donors, trustees and subscribers. We have foundation trusts; why not foundation practices?

A single electronic record will in time offer exciting opportunities to integrate information from different providers and to support more self-care from home. Creative use of IT, particularly the Internet, to communicate with patients can help support a different kind of continuity of care in future – linked to a practice if not a single practitioner. Expert patients and carers will be the most important element in the health care workforce. The central fact (only dimly appreciated by policy makers) remains that health care is seldom 'delivered' or 'provided' but more often co-produced by patients and health professionals working together.

Conclusion

The collectivisation of primary care under Labour marks a move toward managed care under UK-style health maintenance organisations. GPs must resist too reductionist a slide into managed care activities, particularly if this focuses financial incentives and quality assurance on the easily measurable (Roland and Marshall, 2001). Health care is not a commodity amenable to crude, technocratic manipulation. For those at the frontline, the infinite richness of human encounters that make up their working days down the decades have few echoes in the ever expanding datasets beloved of resource allocators. However, PCTs offer an administrative and organisational model to support service integration, for example out-of-hours, more cost-effectively. They are already realising opportunities for virtual integration (across networks of primary care professionals) and vertical integration (with colleagues in secondary care) around which to re-design community-based services.

In conclusion, the power to reconstruct the profession lies principally with the professionals themselves. GPs are best placed to realise the possibilities listed above but hands-on primary care will increasingly be delivered by nurse (general) practitioners. They are paving the way for new forms of primary care management as did their forebears for domiciliary and residential care management a decade ago.

Over the coming years, pharmacists, social workers and others may challenge GPs' monopoly over primary care leadership (Moore, 2000). However, general practice remains the only profession of primary care with a body of specialist knowledge, expertise and relationships exclusive to this setting and of a comparable status to the specialist professions in settings such as hospitals, courts and cathedrals. And it still both owns and controls the assets. Managing the transition will involve trade-offs – for the profession as a whole and for individual doctors – between collective and individual goals. General practitioners have no need to subvert the processes of modernisation. Long after today's structures – these Trusts, those pilots – have disappeared, people will seek the personal care that tomorrow's general practitioners should strive to provide.

Notes

1. Acknowledgements: to Geoff Meads, Diane Plamping and Richard Lewis for helpful discussions and collaboration and to the King's Fund, London for allowing me to draw freely on a publication, Stephen Gillam and Geoff Meads *Modernisation and the Future of General Practice*, London, King's Fund, 2001.
2. The term GMS refers to a range of services governed by the national GP contract and defined in Part II of the NHS Act 1977. PMS practices created by

the 1997 Primary Care Act provide broadly the same services but their legislative lineage is different. PMS pilots transferred from Part II to Part I of the 1977 Act which previously covered only hospital and community services within the NHS.

3. In contract negotiations with the government, the BMA General Practice Committee represents GMS but not PMS GPs. The BMA has been disempowered in its scope for national collective bargaining as a result. As will be seen below, the new contract, first proposed in 2002, borrows from the experience of PMS.

4. This relates also to debates about single-handed practice. The proportion of single-handed practices has steadily declined over the last 30 years. Small practices may struggle to deliver the same range of services that group practices can sustain but there is little evidence that the care they do provide is of poorer quality (see Hippisley-Cox, Pringle, Coupland, Hammersley and Wilson, 2001).

5. For more on the background to the contract negotiations, (see Gillam and Meads, 2001).

References

Ashcroft, J. (2001) 'Releasing the Dividend of "New" Partnerships', in Geoff Meads and Tricia Meads (eds) *Trust in Experience: transferable learning for primary care trusts*, Oxford: Radcliffe Medical Press, 49–68.

Balint, M. (1964) *The Doctor, His Patient and the Illness*, London: Pitman.

Carter, Y., Curtis, S., Harding, G. *et al.* (2000) *National Evaluation of Primary Care Act Pilots – addressing inequalities*, London: The Stationery Office.

Coulter, A. (2002) *The Autonomous Patient. Ending paternalism in medical care*, London: The Nuffield Trust.

Department of Health (1989) *Working for Patients*, London: Her Majesty's Stationery Office, Cm 555.

Department of Health (1997) *The New NHS: modern, dependable*, London: The Stationery Office.

Department of Health (1998) *A First Class Service: quality in the new NHS*. London: Department of Health.

Department of Health (2000) *The NHS Plan: a plan for investment; a plan for reform*, London: The Stationery Office, Cm 4818-I.

Fitzpatrick, M. (2001) *The Tyranny of Health – doctors and the regulation of lifestyle*, London: Routledge.

Florin, D. and Coulter, A. (2001) 'Partnership in the Primary Care Consultation', in S. Gillam and F. Brooks (eds) *New Beginnings – towards patient and public involvement in primary health care*, London: King's Fund.

Forrest, C. (2003) 'Primary Care in the United States. Primary care gatekeeping and referrals: effective filter or failed experiment?', *British Medical Journal*, 326, 692–5.

Gillam, S. (2000) 'Homeward Bound? Just how far have we come in re-directing resources to primary care?', *Health Management*, November, 14–15.

Gillam, S., Abbott, S. and Banks-Smith, J. (2001) 'Can Primary Care Groups and Trusts Improve the Population's Health?', *British Medical Journal*, 323, 89–92.

Gillam, S. and Meads, G. (2001) *Modernisation and the Future of General Practice*, London: King's Fund.

Guthrie, B. and Wyke, S. (2000) 'Does Continuity in General Practice Really Matter?', *British Medical Journal*, 321, 734–5.

Hannay, D. and Mathers, N. (2000) 'General Practice, Management Culture and Market Ideology – bedfellows or culture clash?', *British Journal of General Practice*, 455, 518–19.

Heath, I. (1995) *The Mystery of General Practice*, London: Nuffield Provincial Hospitals Trust, 5–14.

Hippisley-Cox, J., Pringle, M., Coupland, C., Hammersley, V. and Wilson, A. (2001) 'Do Single-handed Practices Offer Poorer Care? Cross-sectional survey of processes and outcomes', *British Medical Journal*, 323, 320–3.

Huntingdon, J., Walsh, N., Barnes, M., Rogers, R. and Baines, D. (2000) 'This is Your Pilot Speaking', *Health Service Journal*, 3 August, 30–1.

Jones, M. (2000) 'Walk-In Primary Care Centres: lessons from Canada', *British Medical Journal*, 321, 928–31.

Le Grand, J., Mays, N. and Mulligan, J-A. (eds) (1998) *Learning from the NHS Internal Market. A review of the evidence*, London: King's Fund.

Lewis, R., Dixon, J. and Gillam, S. (2003) 'Outside Chance', *Health Service Journal*, 8 May, 24–6.

Lewis, R. and Gillam, S. (eds) (1999) *Transforming Primary Care. Personal medical services in the new NHS*, London: King's Fund.

Lewis, R. and Gillam, S. (2001) 'The NHS Plan – further reform of the British health service', *International Journal of Health Services*, 31, 111–18.

Moore, G. (2000) *Managing to do Better. General practice for the twenty-first century*, London: Office of Health Economics.

Muir Gray, J. A. (1999) 'Post-modern Medicine', *Lancet*, 354, 1550–3.

Munro, J., Nicholl, J., O'Cathain, A. and Knowles, E. (2000) *Evaluation of NHS Direct First Wave Sites. Second interim report to the Department of Health*, Sheffield: Medical Care Research Unit, University of Sheffield.

National Health Service Executive (1999a) *Supporting Doctors, Protecting Patients*, London: The Stationery Office.

National Health Service Executive (1999b) *National Surveys of NHS Patients. General practice 1998*, London: Department of Health.

Pietroni, P. (1996) 'The Greening of Medicine', in P. Pietroni and C. Pietroni (eds) *Innovation in Community Care and Primary Health*, Edinburgh: Churchill Livingstone, 15–18.

Roland, M., Holden, J. and Campbell, S. (1998) *Quality Assessment for General Practice: supporting clinical governance in primary care groups*, Manchester: National Primary Care Research and Development Centre.

Roland, M. and Marshall, M. (2001) 'General Practice in an Age of Measurement', *British Journal of General Practice*, 469, 611–12.

Skrabanek, P. (1994) *The Death of Humane Medicine and the Rise of Coercive Healthism*, London: Social Affairs Unit.

Starfield, B. (1994) 'Is Primary Care Essential?', *Lancet*, 344, 1129–33.

Tudor Hart, J. (1988) *A New Kind of Doctor*, London: Merlin Press.

Wilkin, D., Gillam, S. and Leese, B. (eds) (2000) *The National Tracker Survey of Primary Care Groups and Trusts. Progress and challenges 1999/2000*, London: National Primary Care Research and Development Centre/King's Fund.

11

The Future Healthcare Workforce in Pharmacy

Alison Blenkinsopp and Christine Bond

Introduction

There are three main groups of practising pharmacists, working in community pharmacies, in hospitals and in primary care settings. Community pharmacists dispense prescriptions, sell 'over the counter' (OTC) medicines and advise people on medicines and health. Hospital pharmacists have a more clinical role, working closely with doctors and other health care staff to advise on the selection and use of medicines. Primary care pharmacists, a relatively new occupational group, work in both strategic and operational roles advising on prescribing and medicines. There has been an increasing interest in where pharmacists fit in relation to NHS modernisation. Both government and the pharmacy profession itself have been seeking to reposition pharmacists towards roles involving closer working with patients, doctors and nurses. In this chapter, we examine the government and professional policy contexts, consider how and why change is occurring in pharmacy and finally, present a vision for the future.

The policy context

External policy

'Pharmacy in the Future' (Department of Health, 2000), setting out new directions for the profession in England heralded major change for pharmacy in primary and secondary care settings. Pharmacy strategy documents were subsequently published in Scotland, Wales and Northern Ireland.[1] Although there were some differences between the policies of the four home territories, much was common. The general 'direction of travel' was:

- pharmaceutical services that are more patient-centred;
- greater involvement of patients as partners in decisions about treatment and the use of medicines;
- improving access to medicines in primary and secondary care;
- better utilisation of pharmacists' skills though the provision of what has come to be known as medicines management services;
- using skill-mix changes and technological advances to enable pharmacists to spend more time with patients.

The government's implementation programme for pharmacy in England is summarised in Figure 11.1. Key systems changes are the electronic transfer of prescribing (ETP) and introduction of repeat dispensing, where community pharmacists effectively take over management of patients' repeat medication. These changes will both streamline the process of ordering and obtaining medicines for patients and enable pharmacists better to plan and manage their workload. Medicines management and local pharmaceutical services (LPS) are mechanisms to introduce new, patient-focused service models for community pharmacy. Community pharmacy is an independent contractor service with a national contract predominantly based on the number of prescriptions dispensed. Local development of LPS has an analogy with personal medical services (PMS) pilots in demonstrating the government's intention to make services more responsive to local needs. Like PMS contractors, LPS contractors will opt out of the national contractual arrangements (see Gillam, Chapter 10). Pharmacists who become supplementary prescribers will manage chronic conditions and, in the first instance at least, are likely to work in hospital or primary care settings. The implication of the government's commitment to making a wider range of medicines available over the counter is an extended involvement of community pharmacists in advice-giving. Finally, the medicines partnership programme (*http://www.medicines-partnership.org* [accessed 11 June 2003]) seeks to increase patient involvement in decisions and choices about medicines and their use. In line with other government initiatives to increase patient and public involvement, it signals a change in the relationship between pharmacists and patients (Marinker, 1997).

While pharmacy, as these policies and targets demonstrate, is an integral part of the NHS modernisation programme and a substantially wider

Policy	Setting	Target date
Electronic transfer of prescriptions (ETP)	Primary care	National by 2005
Repeat dispensing	Primary care	National by 2004
Medicines management services	Primary and secondary care	National by 2004
Supplementary prescribing	Primary and secondary care	Mid-2003 (first qualifying pharmacists)
Local pharmaceutical services	Primary care	Late 2002 (first schemes)
More prescription only medicines deregulated for over the counter sale	Primary care	Ongoing
Medicines partnership programme	Primary and secondary care	Ongoing

Figure 11.1: Implementation of key government policies relating to pharmacy

Source: Department of Health, 2000.

role for pharmacists is envisaged, there is also controversy. Community pharmacies encompass both the private sector (in their sale of medicines and other goods) and the public sector (in their provision of NHS dispensing services). The government has a wider drive for deregulation as a means of improving services and prices for consumers through greater market competition. The granting of NHS contracts to dispense prescriptions has been subject to restrictions since 1987. Effectively this has made it difficult to open new pharmacies and protected those already existing. The Office of Fair Trading conducted an inquiry and recommended (Office of Fair Trading, 2003) that NHS dispensing contracts should be subject to deregulation, removing the controls on entry to contract that previously existed.[2] Responses to the 2003 Office of Fair Trading consultation on its proposal to abolish control of entry were polarised. On the one hand, it was argued by the Office of Fair Trading and some supermarkets that deregulation could reduce the price of over the counter medicines and could improve access for patients. The contrary argument, put forward in strong terms by those whose priority was wider NHS developments, was that exposing pharmacy services to an open market, would reduce the capacity of the NHS to plan future services. It had the potential to 'destabilise the community pharmacy network and hinder the development of extended role services' (Association of Directors of Social Services, 2003).

Health service policy and initiatives around prescribing are also of direct relevance to pharmacy. Curbing the high and growing cost of prescribing has been high on the present government's agenda. The cost of prescribing in primary care had risen to £2.2 billion by 2002 and its further growth was predicted to outstrip general increases in NHS funding in 2002–3 (Audit Commission, 2003). Controlling the increase in prescribing costs is thus a major challenge for primary care organisations and it is increasingly clear, as the chapter will show, that pharmacists are coming to play a key role in managing prescribing as part of local prescribing teams.

The recent drive to improve patient safety also has implications for pharmacy. Recognition of preventable adverse events, illness and deaths associated with medication (Department of Health, 2001) led to the setting up of the National Patient Safety Agency[3] and has high-lighted the pharmacist's role in improving medication safety in both primary and secondary care. Key issues in improving safety in secondary care are enhancing systems in hospitals, for example, improving medication history-taking and review on admission and communication after discharge (Audit Commission, 2001). In primary care, the need to strengthen systems for monitoring and reviewing medication, particularly for older people and those on medicines of 'higher risk', has become clear. Pharmacists have a central role to play in these areas.

In 1995, the then Conservative government set up a review of prescribing, supply and administration of medicines (Department of Health, 1999). The remit of the review included consideration of which non-medical professionals might prescribe and in which circumstances. The review also made recommendations about procedures for the supply of medicines under patient group directions.[4] The final report (commonly referred to as the Crown report), recommended two categories of new prescribers, 'independent' and 'supplementary'.[5] The implementation of the Crown report brought two significant changes to pharmacy practice. Firstly, patient group directions have enabled pharmacists and nurses to supply certain prescription only medicines for specific groups of patients.[6] Secondly, since April 2003, both pharmacists and nurses can now become 'supplementary prescribers', managing the medication of patients with chronic illness (Medicines Control Agency, 2002).

Policy relating to increasing patient and public involvement in health services is reflected in the move towards partnership in medicine taking. The NHS Medicines Partnership Taskforce was established as part of the NHS Plan Pharmacy Programme and is overseeing work whose purpose is to increase patient involvement in decisions about treatment and to improve patients' access to information and support (Department of Health, 2000).

Internal (professional) policy

Many of the components of government policy on pharmacy were in practice led by the profession itself and we turn now to policy prompted by the deliberations of pharmacists themselves, particularly as mediated through their regulatory body the Royal Pharmaceutical Society of Great Britain (RPSGB). The Society's strategy (Royal Pharmaceutical Society of Great Britain, 1995), and its implementation document (Royal Pharmaceutical Society of Great Britain, 1997) pre-dated the developments described at the beginning of this chapter and identified five core roles for pharmacists to be delivered across primary and secondary care settings:

- management of prescribed medicines;
- management of long-term diseases;
- management of minor ailments;
- promotion and support of healthy lifestyles;
- advice and support for other health professionals.

Prior to development of this strategy, there had been two influential reports, one from the Nuffield Foundation (1986), and the other a joint profession and government review of UK and international roles for pharmacy (Royal Pharmaceutical Society of Great Britain and Department of Health, 1992). Ideas and policies first raised in these internal documents were later echoed in the government's strategy for pharmacy. The more recent policy documents from Scotland, Wales and Northern Ireland have focused rather more on public health. Furthermore, in Scotland there are also plans for selected community pharmacies to become a network of walk in 'healthy living centres', rather than for these to be developed in separate premises as in England.

Another important new role for pharmacists is in the direct prescribing of medicines on the NHS to treat minor ailments. This is discussed in more detail later, but the policy context is considered here. Initially, community pharmacist involvement was in NHS schemes for the management of minor illnesses and this was facilitated by pilot projects where pharmacists were able to treat certain conditions free of charge for people who were exempt from prescription charges. These schemes were established in target areas where low income was a barrier to patients self-medicating. A pioneering scheme in Sefton (Hassell *et al.*, 2001) was adapted and is already being rolled out in 14 PCTs in England and two areas in Scotland. The supply of OTC medicines was followed by the introduction of patient group directions allowing the supply of medicines, some of which were prescription only, to specific patients, for example emergency hormonal contraception and treatment for eye infections.

In addition to the difference in emphasis on the public health role of community pharmacists (Moore, 1999), there is an interesting distinction between Scotland and England in relation to community pharmacy. In Scotland (but not England), there are further plans for pharmacists to become independent prescribers and a clear vision that they will become the main NHS managers of minor ailments (Scottish Executive, 2002). In contrast, the emphasis has been on supplementary prescribing in England with no commitment to implement independent prescribing for pharmacists. There has also been an expansion in the numbers of community pharmacists working on a sessional basis in primary care medical practices (primary care pharmacists) across the UK. However, in Scotland, there have been recent moves to transfer some of the responsibilities undertaken within this setting back to the community pharmacy base, whereas in England, general practice is seen as the key setting for supplementary prescribing. In summary, Scotland presents a wider vision of the community pharmacy as a centre for promoting and maintaining health and beyond the treatment of ill-health.

What are the driving forces for change?

Like other occupational groups within the healthcare workforce, pharmacy is subject to a number of governmental and societal drivers in addition to the aspirations of its own members. Figure 11.2 shows the key driving forces and resisting forces. We are not suggesting that these are equal and opposite, but use the idea to illustrate the range of issues.

Developments in technology are enabling a number of major changes to increase access and convenience for patients, including electronic transfer of prescriptions and repeat dispensing. The potential benefits of these new processes are threefold. Firstly they will reduce inconvenience and multiple visits for patients. Secondly, they will enable pharmacists to plan their workload better, and thirdly they will allow the pharmacist to identify when a patient's treatment requires further review. Although repeat dispensing may appear to be a process change, in fact it has the potential to substantially re-engineer

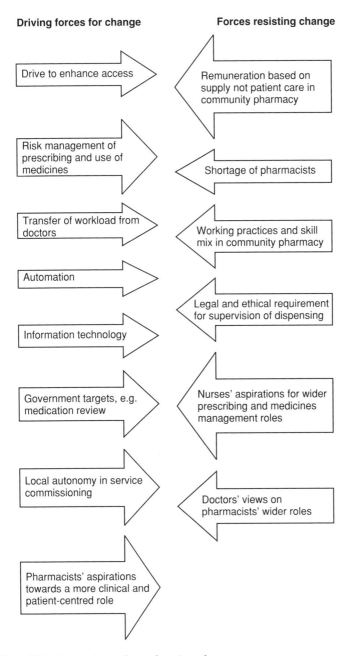

Figure 11.2: Driving forces for and against change

community pharmacy practice. Pharmacists have generally welcomed the introduction of repeat dispensing but have expressed some concerns about the way in which electronic transfer of prescriptions might enable the setting up of large-scale prescription mail order centres.

The major blocks to achieving change in community pharmacy are the allocation of responsibilities between pharmacists and their staff, the current unpredictability of prescription workload and a national contract that rewards supply of medicines rather than one focused on improving patients' medication. The capacity of the pharmacy workforce to deliver is discussed in a later section.

The attitudes and actions of other health professionals influence change in the pharmacy workforce. Until recently, doctors guarded their prescribing territory fiercely. However, the national shortage of doctors and the increased workload resulting from this and other factors has itself acted as a driving force to change medical opinion. Evidence to support this contention comes from the proposed new general medical services contract, which highlights future transfer of management of minor illness and chronic diseases to nurses and pharmacists. Nurses are new prescribers and, while not taking any overt stance for or against prescribing by pharmacists, may see this as unwelcome competition for their own burgeoning professional role.

Figure 11.3 summarises the ways in which roles are likely to change for pharmacists in different sectors. Community pharmacy will be subject to the greatest change. As the trend to self-care continues, with further encouragement from government, sales and associated advice with over the counter medicines will increase for community pharmacists. The public health role of community pharmacists is also set to become wider as part of local health improvement plans. Pharmacists in community, hospital and primary care will be more involved in reviewing and discussing medicines with patients, with a more active role in monitoring by pharmacists in the community. Advice to prescribers is already a key role for hospital and primary care pharmacists and will become so for community pharmacists.

Overall, the changes represent a move away from direct involvement in technical aspects of dispensing, and towards greater direct contact with patients. The vision, however, depends in large measure on workforce availability and how staff skills are developed and utilised, which will be considered in the following section.

	Community pharmacist		Hospital pharmacist		Primary care pharmacist	
	Current	Future	Current	Future	Current	Future
Purchasing of medicine stocks	√	√	√√	√		
Supply of medicines	√√	√	√	√		
Sale of over the counter medicines	√	√√				
NHS prescribing for acute conditions		?√		√		√
NHS prescribing for chronic conditions		√		√√		√√
Monitoring of prescribed medicines		√√				
Reviews of prescribed medicines[1]		√	√	√√	√	√√
Public health activities	√	√√		√	√	√
Advice to patients	√	√√	√	√√	√	√√
Advice to prescribers		√√	√√	√√	√√	√√
Advice to healthcare organisations				√	√√	√√

Figure 11.3: Current and future roles of community, hospital and primary care pharmacists

[1] See Tully and Cantrill, 1999; Mackie *et al.* 1999; Furniss *et al.* 2000.

Workforce supply and demand

The pharmacy labour force

A census of pharmacists registered in Great Britain was undertaken in 2002 (Hassell, Fisher, Nichols and Shann, 2002). There were some 45,000 registered pharmacists in Great Britain at that time and almost 87 per cent responded (39,020). Around 29,000 pharmacists were working within pharmacy, with just over 1000 working outside, and over 5500 not working at all. A further 3400 were working overseas.

Most pharmacists work in the community (retail) pharmacy sector. Here a pharmacist might be a pharmacy owner, a manager, or may work freelance (locum pharmacist). They might work full or part-time and, in the latter case, may combine community pharmacy with

	Number	Per cent
Community pharmacy	22,924	65.4%
Hospital pharmacy	6385	18.2%
Primary care pharmacy	1867	5.3%
Pharmaceutical industry	1739	
Academia	801	
National organisation	217	
Pharmaceutical wholesaling	236	11.0%
NHS management	132	
Other	755	
	35,056	

Figure 11.4: Pharmacists by sector of work 2002

Source: Adapted from Hassell, Fisher, Nichols and Shann, 2002.

another pharmacy job. About one in five pharmacists work in a hospital. Primary care pharmacists (around 5 per cent of the total) work in either a medical practice or a primary care management organisation (for example, a PCT in England). In the former they have an operational, and in the latter, strategic, role. In 2002, there were some 12,000 community pharmacies in the UK (9765 in England, 1141 in Scotland, 704 in Wales and 512 in Northern Ireland (Office of Fair Trading, 2003)). The top three large multiple companies (*Lloyds Pharmacy*, *Boots* and *Moss*) account for 27 per cent of all community pharmacies. The supermarkets *Tesco*, *Safeway*, *Sainsbury* and *Asda* account for a further 502 pharmacies (4.1 per cent).

Just under 14 per cent of pharmacists who were working reported having more than one job, with the percentage varying according to sector of practice. In community pharmacy 16.5 per cent had two or more jobs and for those in hospital, primary care and academia the figures were 22 per cent, 65 per cent and 67 per cent respectively. These figures indicate that most primary care pharmacist posts are not full-time. Primary care pharmacists were most likely to have completed a postgraduate qualification, with 52 per cent reporting having a diploma compared with 34 per cent of hospital and 10 per cent of community pharmacists.

Within community pharmacy, locums were the largest group, at 36 per cent, followed by managers at 28 per cent. Almost one in five (18 per cent) pharmacists were owner-proprietors, although 31 per cent of pharmacists reported working in 'independent' pharmacies. Large multiples were the most frequent job setting in community practice, at 43 per cent, with 15 per cent in small chains and 11 per cent in medium-sized multiples.

Is demand outstripping supply?

Debates about a 'shortage' of pharmacists have been a feature of the last decade. In its response to the Department of Health's discussion document on the pharmacy workforce (Department of Health, 2002) the Royal Pharmaceutical Society stated its view that achieving the necessary levels of recruitment and retention was as high a priority as developing the required levels of competence (Royal Pharmaceutical Society of Great Britain, 2003). Research findings indicate that rather than an inadequate supply of pharmacists, the issue is the ways in which pharmacists have chosen and are choosing to work, and the new opportunities they are taking up (Hassell, Fisher, Nichols and Shann, 2002; Blenkinsopp, Boardman, Jesson and Wilson, 1999). Key changes are that more pharmacists are opting for freelance (locum) work; more 'primary care pharmacist' posts have been established; and the profession has become increasingly feminised. Each of these is discussed briefly in turn.

Regional and national surveys have shown that more pharmacists are opting for a career that offers more flexibility than the traditional full-time community or hospital pharmacy posts. Freelance locum work in community pharmacy is a key component of many such careers (Blenkinsopp, Boardman, Jesson and Wilson, 1999; Hassell, Fisher, Nichols and Shann, 2002) – as the figures above implied. A qualitative study of pharmacists' reasons for career decisions showed that having control over when and where they worked were key factors (Boardman, Blenkinsopp, Jesson and Wilson, 2001). Lack of management responsibility was also commonly cited as a reason for preferring locum work (Boardman, Blenkinsopp, Jesson and Wilson, 2001).

Turning to primary care, the 2002 census showed 1867 (5 per cent) pharmacists reporting working in this sector (Hassell, Fisher, Nichols and Shann, 2002). While there are no baseline national figures, extrapolation from regional data suggests there may have been a 10-fold increase since 1995 and a four-fold increase since 1997 (Blenkinsopp, Boardman, Jesson and Wilson, 2001). At Primary Care Trust (or equivalent) level such posts are strategic, whereas at individual GP practice level they are operational. Given the numbers of primary care organisations, it might be expected that up to 400 primary care pharmacists work at strategic and 1400 at operational level. The latter group are likely to work part-time and are often community pharmacist managers or locums (Hassell, Fisher, Nichols and Shann, 2002; Blenkinsopp, Boardman, Jesson and Wilson, 2001).

Comparison of workforce trends over the period 1964–2001 (Hassell, Fisher, Nichols and Shann, 2002), shows that the percentage of female pharmacists has increased dramatically – from 19 per cent to 52 per cent. Women are likely to work, on average, fewer hours per week than men, to take more career breaks and to prefer flexible working arrangements to allow them to balance family and professional responsibilities. Thus again if retention is considered, employers need to be considering family friendly policies, and workforce planning needs to include an estimate of hourly capacity as well as numbers of individuals. There is also a suggestion that women are less motivated to attain higher managerial positions than men, although this may change in line with an evolving socio-cultural context.

There is growing evidence that pharmacists' skills could be better used. Observational studies indicate that only a half to a third of a community pharmacist's time is spent on professional activities (Fisher, Corrigan and Henman, 1991; Bell, McElnay and Hughes, 1999; Rutter, Hunt, Darracott and Jones, 1998), defined as dispensing, prescription monitoring, patient advice and OTC recommendations. Other activities include administration and paperwork, and although multiple pharmacy groups have economies of scale in this respect, such activities consume considerable amounts of time for independent pharmacies and those in small groups. Ways to address this apparent skill wastage are considered in the next section. The time spent on professional activities has implications for retention in the profession, as other work shows that pharmacists experience greater job satisfaction from more professional roles, such as the advisory roles in general practice (Boardman, Blenkinsopp, Jesson and Wilson, 2001). Conversely, dissatisfaction is associated with low skill utilisation, stress, and long working hours. The last of these particularly leads to tensions between meeting the public demand for longer opening hours, and keeping a healthy motivated workforce. A recent study found that 45 per cent of community pharmacists felt their current professional role was unsatisfying in these respects (King's Fund, 2002).

Making more effective use of the workforce

It is unlikely that there will be any immediate increase in number of pharmacists, and a number of developments is in place designed to mitigate the effects of shortages. Five of these are summarised below, with the first two at a well-advanced stage of development and the next three more speculative.

Pharmacy technicians

Hospital pharmacy responded to increasing demand for pharmacist input at ward and clinic level by developing technicians' skills and accrediting them to check dispensed prescriptions. Community pharmacy has made much less progress in this regard. Technicians are now being considered as a resource for further releasing community pharmacist time. However, a re-interpretation of the RPSGB's current strict interpretation of its supervision requirement is indicated. This currently requires the pharmacist to be personally aware of all transactions involving the dispensing of prescriptions, or the sale of medicines, and has tied the pharmacist to their premises, so that they are unable to provide other services such as domiciliary visits or case conferences with primary care colleagues. A more flexible approach to supervision, which would allow delegation of tasks to a technician, whilst retaining accountability for the technician's actions would free up the pharmacists for other professional activity.

Perhaps as a precursor to this, the RPSGB has now received confirmation from the Government that it can proceed with the regulation of pharmacy technicians which will include registration and a regulatory framework. From 2007, the acceptable entry for technicians will be a national vocational qualification – NVQ level 3. The technician workforce is still likely to be primarily based in the acute sector in the near future, but this will be likely to change as outlined above.

In primary care, also, a new technician role is emerging, that of Prescribing Support Technician. Work includes analysis and audit of prescribing and implementing changes using computerised repeat prescribing systems. Leading edge technicians are now involved in medication review.

Medicines counter assistants

Medicine Counter Assistants (MCAs) have long been the first point of contact for many customers in community pharmacies. However, the recent increase in availability of potent OTC drugs has raised questions about their training and competence to carry out what is really a clinical role, whilst the trained pharmacist often remains out of sight in the dispensary. An initial response to this was the requirement from the RPSGB that by January 1996, all counter staff involved in the sale of medicines should hold an approved qualification (the equivalent of an NVQ (national vocational qualification). All such staff now have to complete a minimum amount of accredited training in identifying correct treatments for specified symptoms and demonstrate an awareness of those occasions when the pharmacist must be consulted. There is now ongoing debate about whether this training should be further enhanced.

MCAs themselves take a pride in their work and have a sense of professionalism and accountabilty which is commendable. Although not always formalised though the supervision protocols which the RPSGB also require, there is evidence that they are particularly concerned about the safety of their actions, and are always ready to seek further advice from the pharmacist. They also believe that as a group they are undervalued and they are unsure of their positions within pharmacy (Hibbert, Bissell and Ward, 2002). This needs to be addressed.

Multidisciplinary teams

Another way of increasing capacity and extending services, again in the community pharmacy setting, is to bring in other trained professionals. Small local initiatives have successfully demonstrated the feasibilty of basing health promotion assistants in community pharmacies, and other examples include doctors, chiropodists and opticians, and social workers. These initiatives are often, but not always time limited projects associated with a targeted campaign. In one such initiative in Scotland, nurses have worked alongside community pharmacists giving flu immunisations to customers who found it more convenient to access this from the pharmacy than from their GP.

Automation

Automated dispensing is well established in the acute sector in the US and continental Europe yet, apart from a few notable exceptions (Pharmaceutical Journal, 2003: 270, 359), has not been fully adopted by hospitals in the UK. Automated dispensing has the potential to free up staff and reduce errors, and there is even greater potential for this if linked to systems of electronic prescribing which are now being proposed. Its lower uptake in the UK is probably largely related to the drivers for introducing automation, which were specific to the health care systems in the host countries, and did not apply to the UK.

If automated dispensing is little used in the hospital service, it is even less used in the community setting, although this too may be set to change. It has recently been announced that one multiple is to introduce robotic dispensing into its pharmacies (*Pharmaceutical Journal*, 2003: 270, 177), and three independent community pharmacies already have systems installed (*Pharmaceutical Journal*, 2003: 270,

106). This may well be an important route in future for releasing professional time.

A practice manager role?

Whereas the use of technicians and MCAs releases pharmacists from the more routine and often technical tasks, the final option presented here suggests employing a manager to take on the administrative and business tasks. This would be akin to the Practice Manager role in General Practice. We are unaware of any current models of this, although to some extent branches of large multiples with non-pharmacist floor managers, may well provide some useful insights.

Progress and the future

In this final section of the chapter, we will present a series of case studies to illustrate progress, ending with a vision of the future.

Management of prescribed medicines and chronic conditions

A shift from product to patient-oriented services has been a feature of UK and international pharmacy literature since the late 1980s. This shift is best illustrated by the concept of 'pharmaceutical care' (Hepler and Strand, 1990) in which pharmacists take responsibility for preventing and detecting patients' medication problems and for implementing a plan to resolve them. In England the term 'medicines management' has featured more prominently and includes a broader range of medicines-related pharmacist inputs at population level as well as pharmaceutical care at individual patient level. The term medicines management also includes services provided by other health care professionals, and a range of medicines management projects are being supported by the National Prescribing Centre. In Scotland, medicines management is used as a term only to refer to the population level and pharmaceutical care is retained at the individual patient level. Despite a high level of international consensus about the direction of travel, however, implementing pharmaceutical care/medicines management has been difficult to achieve.

The concept of pharmaceutical care has been around for over 10 years, and it could be argued that hospital-based 'clinical pharmacy' already encompasses its key features. These are still developing with pharmacist input at admission and in discharge clinics and the sharing of medication information with community pharmacy colleagues at discharge. Community pharmacy practice, however, has not yet universally adopted the practice of pharmaceutical care, although there are beacon projects demonstrating the feasibility and benefits of this approach (Case Study 1).

Legislation to allow supplementary prescribing by pharmacists for chronic conditions was introduced in April 2003. However, before this date there were examples of practice where pharmacists in hospital and primary care were running clinics, as Case Study 2 shows.

Management of minor ailments

Community pharmacists have traditionally given advice on minor ailments to customers purchasing OTC medicines. This role was, until recently, regarded firmly as 'private sector' work. However innovative schemes throughout England and Scotland have integrated this work into the NHS (Case Study 3).

Case Study 1: the community pharmacy medicines management study

The Community Pharmacy Medicine Management project started in 2002. This project involves over 60 community pharmacies, over 1400 patients, and 39 GP practices. These are in nine health authority areas across England, and cover a range of urban and rural locations, deprivation categories and ethnic groups. In the project, consenting patients with coronary heart disease, with the agreement of their GP, attend a community pharmacist of their choice for a formal medicine management consultation. At this appointment, the pharmacist, who has already obtained basic information on medication and medical history from the general practice, reviews the patient's medication. Objectives of the review include an assessment of the appropriateness of the prescription according to current guidelines of best practice, confirming that all of the medicines needed are being prescribed based on the patient's diagnosis, and checking that relevant monitoring tests have been done. The pharmacist also checks the patient's understanding of their diagnosis and treatment, as well as addressing lifestyle issues as appropriate. It is up to the pharmacist to prioritise the interventions, communicate them to both patient and GP and monitor subsequent progress. It is anticipated that there may be subsequent opportunistic interventions and reinforcement of advice at the point of any future pharmacy transactions, whether related to dispensed medicines or OTC purchases. The extent of this will be quantified, as the project has been set up as a randomised controlled trial which is currently being evaluated and will report in 2004 (Community Pharmacy Medicines Management study *http://www.psnc.org.uk/* [accessed 19 June 2003]).

Case Study 2: prescribing in primary and secondary care

A pharmacist working in a GP surgery set up a clinic for patients with hypertension. Together with the GPs and the practice nurse, she developed protocols for assessment, selection of treatment and monitoring of progress for each patient. Prior to the introduction of supplementary prescribing, each prescription recommended by the pharmacist had to be authorised by a doctor. However, the pharmacist can now prescribe in her own right. Other examples of pharmacist-run clinics in primary care include chronic pain management, anticoagulant control, post-heart attack medication and medication review for older people.

Pharmacists in hospitals are running anticoagulant clinics and are increasingly involved in medication review on admission and at discharge. Pharmacist prescribing at discharge is becoming increasingly common. See *http://www.doh.gov.uk/supplementaryprescribing/* [accessed 19 June 2003].

Case Study 3: community pharmacy NHS minor ailments schemes

Transfer of consultations for the management of minor ailments from GPs to community pharmacists improves public access to advice and treatment as well as utilising pharmacists' skills. Affordability of OTC medicines for self-treatment is sometimes a reason why people consult the doctor. Local schemes have now been established in 15 Primary Care Trusts in England and two Health Boards in Scotland. Pharmacists and GPs agree the ailments for which people will be encouraged to visit the pharmacy rather than the doctor for treatment. Those who do not pay NHS prescription charges can obtain certain medicines free of charge from the pharmacy as part of the new service. Evaluation has shown that the pharmacy schemes are well-received by doctors and patients and that they reduce the number of GP consultations for minor illness (Hassell *et al.*, 2001; Anonymous, 2002). More patients get free medicines from pharmacies over the counter (Pharmaceutical Journal, 201: 267, 767–73).

Promotion of healthy lifestyles

A major recent review of the published evidence has demonstrated the potential contribution that community pharmacists could make to improving public health (Anderson and Blenkinsopp, 2003). Smoking cessation (Case Study 4), supply of emergency hormonal contraception, lipid management and drug misuse services were strongly recommended by the review. The review also found that both pharmacists and the public currently see health topics involving the use of medicines as those most suitable for pharmacist involvement, suggesting that further work is needed if the pharmacist's role is to be extended here.

Advice and information for other health professionals

The increasing complexity of medicines and numbers of patients on multiple medications mean that pharmacists' knowledge is likely to be needed more often. Hospital pharmacists have long been consulted by medical and nursing staff about decisions on the prescribing and administration of medicines. Community pharmacists' role as advisers to GPs is increasing through the sessional practice-based work which many are now undertaking, and pharmacists are now in some cases central to strategic decisions on prescribing (Case Study 5).

Adoption of new roles

Until recently little was known about the initiation and spread of innovation in community pharmacy. A recent study of innovation in community pharmacy found that some of the new roles envisaged by the Royal Pharmaceutical Society and government had been implemented (Tann

---

Case Study 4: smoking cessation service

Smoking is said to be the most preventable cause of major morbidity and mortality (associated with cancer, and respiratory and coronary heart disease). Recent understanding, gained from theories of behavioural change, has supported the development of more effective smoking cessation interventions, tailored to the individual's stage of change. These are primarily counselling-based with the addition of pharmacological support as appropriate. The parallel availability of nicotine replacement products over the counter from community pharmacists has made the community pharmacist and his/her staff well placed to support smokers in their quit attempts. Research studies have demonstrated that community pharmacists can effectively provide both intensive (Maguire, McElnay and Drummond, 2001) and brief opportunistic advice (Sinclair *et al.*, 1998, 1999a and 1999b) and that long term smoking cessation status is achieved. Additional ongoing support as provided by commercial schemes such as the Pro change initiative (Anderson and Mair, 2002) is also welcomed by pharmacy customers. At the present time, many community pharmacists across the UK are taking part in locally-funded smoking cessation initiatives, helping the NHS achieve its targets in this important public health area. The recent introduction of Patient Group Directions has also enhanced the service pharmacists can provide by allowing provision of Nicotine Replacement Therapy products outwith their product license, for example to pregnant women, or people with heart disease.

Case Study 5: pharmacists as prescribing advisers

The first pharmacists began to be appointed as prescribing advisers (termed 'Pharmaceutical Advisers') to Health Authorities (HAs) in the mid to late 1980s. At that time most HAs had a Medical Adviser whose role it was to analyse local prescribing patterns and advise on necessary changes. By the time the 105 English HAs were abolished in 2002, most employed at least one Pharmaceutical Adviser, and the role of prescribing adviser was clearly seen as pharmaceutical territory. Almost all of the 300 Primary Care Trusts in England now employ a Pharmaceutical Adviser (sometimes now called 'Head of Medicines Management' or a similar title) to advise on strategy to manage prescribing and medicines management locally. The strategies developed by these pharmacists are often now implemented at GP surgery level by pharmacists who work in an operational capacity on a sessional basis. These pharmacists began by analysing prescribing data and conducting audits of prescribing but are increasingly taking on a clinical role in medication review and supplementary prescribing for individual patients (Mullen, Hassell and Noyce, 2002; Jesson, Wilson and Blenkinsopp, 2002).

---

and Blenkinsopp, 2003). Individual pharmacist innovators were found to be predominantly from independent pharmacies, although the authors acknowledged that innovators within corporate structures may simply be less visible. The research found rich examples of individual innovation in single pharmacies and small pharmacy groups. Networks were found to be critical to the wider spread and sustaining of innovation by enabling pharmacists to adopt worked-up service delivery models. Pharmacists' perceptions about possible negative responses from GPs and the public were important blocks to activity. Pharmacists who adopted innovations varied in their support needs to sustain the new ways of working. In any setting, innovator pharmacists were characterised by a strong sense of professional self-esteem, by effective use of all members of the pharmacy staff, and by effective networking with other health and social care professionals (Tann and Blenkinsopp, 2003). These findings help to explain why major change has been slow to occur in community pharmacy and to offer pointers for the future.

Vision for the future

This chapter has reviewed policy development and implementation in pharmacy. We have identified the future roles envisaged for pharmacists, discussed the factors driving and resisting change, and used case studies to illustrate the types of development that are likely to become more widespread.

In the future, pharmacists will be directly involved in patient care through prescribing, monitoring and reviewing patients' medication. They will work more closely with patients, making decisions about treatment choices and medicines use in partnership. As the transfer of tasks from doctors to other health professionals continues, prescribing will be undertaken by a range of individuals. A patient with multiple diseases and treatments might be seen by a GP, a practice nurse and a pharmacist in a hospital out-patients clinic, all of whom may prescribe for that patient. For patients living in the community, it is likely that the pharmacist will become the only health professional with a full picture of the patient's medication.

With these changes in place, supply of medicines will become more convenient for patients, who will be able to order and obtain their medicines via the internet as well as, or instead of, visits to the pharmacy, with the process being co-ordinated by the pharmacist. All this holds out the prospect of community pharmacies becoming accessible centres for public health services – places offering support for self-care and for patients' self-management of chronic conditions.

Notes

1. Scotland (Scottish Executive, 2002), Wales (Welsh Assembly Government, 2002) and Northern Ireland (Department of Health, Social Services and Public Safety, 2003).
2. Prior to 1987 there had been no restriction on the granting of a contract for NHS dispensing to a pharmacy. Restrictions were introduced for the first time in 1987 requiring primary care organisations only to grant a new pharmacy contract where one was shown to be both 'necessary and desirable'.
3. The National Patient Safety Agency (NPSA) has a remit to improve safety in the NHS through a culture of reporting of, and learning from, adverse incidents and 'near misses'. See *http://www.npsa.nhs.uk/* [accessed 11 June 2003].
4. A Patient Group Direction (PGD) is a written document that authorises the supply of a specific medicine to certain patients under conditions defined in a protocol. PGDs authorise the supply of some medicines by a nurse or pharmacist that would otherwise be 'Prescription Only'.
5. Independent prescribers – professionals who are responsible for the initial assessment of the patient and for devising the broad treatment plan, with the authority to prescribe the medicines required as part of that plan. Supplementary prescribers – professionals who are authorised to prescribe certain medicines for patients whose condition has been diagnosed or assessed by an independent prescriber, within an agreed assessment and treatment plan.

6. In community pharmacy PGDs have been used as the basis of services supplying emergency hormonal contraception and smoking cessation treatments on the NHS.

References

Anderson, C. and Mair, A. (2002) 'Prochange Adult Smokers Program: Northumberland pilot', *International Journal of Pharmacy Practice*, 10, 4, 281–7.

Anderson, C. and Blenkinsopp, A. (2003) *The Evidence Relating to Community Pharmacy's Contribution to Improving the Public's Health: a critical review of the literature 1990–2001*, London: Royal Pharmaceutical Society of Great Britain.

Anonymous (2002) 'No Obstacle to Pharmacists Prescribing', *Pharmaceutical Journal*, 269, 28 September, 450.

Association of Directors of Social Services (2003) ADSS Response to the Office of Fair Trading Report on The Control of Entry Regulations and Retail Pharmacy Services in the UK [online], Association of Directors of Social Services. Available from: *http://www.adss.org.uk/publications/consresp/2003/entry.shtml* [Accessed 19 June 2003].

Audit Commission (2001) *A Spoonful of Sugar: medicines management in NHS hospitals*, London: Audit Commission.

Audit Commission (2003) *Primary Care Prescribing: a bulletin for primary care trusts*, London: Audit Commission.

Bell, H. M., McElnay, J. C. and Hughes, C. M. (1999) 'A Self-reported Work Sampling Study in Community Pharmacy Practice', *Pharmacy World & Science*, 21, 5, 210–16.

Blenkinsopp, A., Boardman, H., Jesson, J. and Wilson, K. (1999) 'A Pharmacy Workforce Survey in the West Midlands: (1) Current work profiles and patterns', *Pharmaceutical Journal*, 263, 4 December, 909–13.

Blenkinsopp, A., Boardman, H., Jesson, J. and Wilson, K. (2001) 'A Pharmacy Workforce Survey in the West Midlands: (3) Primary Care Pharmacists', *Pharmaceutical Journal*, 266, 19 May, 684–7.

Boardman, H., Blenkinsopp, A., Jesson, J. and Wilson, K. (2001) 'A Pharmacy Workforce Survey in the West Midlands: (4) Morale and motivation', *Pharmaceutical Journal*, 267, 10 November, 685–90.

Department of Health (1999) Review of Prescribing, Supply and Administration of Medicines. Final Report [online], Department of Health. Available from: *http://www.doh.gov.uk/prescrib.htm* [Accessed 19 June 2003].

Department of Health (2000) *Pharmacy in the Future: implementing the NHS Plan – a programme for pharmacy*, London: Department of Health.

Department of Health (2001) *Building a Safer NHS for Patients*, London: The Stationery Office.

Department of Health (2002) *Discussion Paper: pharmacy workforce in the new NHS*, London: Department of Health.

Department of Health, Social Services and Public Safety (2003) *Making It Better: a strategy for pharmacy in the community. A consultation paper*, Belfast: Department of Health, Social Services and Public Safety.

Fisher, C. M., Corrigan, O. I. and Henman, M. C. (1991) 'A Study of Community Pharmacy Practice. I. Pharmacists' work patterns', *Journal of Social & Administrative Pharmacy*, 8, 1, 15–24.

Furniss, L., Burns, A., Craig, S. K., Scobie, S., Cooke, J. and Faragher, B. (2000) 'Effects of a Pharmacist's Medication Review in Nursing Homes: randomised controlled trial', *British Journal of Psychiatry*, 176, 6, 563–7.

Hassell, K., Whittington, Z., Cantrill, J., Bates, F., Rogers, A. and Noyce, P. (2001) 'Managing Demand: the transfer of self-limiting conditions from general practice to community pharmacy management', *British Medical Journal*, 323, 21 July, 146–7.

Hassell, K., Fisher, R., Nichols, L. and Shann, P. (2002) 'Contemporary Workforce Patterns and Historical Trends: the pharmacy labour market over the past 40 years', *Pharmaceutical Journal*, 269, 31 August, 291–6.

Hepler, C. D. and Strand, L. M. (1990) 'Opportunities and Responsibilities in Pharmaceutical Care', *American Journal of Hospital Pharmacy*, 47, 533–43.

Hibbert, D., Bissell, P. and Ward, P. R. (2002) 'Consumerism and Professional Work in the Community Pharmacy', *Sociology of Health and Illness*, 24, 1, 46–65.

Jesson, J., Wilson, K. A. and Blenkinsopp, A. (2002) 'Primary Care Pharmacists: a profile', *Journal of Social and Administrative Pharmacy*, 19, 99–104.

King's Fund (2002) *Developing Community Pharmacy: what pharmacists think is needed*, London: King's Fund.

Mackie, C. A., Lawson, D. H., Campbell, A., Maclaren, A. G. and Waigh, R. (1999) 'A Randomised Controlled Trial of Medication Review in Patients Receiving Polypharmacy in General Practice', *Pharmaceutical Journal*, 263, 18 September, R16–17.

Maguire, T. A., McElnay, J. C. and Drummond, A. (2001) 'A Randomised Controlled Trial of a Smoking Cessation Intervention Based in Community Pharmacies', *Addiction*, 96, 2, 325–31.

Marinker, M. (1997) *From Compliance to Condordance – achieving partnership in medicine-taking*, London: Royal Pharmaceutical Society of Great Britain.

Medicines Control Agency (2002) *Consultation letter MLX 284. Supplementary prescribing. Proposals for supplementary prescribing by nurses and pharmacists and proposed amendments to Prescription Only Medicines (human use) order 1997* [online] Medicines Control Agency. Available from: *http://www.doh.gov.uk/supplementaryprescribing/* [Accessed 19 June 2003].

Moore, S. R. (1999) 'Pharmacy's Contribution to Public Health in the 20th Century', *Journal of American Pharmaceutical Association*, 39, 744–5.

Mullen, R., Hassell, K. and Noyce, P. R. (2002) Pharmacists Working in Primary Care: two extreme cases [online] Health Services Research and Pharmacy Practice Conference 2003. Available from: *http://hsrpp.org.uk/abstracts/2002_07.shtml* [Accessed 19 June 2003].

Nuffield Foundation (1986) *Pharmacy: a report to the Nuffield Foundation*, London: Nuffield Foundation.

Office of Fair Trading (2003) *The Control of Entry Regulations and Retail Pharmacy Services in the UK*, London: Office of Fair Trading.

Royal Pharmaceutical Society of Great Britain (1995) *Pharmacy in a New Age*, London: Royal Pharmaceutical Society of Great Britain.

Royal Pharmaceutical Society of Great Britain (1997) *Building the Future*, London: Royal Pharmaceutical Society of Great Britain.

Royal Pharmaceutical Society of Great Britain (2003) Response to the Department of Health discussion paper 'Pharmacy Workforce in the New NHS' [online] Royal Pharmaceutical Society of Great Britain. Available from: *http://www.rpsgb.org.uk/pdfs/pworknewnhs.pdf* [Accessed 19 June 2003].

Royal Pharmaceutical Society of Great Britain and Department of Health (1992) *Pharmaceutical Care and Joint Reports of Royal Pharmaceutical Society of Great Britain and Department of Health,* London: Royal Pharmaceutical Society of Great Britain.

Rutter, P. M., Hunt, A. J., Darracott, R. and Jones, I. F. (1998) 'A Subjective Study of how Community Pharmacists in Great Britain Spend their Time', *Journal of Social & Administrative Pharmacy,* 15, 4, 252–61.

Scottish Executive (2002) *The Right Medicine – a strategy for pharmaceutical care in Scotland,* Edinburgh: Scottish Executive.

Sinclair, H. K., Bond, C. M., Lennox, A. S., Silcock, J., Winfield, A. J. and Donnan, P. T. (1998) 'Training Pharmacists and Pharmacy Assistants in the Stage of Change Model of Smoking Cessation: a randomised controlled trial in Scotland', *Tobacco Control,* 7, 3, 253–61.

Sinclair, H. K., Bond, C. M. and Lennox, A. S. (1999a) 'The Long Term Learning Effect of Training in Stage of Change for Smoking Cessation', *International Journal of Pharmacy Practice,* 7, 1, 1–11.

Sinclair, H. K., Silcock, J., Bond, C. M., Lennox, A. S. and Winfield, A. J. (1999b) 'The Cost Effectiveness of Intensive Pharmaceutical Intervention in Assisting People to Stop Smoking', *International Journal of Pharmacy Practice,* 7, 2, 107–12.

Tann, J. and Blenkinsopp, A. (2003) *Understanding Innovation in Community Pharmacy: an interim report,* London: Royal Pharmaceutical Society of Great Britain.

Tully, M., and Cantrill, J. (1999) 'Role of the Pharmacist in Evidence-based Prescribing in Primary Care', in M. Gabbay (ed.) *The Evidence-based Primary Care Handbook,* London: Royal Society of Medicine Press.

Welsh Assembly Government (2002) *Remedies for Success: a strategy for pharmacy in Wales,* Cardiff: Welsh Assembly Government.

12
The Future Health Workforce: an Overview of Trends

Charlotte Sausman

Introduction

This chapter considers some possible future directions for the health service drawing on a variety of sources collated for a policy futures project.[1] It uses an array of 'visions' of the future, developed by different groups, to suggest how the future workforce might change and what new roles and skills will be required. It then goes on to broaden the scope of inquiry by examining wider trends and issues – from scientific developments and demographic change to political drivers and socio-economic change – that will affect the kind of future that can be achieved. The chapter begins by briefly describing the current health workforce and the ways in which it has been changing.

The present health workforce

The overall shape and size of the health workforce in the UK remains shadowy. There is no doubt that it is large – over a million people are employed in the NHS, which makes it the largest employer in Europe. This workforce includes doctors, nurses, therapists, pharmacists, a range of other health professionals and scientists as well as support staff, managers and administrators. Around three quarters of the NHS workforce work in hospitals. As other chapters in this volume (see also the Appendix) illustrate, the health workforce is significant in terms of its size, and complexity, as well as the fact that staff are working in, and managing, complex organisations with sophisticated technology and procedures in a highly politicised environment.

The health workforce would be significant even it remained static, but many of the issues to be considered concern changes that are taking place – changes in the development of professional groups and their roles, changes in the technology and therapeutic potential of health care, changes in the population and future heath needs and demands, and changes in the economy and society – that will impact on the demand and supply of the health workforce.

Over the last twenty years, the hospital workforce has fallen by around 10 per cent. Hospital nurses have declined in number, although this is largely accounted for by student nurses no longer being counted as nursing staff. Medical, professional and technical staffs have increased significantly (by over 50 per cent) and administrative and clerical staff have grown by 30 per cent. Directly employed domestic ancillary staff account for most of the overall fall, due to contracting out for services such as catering and cleaning (Wanless, 2001: 186–7).

However, the key issue is whether the supply of health workers, and in particular, the professional health workforce, is at a level that will meet demand – in terms of the future health needs of the population, and the expectations of the public. We are currently in a position where the overwhelming issue is a shortage in supply in all professions, and yet there is increasing demand, principally to meet reforms being put in place to improve the NHS. The government is committed to providing significant increases in the professional workforce in order to implement the ten year NHS Plan (Department of Health, 2000). Progress in meeting the Plan's target numbers has been made, although reservations remain (Buchan and Edwards, 2000). Internationally, the UK at present employs fewer doctors and nurses per head of the population than other Organisation for Economic Co-operation and Development countries (OECD, 2001).

There are two questions to be considered. First, will the required increases in supply be achieved in the future? Here, the pattern of international recruitment is important, since the UK relies on foreign nurses to meet current gaps in supply. We also need to consider whether the professionals who are recruited by the NHS will be retained or whether the nursing workforce in particular will continue to lose experienced staff. The second key question is: even if the workforce supply targets are achieved, will they be sufficient to meet the requirements of the future health service? The Wanless report, commissioned by the Treasury to examine future funding requirements of the National Health Service concluded that NHS Plan targets for nursing would meet their future scenarios if they were achieved, but that the planned increase in doctors was 'well short of needs' – by a figure of 25,000 after 20 years (Wanless, 2002: 90).

What are the reasons for these challenges? Nurses are predominantly a female workforce. Over the last 20 years, employment opportunities for women have increased and this has reduced nurses' relative earnings in relation to the workforce as a whole. Such changes are manifested in a nursing profession that is ageing, and older cohorts are not being fully replenished by younger groups. The economic considerations relating to choosing nursing as a profession are felt most strongly in the capital city, which sees staff losses of up to 38 per cent per annum and overseas nurses account for more than one in ten nurses (Buchan, Finlayson and Gough, 2002). Here, competition for skilled workers as well as property prices exacerbates problems for the recruitment and retention of nursing staff.

In contrast, doctors have maintained their relative earnings in relation to the workforce as a whole over the past 20 years (Wanless, 2001: 190). However, the UK still relies on overseas trained doctors to fill gaps in supply. Most of these doctors come from outside Europe, significantly from India, New Zealand, South-east Asia and Africa. The medical workforce, like the nursing workforce is ageing and there are concerns that certain cohorts are not being replenished and that more doctors are taking early retirement. Over half of medical graduates are now women (Young and Leese, 1999) and a third of medical staff in hospitals in 1998 were women (Dowie and Langman, 1999). The growth of female GPs is a significant trend, which also has implications for the future organisation of general practice, given that women express a greater desire to take career breaks and work part time than their male counterparts. This may have consequences for the traditional GP partnership, which may not be seen as a suitable option by women.

The UK is not alone in facing shortages of supply in terms of doctors and nurses. Other developed countries also rely on overseas staff to fill gaps in supply. With a more 'global' labour market for health professionals in the future, and a clear European-wide market as barriers to mobility are reduced, countries may find that they have less control of their health workforce as others to tap into their countries' resources in times of shortage. In this context – many would describe it as a crisis – a range of different agencies and groups have conducted seminars, conferences, commissioned research and policy analysis to think about the future, and produced recommendations about how the situation can be improved. These are considered in the next section.

New arguments, new ideas

The current government's 10-year NHS plan is to reform the health service so that it meets public expectations and so that the requirements of patients are placed in a more central position. There is much talk of re-engineering, establishing critical care pathways and team-work, all designed to focus care around the patient's experience and to ensure as smooth a journey for the patient as possible through the system. This means changing the way groups of staff are organised so that teams of people with different skills and expertise work together because they are concerned with a particular patient, or having a key member of staff who co-ordinates the care of an individual patient, rather than organising in a traditional way around clinical specialties (see Lissauer, Chapter 1). Current developments, for example, include the expansion of the prescribing rights of nurses and in primary care, nurses taking on roles in screening, health promotion and the management of chronic diseases. In secondary care, nurses are taking on responsibility for co-ordination of services such as outpatients' clinics, minor injury services, and cardiology day care. Lissauer (Chapter 1) also reports on community pharmacists working with primary care to run services such as smoking cessation, a trend picked up by the Wanless review (see Blenkinsopp and Bond, Chapter 11).

Professional organisations have produced their own models of care for the future. The British Medical Association Health Policy and Economic Research Unit (2002), in their report on the future health-care workforce, propose changes to nursing roles so that a nurse practitioner becomes the first port of call for patients. In hospitals, nurses will be responsible for the co-ordination of clinical care. The analysis removes the physician role from the changes, the argument being that change leaves physicians to focus on clinical skills. This is a theme running through other reports from professional groups on future roles. For example, the Royal College of Physicians (Royal College of Physicians, 2000) recommended the future expansion of existing nursing roles, of the consultant grade, and the creation of a new post of 'health care practitioner' to complement the work of nurses. It has also advocated the use of physician assistants to assist in the burden of work on doctors, a model developed in the United States (Hutchinson, Marks and Pittilo, 2001; Mittman, Cawley and Fenn, 2002). An approach centred around the patient, however, would involve re-orientating all roles involved.

The changing role of nurses and nursing is key to all visions of future health care. Multi-skilling and a flexible healthcare workforce are required and most change is envisaged in the nursing workforce. The Royal College of Nursing has addressed the future nurse in several publications and recently opened a debate on the issue amongst its members (Naish, 2003). Nursing organisations rightly want to shape the debate about the consequences of change for the future identity of nurses and to consider implications for the definition of 'nursing', when nurses are extending their role into new areas whilst retaining responsibility for basic nursing care. Will nursing become a generic or specialist role in the future? Does the extension of roles mean placing medical knowledge and medical skills above traditional nursing skills in a hierarchy? Nursing organisations are searching for a preferred future for the nursing profession that allows new roles to be developed that improve patient care and develop nursing skills whilst at the same time maintaining the coherent identify of the nursing profession (Royal College of Nursing (Great Britain), 2003; see also Williams, Chapter 5).

The National Health Service Confederation (2000) set out a vision of the future workforce where services are organised around patients and their diseases or injuries rather than as at present around occupational groups. The Confederation advocated an increase in staff levels but also changes in workforce categories, such as 'doctor' being a training period with less emphasis on service delivery, clear competence-based career stages for consultant nurses and other professionals and assistants to provide various levels of support.

The recommendations of the 'The Future Healthcare Workforce' team (Future Healthcare Workforce, 1996; Future Healthcare Workforce, 1999) are based on the notion of a 'generic carer', responsible for the majority of patient care, with some carers functioning at a professional level and others as support workers. Future doctors, therapists and scientists are projected to carry out more focused roles specific to their knowledge and skills, with some of their current functions being provided by this generic worker. The main thrust of their thinking is towards an increased role for support workers by 2005:

> We anticipate that there will be a spectrum of roles in the future and a major expansion in the numbers of 'non-professional' staff. As an indication of the degree of change that we are confident is both desirable and achievable we envisage that, by the year 2005, support staff will account for 40 percent of the 'generic carer' workforce. In

comparison, support workers account for only 28 percent of the nursing & midwifery core workforce at present. (Future Healthcare Workforce, 1996: 81)

Such a model has proved controversial. Nursing organisations feel that the trend towards generic skills will hit nurses, who will lose their accumulated skills, knowledge and status. Such is one of the real tensions within debates about the future workforce, between demands for professional groups to be flexible and change the way they train and work in the interests of patient-focused care, and the preservation of highly valued professional status, practices, training and ethos developed by the professions. Any re-orienting of organisational processes in the future will have to be successful in dealing with these tensions as well as with the aspirations of 'unqualified' nurses (see Thornley, Chapter 8).

One of the most comprehensive assessments regarding the future of health care is provided by the Wanless review, which was commissioned by the Treasury to investigate long-term resource requirements in health care. The review produced its final report in 2002 and it is worth looking at its analysis in some detail, both because it considered the future of health care in broad terms and also because its recommendations have been picked up government and will be used to inform government policy.

Wanless (2002) examined a wide array of factors likely to affect the demand and supply of health services in the future. They include the demographic picture and the health status of the population. They also include the demand for health services for a given need – where, to date, experience has shown that healthier, more affluent populations consume more health services rather than less. Other important factors are directly related to the health service. They include investment in technology, both medical advances and information technology; human resources and how the workforce is deployed; and finally, whether there productivity gains are likely in the future.

The Wanless review took projections of these factors and translated them into three scenarios in order to give a picture of how the dynamics might change. The three scenarios are described in Figure 12.1. In the three Wanless scenarios, there is similar investment into the service. They differ in terms of the response of the health service and how health care needs and demands change in the future. They therefore present alternative pictures of how the service could change in the future for a given level of investment. It is not the amount of money that is invested – but how it is deployed – and how we as consumers of health care may change in our relationship with the health service, our demands on it, and our engagement with the service regarding own health status.

In the *solid progress* scenario Wanless describes people being more 'engaged' in relation to their health, which causes life expectancy to rise, health status to improve and people use the primary care system more appropriately. The health service is described as 'responsive' in this scenario, where there are high rates of technology uptake and a more efficient use of resources than at the present. In the *slow uptake* scenario, our engagement with the service does not change, life expectancy rises by a small amount and health status is not improved. In terms of the health service response, there is low technology uptake and low productivity. In the *fully engaged* scenario, public engagement makes the most dramatic improvement, health status improves considerably, life expectancy increases and people have confidence in the health service. The health service responds well, with a focus on disease prevention.

While the Wanless review does not provide detailed workforce data based on its analysis (it recommends that NHS workforce planning bodies should undertake this exercise), several important trends are identified. Overall, the three scenarios will require an increase of about 300,000 staff over 20 years, which includes more doctors (62,000), more nurses (108,000), more therapists and scientists (45,000) and health care assistants (74,000) (Wanless, 2002: 88). The report predicts an increase in primary care activity in the future that will require a doubling in the demand for GPs. This is even with a development of primary care that shows increased prevention and better chronic disease management with more nurse-led services.

'Solid progress'	'Slow uptake'	'Fully engaged'
People live longer with even split of extra healthy years and ill-health; better skill mix in NHS; good take-up of technology; general improvements in public health and self care; higher expectations lead to higher demands on service.	Increased life expectancy with longer periods of ill-health; little improvement in public health or narrowing of health inequalities; small productivity gain from better deployment of staff or use of technology.	Increased healthy life expectancy; major improvements in public engagement with health – better care of own health and higher demands on services; responsive NHS makes use of technology and staff.

Figure 12.1: Three future scenarios for the NHS

Source: Wanless, 2002.

Both in the *solid progress* and *fully engaged* scenarios, increased GP visits are predicted. Wanless projects that increases in doctors and nurses are required to achieve each of the future scenarios as well as skill mix changes – for example, by 20 per cent of GP and junior doctors' work being shifted to nurse practitioners, and some nurses' work being carried out by healthcare assistants. Wanless does not consider in any detail possible configurations of staff in the future along these lines, but focuses on the resource implications, noting that if, for example, GP and junior doctor work is transferred to nurse practitioners, this will ease pressure on GP demand, but have a knock-on effect on nurse supply.

So, what we can discern from Wanless is that overall increases in staff are required to meet future expectations of the service, and here, it is doctor numbers that are particularly lacking. Wanless notes that significant change in the skill mix of the health workforce is required, with a greater role for nurse practitioners and health care assistants. What is key to the achievement of the more desirable of the three future scenarios is the relationship between the service and the public, and the response of the service to the future demands placed upon it.

Drivers of workforce change

How likely is it that the required futures set out by Wanless and others will be achieved and what are the factors affecting this? Four groups of factors will be considered: technology and scientific developments, demography and disease, political drivers, and wider social and economic change. In considering each of these, examples of how future health care – and the hence the future workforce – might be different will be given.

Technology and scientific developments

It is difficult to do justice to the range of medical and technological advances that are being made – given increasing therapeutic potential, new knowledge about preventive strategies and greater technical expertise in health. A few examples are: developments in biotechnology (using biological processes to make products for treatment) such as bio-pharmaceuticals, which are being used in areas such as the treatment of brain tumours and slowing the progression of Parkinson's Disease; bioengineering which involves advances in cell biology and plastic manufacture to produce artificial organs including kidneys, lung and heart; minimal access and image guided surgery; and transplantation developments focusing on the elimination of organ rejection (Robert, 1999). There are also significant possible applications from advancing genetic knowledge; by 2010 individualised medicine from pharmaco-genetics may be apparent (Foresight, 2002; The Institute for Alternative Futures, 2003).

There is an increasing role for technology in health care both in developing the services and treatment offered and in influencing the settings in which treatment and care take place. For example, there are developments in cognitive therapy and web-based or IT-based self-administered therapy for simple depression, panic disorders, and phobias. This suggests that for a number of conditions 'information-ists' will be able to create software that will cover possibly 25–30 per cent of what GPs do now. It is predicted that by 2019, $1000 dollars will buy a machine with the computing capability of the human mind. Interactions with it will be via gestures and voice (Kurzweil, 2001). Technology via Personal Data Assistant (PDAs) and hand-held computers will be used to provide information on health issues on virtually any dimension. Robots can already be used for a variety of tasks including dispensing in hospitals and surgery.[2] The Technology Foresight Programme predicted in the mid-1990s that by 2010–14, 10 per cent of surgical interventions could be carried out by robotic techniques (Robert, 1999).

For the workforce, such developments require the development of new skills and new knowledge. New surgical techniques, telemedicine, evidence-based-medicine (EBM), on-line health services, and electronic health databases will require specific skills from staff such as highly specific technology skills in certain areas; research skills (EBM, genetics, use of databases) and data and information management. As well as a demand for new skills from the health workforce, the impact of new technology and scientific developments will change existing roles from one professional group to another, and will need to influence the future education and training of professionals. Figure 12.2 illustrates how genetics is impacting on health professionals.

The future location of care will also be influenced by scientific and technological developments. Figure 12.3 summarises some the likely impacts. Technologies are being developed which allow self-diagnosis and self-treatment and home care. The Wanless review predicts initial diagnosis being received in future in a variety of settings, facilitated by developments in technology. General and less specialised medicine and surgery will move out of large hospitals and hospitals will focus on specialist treatments.

- Some physicians in all medical specialties must gain special expertise in genetics.
- The UK should plan for greater numbers of medical geneticists.
- Genetic nurses and associates will lead educational programmes and be involved in patient care and counselling. Arrangements should be made to establish accredited training programmes for these groups.
- In-service training will need to be implemented for all health professionals on the implications of genetics. Training should be multi-disciplinary and include basic genetic knowledge, ethical, social and legal aspects, and issues around the impact of genetic testing – on individuals and families.
- The UK must develop the specialty of public health genetics and increase the numbers of public health professionals trained in genetics. Training in public health genetics should be open to a wide range of health professionals.
- GPs and the primary care team will need to have some knowledge or training in genetics and be capable of providing counselling and support services. Primary care would also be the site of genetic testing, reading a patient's 'genetic chip' and treating with pharmacogenetics.

Figure 12.2: Recommendations from Nuffield Trust genetics scenario project regarding health professionals and the impact of genetics

Source: Zimmern and Cook, 2000.

- A greater concentration of specialist expertise and equipment in a smaller number of larger centres dealing with complex cases, driven by the increasing sophistication of medicine.
- More diagnosis, treatment and monitoring taking place outside the hospital, including increases in self-diagnosis and home care.
- More conditions being treated locally in small centres linked telemetrically to specialist centres.
- Increasingly blurred distinctions between primary, secondary and tertiary care.
- Reduction in length of hospital stay.

Figure 12.3: How the location of health care may change

Source: Dargie, Dawson and Garside, 2000.

Future studies conducted in the past tell us how over-optimistic projections of the impact of science and technology can be. Already, the 'big-bang' impact of discoveries relating to the human genome are being revised in favour of a more gradual, long-term impact on the treatment of diseases. Scientific discoveries are being made at a dramatic rate, but it is their application to treatments that is the crucial issue, and one that requires cautious projections. For several years, futures studies have talked about developments such as 'smart credit cards' that will hold an individual's medical history, that can be accessed by health professionals via networked computers, or technology in the home that will enable us to monitor our own health status – heart rate, blood pressure, insulin levels – and connect to a health professional via television and email. The technology for such developments already exists, but it is the application that is more uncertain. Connecting health organisations up to an NHS 'network', and the use of computer rather than paper records is taking years longer than predicted – even from very recent projections (Simons, 2003).

The usefulness of technological developments is key to their success. Computer and chip technology had limited application outside large corporations until devices were developed that were both powerful and small. Today it is smaller technology that is more clever and more versatile – think of implants to enhance muscle tissue or nanotechnology, the scientific development of tiny molecules, many times smaller than the atom, that can be used to carry drugs through the blood stream in order to attack tumours. Few predicted the impact of mobile phone technology or the internet – that have thrived on small chip development. Fashion and consumer tastes must also not be ruled out. We can now produce smaller cars that are energy efficient – lowering fuel bills and reducing the negative impact on the environment – and yet it is bigger cars, and multiple person vehicles and trucks that are currently fashionable (Associated Press Newswires, 2003).

Demography and disease

Ultimately, it is patients who create the demand for health services. The overall burden of disease has shifted from the young to the old and from communicable to chronic diseases. Non-communicable diseases will represent the main burden of mortality and morbidity in the future. Within that group, deaths from respiratory diseases are increasing and there are adverse trends in smoking and obesity, which will be important determinants of future disease patterns in the UK. A rise in the incidence of cancer is projected for the future, which is associated with the ageing population. Latest figures from WHO show that global cancer rates could increase by 50 per cent to 15 million new cases by 2020 (World Health Organisation, 2003). In the UK, lung cancer and breast cancers are projected to pose the largest burden for women in 2015. For men, it will be prostate cancer, colon cancer and lung cancer (East Anglian Cancer Intelligence Unit, 1997).

The UK also has significant mental health problems amongst its population – from depression, which is one of the most common reasons for visiting a GP, to the 1–3 per cent of the population who suffer from severe mental problems (World Health Organisation Regional Office for Europe, 1999). Finally, there are chronic conditions that will pose a greater threat to health than in the past, such as asthma and diabetes. Research by the Department of Health also suggests that if current trends continue, by 2010 a quarter of the population will be grossly overweight (Hetherington, 2003).

There are several implications for the future workforce from the known trends in the burden of disease. First, the prevention and treatment of chronic diseases is likely to be a key function of future primary care. Obesity and diabetes are examples of conditions that can be treated in primary care in addition to services such as genetic testing, diagnostic and treatment centres and vaccination. A recent example of changes in treatment has been the prescribing of cholesterol-reducing drugs, statins, to combat heart disease, where annual prescriptions have increased 30 per cent in the last three years. A million people are now estimated to be taking statins, saving 6000 lives per annum and relieving pressure on the hospital sector. Primary care's preventive role in the form of anti-smoking campaigns, encouraging people to take more exercise and improving diet is also important. Here it is envisaged, as in the Wanless review, that nurses will be taking on new roles in the prevention and treatment of chronic disease, in prescribing and in helping patients through treatment programmes. Some GP roles are likely to become more specialised in the future as practices undertake specialist services.

Second, the interrelated nature of conditions associated with ageing and chronic disease requires well-integrated services. Figure 12.4 below gives an example of how primary care might look in the future in such a scenario.

Third, if the goal of health policy is to improve population health and tackle health inequalities, health services need to be able to respond to the combined risk factors that affect individuals and populations, and responsibility needs to be extended to businesses, schools and other community settings. Health Action Zones, along with schemes such as Neighbourhood Renewal and the Beacon Scheme for local government, were established by the current government as collaboratives to improve local population health and reduce health inequalities, although since they were established some key local organisations have either been reorganised or abolished.[3]

Finally, avoidable deaths from cancer and heart disease suggest a more appropriate mix of services in the future of preventive and curative, and community-based and hospital-based treatment. (Dargie, Dawson and Garside, 2000). The Wanless Report adopts the use of National Service Frameworks to tackle the main burden of disease – namely coronary

---

- Treating chronic disease (obesity, diabetes).
- First port of call for genetic services (testing, screening, diagnosis, counselling).
- Diagnosis and treatment.
- Vaccination.
- Prevention.
  - Anti-smoking campaigns.
  - Encouraging people to take more exercise.
  - Improving diet.
- Making booked hospital appointments.
- One-stop shops for advice, treatment and prescriptions.
- Integrated case management.
- Mobilisation of health care assistants to work alongside doctors and nurses.
- Evolution of nurses into medical practitioners and doctors into GP specialists.
- GP specialists conducting eye surgery, minor plastic and orthopaedic procedures and diagnostic services such as endoscopies.

Figure 12.4: Possible future roles of primary care

Source: Wanless, 2002; Hetherington, 2003; British Medical Association Health Policy and Economic Research Unit, 2002.

heart disease, cancer, renal disease, mental health and diabetes. They predict that the future focus will be on lifestyles, disease prevention and screening, which will put much more emphasis in the future on the expanded role of primary and community care.

Of course there are other implications for the changing pattern of disease and treatment. Figures from the Department of Health show that prescription costs rose by over 10 per cent for both the primary and secondary sectors in 2002–3, with statins accounting for 20 per cent of the increase (*Health Service Journal*, 2003). The Wanless review predicts an increase in annual spend on statins from the current level of £700 million to £2.1 billion in 2010 and this includes the assumption that all statin patents expire by 2010 (Wanless, 2002: 23).

Political drivers

We are currently in a period of sustained reform of the health service. There also appears to be something of a consensus about the direction of reform, if debate over how the system is funded is put to one side. Speeches by the Health Secretary Alan Milburn in 2002, mention mixed provision, a more diverse range of provider organisations and making use of spare capacity in the private sector in order to reduce waiting times (Timmins, 2002). Notwithstanding controversies over the development of Foundation Trusts, this is intended to be an important model of public service delivery in the future, with greater freedom from central government control and an ownership structure that includes local residents as 'members'.

It is likely that we will see greater involvement of the private and voluntary sectors in the provision of public services in the future. The private sector already participates through the funding of scientific and medical research; through the pharmaceutical industry; in the funding of private finance initiatives and public-private partnerships; and in existing provision through NHS pay beds, filling spare capacity through the NHS Concordat, and in the provision of long-term care for older people. It also supplies the health service with human resources, advice and consultancy, and the provision of significant non-clinical services – information technology, equipment, cleaning and laundry services for example. The voluntary sector is also a significant provider of public services within the welfare state, engaging with local authorities particularly in the provision of specialist services.

Market mechanisms are increasingly applied within the public sector. This takes the form of contracts used to specify relationships with a price for services provided, the separation of purchasers and providers, encouraging competition between similar organisations, and the creation of market incentives to try to improve performance. Fee for service contracts for consultants in the health service, for example, have been advocated (Le Grand, 2003).

Like other public sector workers, health sector workers have seen some changes to their terms of conditions of employment, but could see more decentralised pay structures so that pay is more related to demand and supply; elements of performance-related pay; individual appraisal and performance review; and job specifications closely defined by organisational requirements. One of the implications of such a trend is a constraint on inter-organisational working (such as the use of clinical networks), if there is an increasingly competitive environment.

At the same time as the public sector is 'opened up' in terms of new forms of ownership, new providers and new operating mechanisms, public service organisations – particularly in the health sector – increasingly have their activities scrutinised by a variety of bodies. There has been a proliferation of audit and inspection bodies and mechanisms by which organisations are held to account, financially and on the quality of services. Organisations are now required to work to National Service Frameworks that detail organisation and treatment in particular fields. The National Performance Assessment Framework rates NHS organisations across a range of performance indicators in areas such as waiting lists and productivity measures and organisations are held to account by bodies such as the Commission for Health Improvement, the Audit Commission and the National Audit Office. Those that do not achieve a required standard are liable to direct intervention by government, including the possibility of replacement of the senior management by external managers who have a proven record of success.

In part, the increase in regulation, audit and inspection of public services has been a response by government to the charge that despite substantial recent investment in public services, the British public believe that public services are failing. The government has promised more responsive public services and access to services via new mechanisms such as the Internet. Staff in health organisations too are becoming subject to greater external scrutiny, with curbs on traditional areas of autonomy and control. For example, NHS trust chief executives are now responsible for clinical standards in their organisations, with a duty of quality set out in the Health Act 1999, and several heads have resigned or been removed from post when there are failings in this area. The implications of the Kennedy report into Bristol Royal Infirmary (Department of Health, 2001), recommending that health professionals undergo appraisal, continuing professional development and revalidation to ensure that they remain competent to do their job are being felt. Published standards of care and a systematic mechanism for monitoring the clinical performance of healthcare professionals or of hospitals are also increasingly now in place. Such developments are likely to lead to the increased external inspection and regulation of professional work, as well as bringing the responsibilities of clinicians and managers closer together in terms of accountability for organisational outcomes.

In addition to political drivers that are within the remit of the UK government, global developments and those at the European level will also impact on the future health workforce. Alongside the internationalisation of the medical and nursing labour markets, the European Union is extending its involvement in health care decisions. Rulings on entitlements, financial responsibilities and liabilities could have significant impact on health care services in the future. For example, there could be a future ruling on patients' direct access to specialists, something which has always been controlled by general practitioners in the UK. This would have a dramatic effect on the service. UK health policy is diversifying with devolution. Scotland and Wales are developing their own models for health provision and Scotland has made a landmark decision in support of free nursing care for older people.

Wider social and economic change

Finally, the health workforce will be affected in the future – as it is now – by more general developments in society and work. When we think of the current retention problems within the nursing workforce because of the increasing opportunities being offered to female workers, there are several trends that might impact adversely on the ability to recruit and retain the health workforce of the future.

Projections by the Government Actuary's Department show that women will make up 46.1 per cent of the labour force in 2011, when they accounted for 44.2 per cent in 1997. The labour force will be older in 2011 and with higher activity rate for those of working age (Armitage and Scott, 1998). Demographic change may lead to different lifetime career structures in the future. With average life expectancies moving towards 80 and an ageing population, the statutory retirement age of 65 looks unlikely to be sustained in the future, even on purely financial grounds, because of the pressure on pension funds. At the same time, with a healthy retirement of perhaps 20 years, people may think differently about how they wish to spend their post-65 years. Financial institutions and employers will also need to think differently about the available workforce in the future.

The UK continues to shift towards a service-based economy. In their report on the 'new economy', consultants Business Strategies (Business Strategies, 2001) observe how some organisations are moving towards networks, away from hierarchy to horizontal cooperation. Such organisational structures are required to adapt rapidly to new external factors and to changing business scenarios. In terms of workforce, communication, team working, problem solving, self-organisation, and self-directed learning are skills required. As a consequence of the demands of flexibility, work and home are no longer viewed as separate. Organisations increasingly operate with flexible arrangements, but also demand flexibility from their workforce. Both the self-employed and part-time workforce are increasing. Workers can no longer rely on long-term employment in the same industry and workers can no longer rely on their employer for career planning, training and personal development.

The Joseph Rowntree Foundation (1996) drew attention to the increasing numbers of households who now have no earners at the same time as an increase in households with two or more working, which it found unusual among industrialised countries. There are growing numbers of men who are unemployed or have taken early retirement and the concentration of social housing has created communities where only a small minority work. Some commentators observe an increasing divide between those who have choice in work time and working hours – facilitated by technology – and those who do not (Reeves, 2001). Health and education are seen as sectors where people now have much less control of their working time and hours than other sectors. Lack of time and lack of control over working time has a negative impact on family life.

What will be the consequences of these developments for the future NHS workforce? Two immediate issues emerge. First, there will be greater competition for recruits in the service sector, particularly skilled workers. If technology and consumerism have their predicted impact, questions can be raised about where the future supply of health sector staff will come from. In addition to service developments that will place an increased demand for skilled staff, several studies (Carers UK, 2002; Knickman and Snell, 2002) predict a smaller pool of informal carers in the future, as a consequence of the ageing population and social change. This will make more demands on the formal care system. The ageing health workforce will require sustained improvements in recruitment and retention – but the NHS is traditionally seen as a rigid career, which may not offer the benefits in terms of flexibility and pay that other skilled, service sector professions provide. However, it may benefit from being a secure career in times of rising insecurity, something that may be exacerbated with recession. Finally, a broader policy issue is that of interest in the health effects of work, such as the effect of unemployment on health, and the health and social effects of reduced job security. Some studies show increased stress and mental illness amongst the health workforce (Williams, Michie and Pattani, 1998).

Conclusion

The primary question in relation to the future health workforce is: what will we want the health workforce to do in the future, how, and where? This review of those studies that have looked to the future concludes that it is likely that service patterns will change over time, requiring different organisation of staff and new skills. Many studies point towards services being organised around the patient in the future. New services such as NHS Direct and walk-in clinics are already providing new roles. In general, technological developments are likely to continue to shift services out of hospitals, which means staff treating different conditions and learning new skills in the community and primary care.

Looking outside the service, it seems that the future health service will have less control over the supply of workers than in the past; trends suggest that future labour markets will be more international. If so, the health sector will be competing with other industries for a skilled, educated workforce and there are some areas where there will be stiff competition. Demographic change may also lead to shortages in supply along with increases in demand, particularly in relation to women, who account for a significant proportion of the health workforce, both in nursing and increasingly in medicine. There are real challenges for the future in the supply and retention of staff in the health sector and this review shows that the health sector will need to deliver on making a career in the health service an attractive one in the future. If it does not do so, expectations for results from current reforms will not be met.

Notes

1. The Policy Futures for UK Health Project is funded by the Nuffield Trust, to look at future trends and issues. The author is the principal researcher on the project. Further details and publications can be accessed from the website: *http://www.jims.cam.ac.uk/research/health/polfutures/polfutures_f.html* [Accessed 16 May 2003].
2 Information on future technological developments from personal communication, Professor Don Detmer Gillings, Professor of Health Management, the Judge Institute of Management, Cambridge May 2003.
3 For details of current Health Action Zones see *http://www.haznet.org.uk/* [Accessed 16 May 2003].

References

Armitage, B. and Scott, M. (1998) 'British Labour Force 1998–2011', *Labour Market Trends*, 106, 6, 281–98.

Associated Press Newswires (2003) 'Big Three Automakers' Sales Decline in April; some foreign carmakers post record results', *Associated Press Newswires*, 2 May 2003.

British Medical Association Health Policy and Economic Research Unit (2002) *The Future Healthcare Workforce Discussion Paper 9*, London: British Medical Association, 12.

Buchan, J. and Edwards, N. (2000) 'Nursing Numbers in Britain: the argument for workforce planning', *British Medical Journal*, 320, 7241, 1067–9.

Buchan, J., Finlayson, B. and Gough, P. (2002) *In Capital Health? Meeting the challenges of London's healthcare workforce*, London: The King's Fund.

Business Strategies (2001) *New Economy, New Skills* [online], available from: *http://www.business-strategies.co.uk* [Accessed 16 May 2003].

Carers UK (2002) *Without Us? Calculating the value of carers' support*, London: Carers UK.

Dargie, C., Dawson, S. and Garside, P. (2000) *Policy Futures for UK Health: 2000 report*, London: The Stationery Office.

Department of Health (2000) *The NHS Plan: a plan for investment, a plan for reform*, London: Department of Health.

Department of Health (2001) *Learning from Bristol. The report of the public inquiry into children's heart surgery at the Bristol Royal Infirmary 1984–1995*. Cm 5207(1), London: The Stationery Office.

Dowie, R. and Langman, M. (1999) 'The Hospital of the Future: staffing of hospitals: future needs, future provision', *British Medical Journal*, 319, 7218, 1193–5.

East Anglian Cancer Intelligence Unit (1997) *Report of Cancer Incidence and Prevalence Projections*, London: Macmillan Cancer Relief.

Foresight (2002) *Foresight Consultation 2002* [online], available from: *http://www.foresight.gov.uk/* [Accessed 16 May 2003].

Future Healthcare Workforce (1996) *The Steering Group Report*, Manchester: University of Manchester.

Future Healthcare Workforce (1999) *The Second Report*, Manchester: University of Manchester.

Health Service Journal (2003) 'Cash Top-up Boosts Stats' *Health Service Journal*, 3 April 2003, 7.

Hetherington, P. (2003) 'Is the Move towards Primary Care the Future of the NHS?', *Guardian*, 26 March 2003.

Hutchinson, L., Marks, T. and Pittilo, M. (2001) 'The Physician Assistant: would the US model meet the needs of the NHS?', *British Medical Journal*, 323, 7323, 1244–7.

Institute for Alternative Futures (2003) *http://www.altfutures.com/* [Accessed 16 May 2003].

Joseph Rowntree Foundation (1996) *The Future of Work: contributions to the debate*, York: Joseph Rowntree Foundation.

Knickman, R. and Snell, E. K. (2002) 'The 2030 Problem: caring for ageing baby boomers', *Health Services Research*, 37, 4, 849–84.

Kurzweil, R. (2001) *The Age of Spiritual Machines: how we will live, work and think in the new age of intelligent machines*, New York: Texere Publishing.

Le Grand, J. (2003) 'Being Schooled in Success', *Health Service Journal*, 16 January 2003, 18–20.

Mittman, D. E., Cawley, J. F. and Fenn, W. H. (2002) 'Physician Assistants in the United States', *British Medical Journal*, 325, 7362, 485–7.

Naish, J. (2003) *The Future Nurse*, London: Royal College of Nursing.

National Health Service Confederation (2000) *The Emerging Vision of the Future Workforce*, London: National Health Service Confederation.

Organisation for Economic Co-operation and Development (2001) *OECD Health Data 2001: a comparative analysis of 30 OECD countries*, Paris: Organisation for Economic Co-operation and Development.

Reeves, R. (2001) 'We Should all Become Time Lords', *New Statesman*, 31 July.

Robert, G. (1999) *Science and Technology Trends and Issues Forward to 2015: implications for health care. Technical series, policy futures for UK health*, London: The Nuffield Trust.

Royal College of Nursing (2003) *Imagining the Future: nursing in the new millennium: a summary report of the views of nurses involved in the RCN 'futures' project*, London: Royal College of Nursing.

Royal College of Physicians (2000) *Hospital Doctors Under Pressure. New roles for the healthcare workforce*, London: The Royal College of Physicians.

Simons, M. (2003) 'NHS Faces Planning Blight Fear after £250m Project Cancelled', *Computer Weekly*, 28 April.

Timmins, N. (2002) 'A Time for Change in the British NHS: an interview with Alan Milburn', *Health Affairs*, 21, 129–35.

Wanless, D. (2001) *Securing our Future Health: taking a long-term view: interim report*, London: HM Treasury.

Wanless, D. (2002) *Securing our Future Health: taking a long-term view: final report*, London: HM Treasury.

Williams, S., Michie, S. and Pattani, S. (1998) *Improving the Health of the NHS Workforce*, London: The Nuffield Trust.

World Health Organisation (2003) *Global Cancer Rates could Increase by 50% to 15 Million by 2020* [online], available from: *http://www.who.int/mediacentre/releases/2003/pr27/en/* [Accessed 16 May 2003].

World Health Organisation Regional Office for Europe (1999) *Health 21: health for all in the 21st century*, Copenhagen: World Health Organisation.

Young, R. and Leese, B. (1999) 'Recruitment and Retention of General Practitioners in the UK: what are the problems and solutions?', *British Journal of General Practice*, 49, 447, 829–33.

Zimmern, R. and Cook, C. (2000) *The Nuffield Trust Genetics Scenario Project: genetics and health policy issues for genetic science and their implications for health and health services*, London: The Stationery Office.

Appendix: Sector Workforce Development Plan – Skills for Health[1]

The sector and its workforce

Employment levels and trends

Overview of the sector

The key characteristics of the health sector are summarised below:

- *large and complex* sector with a wide range of both employers and occupations. The size is reflected in the spending on health care – spending on the NHS is over £50 billion a year (set to rise to £69 billion by 2005), investment in health care insurance and independent provision is estimated to be about £8 billion a year and there is a large, if uncosted, spend through voluntary organisations;
- *steady growth in the workforce* (c.1% per annum) which is set to continue;
- *predominantly female workforce*;
- *large number of part-time workers* with the numbers (headcount) of the workforce 19% higher than the WTE. Part-time opportunities are being gradually increased;
- *age structure*: the majority of the workforce is concentrated between 25–54 years;
- *ethnic mix*: 7% of the English NHS Hospital and Community Health Services nonmedical workforce is from ethnic minority groups (data not available for Scotland, Wales and Northern Ireland). Ethnic minorities represent a much higher proportion of medical and dental staff and pharmacists (for example Asian staff account for 18% of the total medical and dental workforce);
- *supply* problems: the sector is experiencing major supply problems and is implementing strategies to ensure that supply better matches demand;
- *professional roles*: the data in this section is presented in terms of conventional professional and other descriptions. This is the only form in which data is available. However, there is a rapid trend towards blurring and change to traditional role boundaries in many parts of the sector and traditional descriptions increasingly do not reflect the reality of what people do.

Health sector map

This is an extremely large and complex sector with about two million employees and independent contractors/practitioners. It is estimated that there are about 50,000 practitioners of complementary and alternative medicine (CAM) within this total. The development of the map is complicated by the wide range of employers (for example, the NHS and the independent and voluntary sectors). The data for each of these sectors is drawn from large numbers of organisations with independent employer status – the NHS, for example, has 122 health authorities or boards and 464 trusts. A large number of health care professionals work as self-employed practitioners or as partners or staff of group practices or private clinics. The diversity of the workforce with its wide range of occupations presents another challenge.

The sector has been sub-divided as follows for mapping:

- *National Health Service hospital and community health services* (referred to as NHS in this document): staff in health authorities, hospitals and community services;
- *general medical and dental practice*: general medical and dental practitioners and other practice staff;
- *independent*: private nursing homes, hospitals and clinics;
- *private and retail*: healthcare professionals working in surgeries or retail outlets (for example, pharmacists, opticians), self-employed practitioners (for example, physiotherapists) and complementary and alternative medicine practitioners;
- *voluntary sector*: paid employment only included.

Size and structure of workforce

The health sector currently employs around two million people (headcount) across a wide range of occupations (see Table A.1):

- National Health Service   1,273,837
- general practice   131,898
- independent sector   394,976
- private & retail   168,909
- voluntary sector   33,000
- *total*   *2,002,620*

The workforce can be divided into 4 broad categories. 46% are clinical practitioners and scientists; 30% work in clinical and technical support; 20% in management and administration; and 4% in estates and maintenance functions. These figures have been derived from Table A.1 and information on the composition of the first two staff groups is outlined below.

Clinical practitioners and scientists:
- medical and dental staff;
- nurses, midwives and health visitors;
- allied health professionals: physiotherapists, dieticians, radiographers, podiatrists/chiropodists, occupational therapists, speech and language therapists, art, music and drama therapists and orthoptists;
- complementary and alternative medicine practitioners;
- scientific and professional staff: clinical psychologists, psychotherapists, pharmacists, pathologists, health care scientists;
- ambulance paramedics.

Clinical and technical support:
- ambulance personnel excluding paramedics;
- healthcare assistants: usually trained to NVQ 2/3 to work in support of professional staff in clinical areas (either hospital or community);

Table A.1:   Health sector workforce: headcount

Staff groups	NHS	Gen. practice & gen. dental	Indep. sector	Private & retail	Vol. sector
Medical	93,143	37,021			
Dental	4,843	21,077		4,000	
Total medical and dental	*97,986*	*58,098*		*4,000*	
Nursing, midwifery & HV qualified	401,238	12,827	92,532		9,900
Nursing, midwifery & HV unqualified	153,291		144,453		
Total nursing, midwifery & HV	*554,529*		*236,985*		
Allied health professionals qual.	65,942	2,251	15,799	10,970	
Allied health professionals helpers	11,171				
Total allied health professionals	*77,113*		*15,799*		
Complementary medicine pract.				50,000	
Scientific & professional	36,825		7,000	40,736	
Scientific & professional asst/tech	44,060		900		
Total scientific & professional	*80,885*		*7,900*		
Healthcare assistants	27,208		3,950		
Support staff	119,824	637		40,000	23,100
Ambulance staff	20,052				
Mgmt & administration	*236,240*	*59,988*	*102,694*		
Works, maintenance and ancillary	60,000		31,598		
Total	*1,273,837*	*133,801*	*394,975*	*171,708*	*33,000*

Notes on employment sectors: (a) NHS hospital and community health services.
(b) General practice: general medical practitioners and other practice staff plus general dental services (dentists only).
(c) Independent sector: private nursing homes, hospitals and clinics.
(d) Private/retail: pharmacists & opticians in retail outlets and academia, self-employed healthcare professionals, and complementary medicine.

- nursing auxiliaries and helpers to allied health professionals;
- assistants to scientific and professional staff;
- technicians: for example, medical physics, pharmacy, pathology, dental, physiological measurement;
- other support staff: for example, ward hostesses and housekeepers.

The health sector map is outlined in more detail on pages 246–7.

Data sources and gaps

The mapping exercise was complicated by the numbers of employers and by the complexity of the workforce itself. The following notes show the sources of the data and identify a number of gaps:

NHS hospital and community services: the figures are based on 1999 data obtained from the NHS Executive in England, Scotland, Wales and Northern Ireland. The English data is published annually (separate Statistical Bulletins for non-medical and medical and dental staff). Estimates were developed for three groups for which data was not available:

- *maintenance and ancillary services*: craftsmen, caterers, porters, domestics, etc. The services provided by these staff groups are largely contracted out. In England the number of NHS employees in this category dropped from 178,430 in 1984 to 12,340 in 1999. During this period improved technology and efficiency gains will have reduced the staffing requirement. An estimated figure of 60,000 has been included;
- *bank and agency nursing*: an estimate of 10,000 has been included for bank and agency nursing. This estimate is supported by an RCN review of the nursing labour market in 2000, which identified 6,730 wte agency staff alone. It should be noted that a number of bank and agency staff are NHS employees and will already have been included in the figures;
- *locum medical and dental staff*: this data is no longer collected nationally. In 1996 locum staff represented 5% of the in-post figure and an estimated figure of 4660 locum staff has been added on this basis. It should be noted that a number of locum staff are NHS employees and will already have been included in the figures. No provision has been made for locums in general practice.

General medical and dental practice: the figures are based on 1999 data from the English data for general practice which is published annually: 'Statistics for General Medical Practitioners in England'. Figures for other practice staff (for example practice nurses and administrative and clerical staff) were available for England only. The English figures were increased by 20% to provide an estimate if the UK total.

Private nursing homes, hospitals and clinics: the figures are drawn from a Statistical Bulletin ('Community Care Statistics 2000') published annually by the Department of Health in England. The only data available was for nursing staff in England. Estimates were developed as follows:

- an estimate for other non-medical staff groups was based on the following staff group mix: nursing and midwifery 60%, allied health professionals 4%,

Health Sector Map

NHS (Hospital and Community)	
Medical and Dental	Hospital (all grades) Public health medicine Community health services
Nursing, Midwifery & Health Visiting	Professionally qualified Unqualified staff and HCAs
Allied Health Profs. Professionally Qual. HCAs and Helpers	Physiotherapists Occupational therapists Dieticians Chiropodists/ Podiatrists Orthoptists Radiographers Diagnostic radiographers Therapeutic Art/music/ therapists Multi-therapists Speech and language therapists

Other Development	
NHS General Practice & General Dental Services	Gen. medical practitioners (all grades) Dentists (all grades) Practice nurses Dental nurses and hygienists Other direct patient care Management and A&C
Independent Sector (Private Nursing Homes, Hospitals & Clinics)	Medical and dental Qualified and unqualified nurses Allied health professionals Scientific and professional Management and A&C Works, maintenance and ancillary

scientific and professional 3%, healthcare assistants 1%, management and administrative and clerical 25% and works, maintenance and ancillary 7%. Medical staff have not been included since the majority of this group are also employed in the NHS;

• the UK figure was estimated at 20% higher than the English figure.

Complementary medicine: a report presented by the University of Exeter to the House of Lords Committee on Science and Technology in 2000.

Voluntary sector: estimates obtained from the Voluntary Sector NTO.

Private and retail: the figure for pharmacists working in retail outlets and academia was obtained from the Royal Pharmaceutical Society of GB. The figures for other professional staff (physiotherapists, speech and language therapists, clinical psychologists, chiropodists, optometrists, and opticians) employed in retail

Health Sector Map (*continued*)

NHS (Hospital and Community)   Other Development

Scientific & Professional	Clin. Psychologists Psychotherapists
Professionally Qual.	Medical physicists Pharmacists
Scientists	Pathologists
Technicians	Dental technicians

Management and Administrative & Clerical	Managers – (on senior manager grades) Administrative staff Secretarial and clerical staff

Works Maintenance Ancillary	Works officers Maintenance craftsmen Main groups: domestic, catering, portering

Private & Retail	Pharmacists and technicians Opticians Pharmacy and opticians' retails assistants Dentists Dental nurses Dental hygienists Dental management and A&C Physiotherapists Speech and language therapists Chiropodists/ Podiatrists Complementary and alternative medicine Practitioners clinical psychologists Dieticians/nutritionists
Voluntary Sector	Paid employees employed on hospital activities Estimates of nurses and helpers

outlets or clinics or as self-employed practitioners were estimated from the numbers on the register as follows:

- minus 20% to take account of those working overseas or not working;
- minus the headcount for the NHS and General Medical and Dental Services.

The gaps that it has not been possible to fill for this mapping exercise are:

- locum general practitioners;
- locum pharmacists and agency administrative & clerical staff in the NHS;
- dental nurses, hygienists and reception staff;
- nutritionists working privately;
- clinical professionals employed in academic posts.

The health sector map does not include health professionals working in other sectors (for example, social services, occupational health, school health, armed services, prison service). These staff will have skill sets specific to the sector where they are employed as well as general professional skills and this plan does not purport to cover these.

Trends in the workforce

There is steady growth in the health sector workforce. NHS employees in England have increased by an average of 1% a year since 1995 and the rate of growth increased to 2% between 1998–99. The fastest growth rates are for clinical professionals with medical staff and therapists increasing by 3% and 4% a year respectively. This expansion reflects the steady upward trend in demand for services (3% in the acute sector and 1% a year in primary care).

This rate of growth in NHS staffing should be at least maintained if not increased. The government projects significant increases in clinical practitioners in England by 2009: 12,000 consultants, 3,000 GPs, 59,600 nurses and over 9,000 allied health professionals. The clinical support workforce is also likely to increase. Scotland, Wales and Northern Ireland are also developing expansion plans.

Demographics of the workforce

This section describes the characteristics of the NHS workforce since the detailed data required is not available for all employment categories. However, the NHS employs around 64% of the total workforce, so its characteristics may be assumed to be broadly indicative of the workforce as a whole.

Gender

The main characteristics are:

- the NHS workforce is predominantly female (see Table A.2). In England, 79% of the total non-medical workforce is female. The majority of hospital medical staff (66%) is male but the number of female staff is increasing rapidly – the average annual growth of all staff is 3.1% a year but female staff are growing by 5.6% a year. Nursing and therapy staff are predominantly female: qualified nurses 88% and allied health professionals 86%;
- figures for general practice in England show similar trends to hospital medical staff: 68% of GP principals are male but 56% of GP registrars are now female;
- the gender breakdown for the NHS workforce in Wales is similar with females accounting for 78% of the total workforce. The figures for nurses and allied health professionals (91% and 87% respectively) are broadly similar to England;
- the figures for Scotland are similar to England and Wales but there are slightly higher numbers of females in the workforce: for example, 91% of allied health professionals and 94% of healthcare assistants are female;
- the staff groups with the highest number of males (across the UK) are ambulance staff, medical and dental staff and managers.

Table A.2:   NHS workforce: gender breakdown

Occupation	England		Wales		Scotland	
	Female	*Male*	*Female*	*Male*	*Female*	*Male*
Medical staff	34.0%	66.0%	32.3%	67.7%	38.9%	61.1%
Dental staff	43.8%	56.2%	38.5%	61.5%	35.7%	64.3%
Total medical & dental	*35.3%*	*64.7%*	*32.7%*	*67.3%*		
Nursing, midwifery & health visiting						
• Qualified	87.7%	12.3%	91.0%	9.0%		
• Unqualified	85.3%	14.7%	86.9%	13.1%		
Allied health professionals			86.7%	13.3%	91.4%	8.6%
Allied health prof. helpers			90.0%	9.1%	93.2%	6.8%
Total allied health professionals	*86.1%*	*13.9%*	*87.4%*	*12.6%*		
Scientific & professional			60.0%	40.0%	67%	33%
Scientific & professional assistant/tech			71.0%	29.0%	67.3%	32.7%
Total scientific & professional	*75.0%*	*25.0%*	*66.0%*	*34.0%*		
Healthcare assistants	83.4%	16.6%	72.5%	27.5%	93.5%	6.5%
Support staff	65.5%	34.5%	72.1%	27.9%	77.1%	22.9%
Ambulance staff	24.2%	75.8%	10.8%	89.2%	20.8%	79.2%
• Administrative managers	52.3%	47.7%	43.9%	56.1%	48.8%	51.2%
• Clerical and administrative staff	85.7%	14.3%	85.7%	14.3%	87.5%	12.5%
Estates staff			5.3%	94.7%		
Total			*77.7%*	*22.3%*		

Age structure

The age structure for selected NHS staff groups is shown in Table A.3 (the examples are drawn from England, Wales and Northern Ireland):

- the majority of the workforce is concentrated in the age bands between 25–54 for example, 83% of the total workforce in Wales is in these age bands;
- the low number of under-25s is to some extent explained by the years of study required for professional qualifications, but may also reflect a changing age profile among students. However, the figures demonstrate scope for increasing the numbers of clinical support staff in this age band in line with increased education and training opportunities for this group;

- the lower figures for those aged 55–64 (only 6% of English nurses are in this age band) reflect a tendency towards earlier retirement. The numbers in the older age bands are even lower in Northern Ireland with only 3% of nurses aged 55 and above and only 9.7% aged 50 and above. These figures make the case for the development of retention and recruitment strategies aimed at this age group.

Table A.3:   NHS workforce: age structure

England	<25	25–34	35–44	45–54	55–64	65 & >	Not known
Medical	4.4%	35.4%	30.0%	20.3%	9.5%	0.7%	–
Dental	2.5%	28.9%	31.5%	24.8%	11.4%	3.9%	–
Nursing, midwifery & health visiting							
• Qualified	4.4%	29%	33.3%	22.8%	6.4%	0.1%	3.9%
• Unqualified (assistants)	7%	19.1%	23.9%	25.9%	13.8%	0.1%	10.1%
Allied health professionals	11.5%	33.8%	27.0%	20.1%	7.4%	0.1%	0.0%
Scientific and professional staff	10.6%	30.3%	28.6%	22.7%	7.4%	0.2%	0.3%
Healthcare assistants	11.6%	22.3%	24.6%	22.6%	9.1%	1.2%	8.7%
Wales	<25	25–34	35–44	45–54	55–64	65 & >	Not known
Nursing & midwifery qualified	0	26.5%	36.4%	23.9%	8.5%	0.1%	4.6%
Total NHS workforce	0.2%	25.5%	32.4%	25.3%	10.5%	0.4%	6%
Northern Ireland	<25	25–34	35–44	45–54	55–64	65 & >	Not known
Nursing, midwifery & health visiting	23.5%	42.5%	24.3%	6.7%	2.6%	0.4%	0

Part-time employment

Part-time working is significant within the sector:

- the NHS already provides a wide range of part-time opportunities, which is demonstrated by the variation between headcount and WTE: the total headcount of 1,269,177 is 19% higher than the WTE of 1,027,786;
- the trend towards part-time working extends to all staff groups – for example, the proportion of GP Principals in England working part-time increased from 5% in 1990 to 17% in 1999 and 13% of senior hospital medical staff now work part-time;

- the level of part-time working is consistent with a predominantly female workforce. However, there are clear indications that male staff are also seeking more opportunities for flexibility in working arrangements;
- the provision of flexible, part-time opportunities is likely to increase further in the future as a result of recruitment and retention initiatives in the NHS. Many parts of the independent sector have traditionally provided scope for flexible employment.

Ethnic mix

Table A.4 provides some information on ethnic origin:

- there is a strong drive to draw from all sectors of the population;
- the ethnic mix of medical and dental staff has changed significantly in recent years, with high levels of Asian recruits. Asian medical and dental staff now account for 18% of the total (18.4% of medical staff and 9.9% of dental staff);
- 7% of non-medical staff in the English NHS is from ethnic minority groups. Although this figure is broadly in line with the working population of England as a whole, it is recognised that there is scope for additional recruitment from ethnic minority groups (both to training places and employment);
- the ethnic minority population is unevenly distributed – there are some areas where the NHS does not reflect the ethnic mix of the population very closely, although this is a target for NHS organisations;
- one of the areas of work where ethnic minorities are least represented is in ambulance services.

Table A.4: NHS workforce ethnic mix (England)

Staff group	White	Black	Asian	Other	Unknown
Medical	67.4%	3.8%	18.4%	8.3%	2.2%
Dental	78.8%	3.0%	9.9%	4.9%	3.5%
Nursing, midwifery & health visiting:					
• Qualified	86.8%	4.7%	1.6%	2.3%	4.6%
• Unqualified (assistants)	82.5%	4.8%	0.9%	2.0%	9.8%
Allied health professionals	94.3%	1.6%	1.6%	1.3%	1.3%
Scientific and professional staff	90.8%	2.5%	3.0%	1.9%	1.7%
Healthcare assistants	90.6%	4.6%	1.5%	1.7%	1.7%
Ambulance staff	97.8%	0.6%	0.3%	0.5%	0.7%
Administration and estates staff	92.9%	2.5%	1.8%	1.1%	1.7%

Note

1. This is an excerpt from a report commissioned and published in June 2001 by Healthwork UK, the then Health Care National Training Organisation. It represented the first UK-wide examination of the size and shape of the workforce and its training needs. Alongside the detailed estimates of workforce size set out here, the report considered responsibilities for education and training, development needs, priorities for action and outcome measures. The full report was transferred to the web-site of Skills for Health, the successor body. It can be found at *http://www.skillsforhealth.org.uk/pdf_files/sw_dev_plan2.pdf.* Updating and further development of this work into a full market assessment was commissioned and due to be presented to the Board in the summer of 2003. Those interested should visit the Skills for Health web-site for further information. This excerpt is reprinted with minor amendments with the permission of Skills for Health.

Index

A&E departments,
  admissions, 80
  nurses, 73
  systems theory, 75
acupuncture, 162
alternative therapies *see*
    complementary and alternative
    medicines
ambulance personnel, 73, 80, 81–2
Ambulance Service Association, 81
Arthritis Care, 42
Aruyvedic medicine, 162
Audit Commission, 42, 72, 73, 81,
    236
automation,
  IT *see* information technology
  pharmacy, 212–13
  robotics, 11, 212, 230

Balint, Michael, 181
Bandura, A., 42
birthing centres, 89
Blenkinsopp, Alison, 11, 199–221,
    225
Bond, Christine, 11, 199–221, 225
Bradshaw, A., 155–6
Bristol Royal Infirmary, 6, 116, 187,
    236
British Medical Association (BMA),
    21, 161, 225
business process re-engineering, 25
Business Strategies, 237

Calman-Hine Report (1995), 71
Cameron, Ailsa, 9, 68–86
carers,
  care policy, 58–60
  census data, 49
  coercion/co-operation, 57
  communication, 62
  crisis situations, 61
  dementia, 55
  DIPEx, 62

  direct payments, 54
  equal partnership, 55
  family carers, 55–8
  future prospects, 63–4
  HCAs *see* health care assistants
  holistic approach, 10, 54
  informal carers, 50–5
  intimacy, 58
  lobbies, 50, 51
  mental health, 58, 59
  National Strategy for Carers, 52
  new technologies, 62
  personal connectivity, 57–8
  producers of care, 33
  professionalisation, 9, 49–67
  relationships, 60–1
  role erosion, 57
  sharing expertise, 62
  skills training, 61–2
  training needs, 55
central standard-setting, 3
Centre for Information Therapy, 37
Changing Workforce Programme, 9,
    15, 27, 83
Changing Workforce Project, 8
Chief Dental Officer, 106, 116
Chief Medical Officer (CMO), 116,
    126–7, 131
chiropodists, 15
chiropractors, 161, 162
chronic diseases,
  nursing, 96, 202
  self-management, 29, 42–3
Chronic Disease Self-Management
    Course (CDSMC), 29
clinical practitioners, 4
Commission for Health Improvement
    (CHI), 3, 5, 119, 236
Commission for Patient and Public
    Involvement in Health (CPPIH),
    132
communication,
  carers, 62